# CONTENTS

# Chapter 1

# PREPARING TO PLANT

**Many astute gardeners attribute their green thumb to good soil. They know that garden success starts in the ground.**

## GET READY TO PLANT

After moving into a home in either a new or an established neighborhood, gardeners are frequently disappointed to discover that the soil is causing landscape plants to struggle for survival. The soil may be full of clay, compacted, too acidic, poorly draining, eroding, or lacking in organic matter.

With a little knowledge and determination, you can use soil amendments to improve poor soil and make your landscape flourish. Soil amendments are materials that are mixed into the topsoil to promote healthy plant growth. Plant food is not usually classified as a soil amendment because its primary function is to supply nutrients. Some soil amendments, such as lime, change the soil pH. Others, such as compost, supply nutrients but they are most

important as soil conditioners providing bulky organic materials that improve soil structure. When soil structure is improved, air and water move through the soil more readily, enhancing root growth and plant health.

Most garden and landscape plants perform best in soils high in organic matter. These soils are loose and easy to dig and plant in. They contain a large number of earthworms. You won't see a dramatic change during the first year after you add soil amendments to a difficult soil. But over three to five years of regular incorporation, you will witness significant improvement in soil conditions and plant growth. Because organic matter is used up through oxidation, especially in warm climates and where soils are frequently tilled, it should be added to the soil every year.

## YOUR SOIL'S PROFILE

If you were to dig and remove a 2- to 3-foot-deep slice of your backyard, you would expose your soil's profile. The top 4 to 8 inches of the slice is topsoil—dark and fertile due to organic matter. Below the topsoil, the profile changes gradually in color and texture, depending on the soil's origin. Many gardeners find that their subsoil increases in clay content and stickiness with increasing depth. Subsoils heavy in clay may restrict the flow of water and air and the growth of plant roots. The rooting depth for most home garden plants rarely exceeds 4 feet.

Soil texture is an important aspect of the soil. It affects drainage, root growth, and plant stability. To test texture, squeeze a handful of lightly moistened soil. Any soil with good texture forms a ball that can be easily broken apart with your fingers. Very sandy soil will not form a ball. (It will dry out and leach nutrients rapidly.) Heavy, clay soil forms a sticky ball that does not break apart. (It tends to pack down and suffocate roots.)

**Squeeze soil between your thumb and forefinger: A long, ribbon indicates a clay soil.**

## TROUBLESHOOTING SOIL PROBLEMS

The first step toward correcting a soil problem is identifying the specific cause.

| Problem | What Can Be Done? |
|---|---|
| **No topsoil** The topsoil may have washed away or was removed during construction. | ▪ Purchase topsoil. (See page 7.)<br>▪ Mix purchased topsoil with the existing topsoil.<br>▪ Make raised beds and fill them with a mixture of purchased topsoil and compost. |
| **Heavy, unmanageable clay soil** | ▪ Loosen soil with a garden fork; work lots of organic matter into the top 12 inches of soil. |
| **Compaction** Driving machinery and vehicles on clay soils results in poor root growth, drowned roots, and root diseases. Hardpan is compacted soil impervious to water, air, and nutrients; it can occur at any depth and inhibits root growth. | ▪ Physically loosen the subsoil or break open the hardpan and add organic matter.<br>▪ Plant in raised beds.<br>▪ Plant a deep-rooted cover crop.<br>▪ Plant a permanent, well-adapted ground cover. |
| **Poor drainage** To test drainage, dig a hole 12 inches deep and 8 inches in diameter. Fill it with water. Fill it again 12 hours later. All the water should drain out within 2 to 3 hours. | ▪ Grow plants adapted to wet soil.<br>▪ Regrade the area to eliminate low spots.<br>▪ Install drainage tile. |
| **Erosion** Rainwater can quickly wash away topsoil. | ▪ Install splash blocks or drainpipe under downspouts.<br>▪ Plant bare soil with a cover crop, ground cover (from turf to trees), or mulch.<br>▪ Terrace sloped ground that is cultivated. |
| **Low fertility** Many soils are naturally low in fertility. | ▪ Add organic matter: 3 to 4 cubic yards per 1,000 square feet (4 to 5 bushels per 100 square feet).<br>▪ Fertilize according to product directions. |
| **Extremely low or high pH** Extreme pH can cause nutrient deficiency and nutrient toxicity. | ▪ Test soil and adjust pH according to the results. |

**For a representative sample, dig trowel-size samples from several places and mix thoroughly in a clean container.**

**Apply thoroughly composted manure to planting beds to boost soil fertility.**

**Use a garden fork to dig the composted manure into the top 12 inches of soil.**

# SOIL TESTING

**H**ealthy soil is one of the keys to growing edible crops successfully. A simple and inexpensive test of your garden soil will help you make decisions about adding plant food and other amendments.

A basic soil test measures pH (the degree of acidity or alkalinity in the soil), phosphorus, potassium, and organic matter (a measure of nitrogen availability). Soil pH affects the availability of nutrients for uptake. A neutral pH is 7. Above 7, the soil pH is alkaline; below 7, it is acidic. Most edible plants grow best in slightly acidic soil—a pH between 6 and 7. Asparagus and onions grow well in alkaline soils with a pH up to 8; potatoes and radishes thrive in highly acidic soil, as low as 4.5. If the soil pH is not appropriate for the crop grown, nutrients in the soil won't be available to the plants.

Lime reduces acidity (raises pH); sulfur increases it (lowers pH). Testing the soil before applying either one helps to determine which type and how much of either application is needed if any. Some soils may be deficient in phosphorus or potassium, which are necessary for plants to bloom and fruit. Additional tests are available to assess the need for any mineral amendments needed for optimum gardening.

A soil test every three to five years is usually often enough for most home gardens. If you routinely plant a crop not typically grown in your geographic area, have the soil tested annually. If a problem arises during the growing season that points to a soil fertility issue, have the soil tested immediately. Otherwise, take the soil sample in autumn so you have time to incorporate any needed amendments before the next spring planting season.

Use a trowel to take samples from the soil. Remove any surface debris, then dig to a depth of 8 inches. Taking samples from more than one area of the garden helps you decide where to locate specific crops and provides

Testing garden soil measures its acidity or alkalinity and helps to determine which nutrients need adjustment, if any. Using clean tools, place each sample in a separate, labeled container.

comparisons when diagnosing plant health problems. Draw a diagram of your garden and label the areas where you took the samples. Place each sample in a separate clean, dry container (plastic bag).

Take several samples from various locations and mix them together to get a representative sample of the whole area. In garden beds, take samples between plants, but avoid collecting any plant foods and mulches.

Contact your local extension agent for a list of laboratories that provide soil testing in your area. The laboratory you choose will provide instructions on how to package your samples for mailing or delivery as well as information on how to interpret the results.

**1**

Home soil test kits are less precise than the results from commercial laboratories, but they can provide rough estimates of needs.

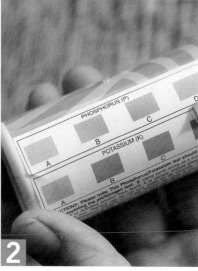

**2**

You will need to interpret the results on your own if using a home soil test kit.

# IMPROVING SOIL

**Coir** is made from coconut fibers. It is used in commercial soil potting mixes to help prevent overwatering and underwatering. Coir improves the water holding capacity of soil mixes and reduces shrinkage that causes the soil to pull away from the sides of the container. Reduced shrinkage results in easier watering because water will soak in to the root ball rather than run down the gap between the root ball and the pot.

**Compost** is made from decayed organic materials such as straw, grass clippings, newspaper, leaves, fruit and vegetable food wastes, spent plants, hay, chipped brush and trees, and farm manures. Compost holds 225 percent of its weight in water and, unlike peat moss, does not repel water when dry. Compost is not nutrient dense— it may contain only 1 percent nitrogen by weight—but it slowly releases a wide range of nutrients essential for plant growth. The pH of most compost is in the 6.6 to 7.2 range. Compost is the most important and frequently used soil amendment. It is easy to make at home and provides long-lasting benefits. Incorporate it into soils prior to planting, spread it over turf and beds of perennials and annuals (top-dressing), and use it to grow plants in containers.

**Composted manure** (check with nearby farms) helps build good soil. Ask for manure that has been mixed with bedding material and allowed to compost for at least two months. Farm manures usually contain 3 percent or less of each of the three main nutrients found in plant fertilizers— nitrogen, phosphorous, and potassium.

**Gypsum** is calcium sulfate. Apply gypsum to heavy, clay soils that are high in sodium to improve soil structure and add calcium and sulfur without raising the soil pH. It also ties up excess magnesium. Gypsum can help leach out sodium when mixed into the top few inches of a soil with a high salt concentration. This can help prevent the burning of plant roots from excess salts.

**Humus** is produced slowly from the decomposition of organic matter in soil. Adding compost and other organic materials to soil will increase the humus content. Humus holds water and nutrients, aids soil aggregation, and contains huge microbial populations. It can be purchased in bags; the quality will vary.

**Organic mulches** such as straw, newspaper, and grass clippings can be tilled into the soil at the end of the growing season. Others, such as shredded pine bark and hardwood chips, are not incorporated, but they act as soil amendments by slowly decomposing in place.

**Peat moss** is partially decomposed sphagnum moss mined from bogs. It absorbs 10 to 20 times its weight in water, but it repels water when it's dry. Peat moss contains little nutritive value but has a high nutrient-holding capacity. It is very acidic and is often mixed into beds prepared for plants in the blueberry, azalea, and rhododendron family.

**Sand** can be used in small areas to improve clay soils and create better growing conditions for certain types of plants, such as Mediterranean herbs and cacti. Only sharp builder's sand should be used; add enough so that the soil is 50 percent sand. Smaller amounts of fine sand can cause clay to set up like concrete.

**Sawdust** that is well aged and decayed can be added to soil. Fresh sawdust can tie up nitrogen as it decomposes.

**Topsoil** can be purchased by the bag or in bulk. Quality can vary widely. Inspect topsoil prior to purchase and delivery, and ask about the soil's history. Where did it come from? Have tests been performed for pH and nutrient levels and for heavy metals such as lead and cadmium? Blended topsoil and leaf compost mixes are excellent for an instant raised-bed garden. You can purchase them by the cubic yard in many areas.

**Water-absorbing polymers** are sold as granules that can absorb 300 to 400 times their weight in water. As soil dries, stored water is released slowly back into it. Polymers' cost-effectiveness has not been demonstrated for outdoor garden use, but they are useful in containers.

Tilling in high-quality organic amendments will loosen and enrich your garden soil.

**1** Add at least one inch of compost each year to beds.

**2** Mix the compost into the top 4 to 8 inches of soil.

## IMPROVING SOIL WITH COVER CROPS

Does your garden need more compost than you can manufacture in one season? Consider cultivating green manure cover crops as a way to improve soil texture and fertility while the garden rests during the winter. If you are a four-season gardener, think about dividing your plot into two or more sections, so you can grow cover crops in one or more of them while the others produce food crops.

Grow fall-seeded legumes where winters are warm.

Winter rye and buckwheat are good cover crops in northern zones.

### GREEN GOLD

Growing cover crops and tilling them in as green manure (not yet decomposed) adds organic matter and nutrients to the soil. The crops themselves keep the soil aerated and protected from erosion, and also help discourage weed growth. Cover crops grown between rows of fruit trees help to prevent soil erosion and protect the tree roots. Some cover crops produce flowers that attract honeybees, which benefit the whole garden.

### WHAT TO PLANT

Choose cover crops based on where you live and the type of soil you want to improve. Winter rye, buckwheat, rye grass, and legumes, such as soybeans, are commonly grown as cover crops in northern zones. In warmer climates, fall-seeded legumes (hairy vetch and bigflower vetch), crimson clover, and alfalfa are popular choices; rye and oats are good nonlegume choices. Legumes are the preferred cover crop for soil enrichment.

Bacteria in nodules on the roots of legumes convert nitrogen in the atmosphere into nitrogen in the soil, where it remains available to crops planted after you till in the cover crop.

To speed up the nitrogen-fixing process, dust your cover crop seeds with rhizobium, a bacterial inoculant. For smaller gardens where growing space is limited, quick-growing rye, hull-less oats, millet, or wheat may be a better choice than legumes. Oilseed radish, a type of mustard, grows quickly in cool weather and is a good choice for compacted soil or dry conditions.

In northern climates, plant a nonlegume cover crop in autumn when the harvest is over. It will have time to sprout and grow before dying in winter. Till it under in early spring. Wait a few weeks to be sure it has all decomposed, and then begin planting your vegetable crops.

In warm-winter areas, sow cover crops in summer and till them under in fall, a few weeks before planting.

For an appealing late-season cover crop that attracts beneficial insects, grow sunflowers (*Helianthus annuus*) every third or fourth year.

For help in deciding which cover crop will work best in your garden, contact the cooperative extension agent or horticultural specialist in your area.

### WHEN TO TILL

You can turn under a cover crop anytime, but for it to be considered green manure it needs to be tilled when it is still green—usually just as the buds are about to open, when the crop is about a foot tall. If you're on vacation when the plants blossom, don't despair. As soon as you have a chance, till under the entire mature crop, adding composted manure to aid decomposition.

In the South, you may be able to plant again in the same year. If you need to till under a mature crop but also need to plant again soon, cut the crop using a lawn mower and compost the clippings. Then, till the remainder into the soil. You can plant again in a few weeks.

**1** Clear the plot of vegetation.

**2** Broadcast quick-growing rye seed.

**3** Rake it into the soil and then water.

# PLANNING TO PLANT

## CHOOSING THE RIGHT TIME

Most soil preparation is done during spring and fall because most planting takes place at that time. Balmy spring days stir gardeners to go outside and play in the dirt. But too often they work the soil when it is too wet. This can force sticky clay particles together, damaging the soil structure. The soil then dries into hard, unmanageable clods. Avoid this with a simple field test: Shape a handful of garden soil into a ball and bounce it a few times in your hand. If it breaks apart, the soil is dry enough to dig. If the ball stays intact, you should wait before planting. On the other hand, tilling during hot, dry weather can turn some soil into a dusty powder. Till a day or two after a rain if possible.

## SITE SELECTION

Among the many factors to consider when choosing a site for vegetables, fruits, and herbs, beauty and access should be at the top of your list. What place in your yard lends itself to the charms of a kitchen garden? Where will fruit trees look best in your current and future landscaping plans? Are these places within convenient reach from your house?

Achieve the harvest of your dreams no matter how limited your growing area. Creative design and careful planning will earn you amazingly tasteful results. Many edibles, such as apple and cherry trees, are ornamental as well as productive and make outstanding landscape plants. Take advantage of the ornamental uses of herbs too and weave them throughout the landscape where they'll add diversity. Herbs make ideal planting partners with annuals, perennials, and fruit trees. Use them to form tidy edges and to attract pollinators to the garden.

Of course, the most important factor when considering sites for your edible plants is ensuring that each location meets requirements for the plants to thrive and yield a harvest. Most of these plants fare best in full sun, with adequate air circulation, and good drainage. If your location does not have full sun all day, plan to give plants as much southern and western exposure as possible.

Despite your eagerness to get as much out of your plantings of fruits, vegetables, and herbs, you may want to begin small, adding plants as you become more comfortable with their care regimen. Most home gardeners begin by planting too many plants and by placing them too closely together. Begin with a plan and a handful of plants. Plant what you know you will use. Add more later as your confidence and experience levels grow. This will save you time, money, and frustration over the long run.

**A productive garden doesn't need to occupy acres of land to provide you with fresh, delicious produce. Raised beds work well.**

## WORKING WITH DIFFICULT SITES

Certain sites require extensive modification to ensure favorable growing conditions for plants.

**Reclaim neglected areas:** Much work is required to rid an area of weeds, brambles, and small woody plants. It may take a combination of cutting, digging, and herbicide applications before the soil can be prepared.

**Compacted soils and lack of topsoil:** Raised beds are a good option for gardeners with problem soil. Loosen the existing soil in the proposed bed with a garden fork and surround it with an enclosure 6 to 12 inches high. Purchase good-quality topsoil that has been mixed with compost and fill the enclosed area. For more details, see page 13.

**Slopes:** Create a flat, terraced area for flower and vegetable beds that require soil preparation each year.

**Poor drainage:** Underground streams, high water tables, and impervious soil layers can create drainage problems. Sometimes it's best to simply grow plants adapted to wet conditions. To correct poor drainage, cut an 18- to 24-inch-deep trench from a point above the poor drainage area to a point below the area. Shovel 2 inches of coarse gravel into the bottom of the trench and lay 4- to 6-inch-diameter perforated plastic drainage pipe on top. The pipe should slope slightly to allow gravity to carry water through it. Cover the pipe with 2 inches of coarse gravel and backfill with soil. The pipe should end near a storm drain or dry well. Consult a landscape architect, landscaper, or building contractor for difficult situations.

# Chapter 2

# PLANTING

**Planting is one of the most satisfying acts of gardening. Proper planting techniques have a profound impact on the beauty and productivity of the home garden and orchard.**

## CHOOSE THE BEST PLANTS

Small gardens can produce abundant food crops all summer. If you choose and plan well, you can grow vegetables throughout the year by selecting crops that are adapted to each season and by planting over a longer period than usual.

Study seed and plant catalogs, books, and cooperative extension bulletins to determine which crops are most suitable for your region. Focus first on those you can plant in late winter or early spring, such as lettuce and broccoli, and then consider what you'll plant in their places in summer or fall. When hardy, herbs and most fruits produce a crop year after year. Some fruit varieties are not self-fruitful, meaning they must be cross-pollinated by another closely related variety nearby, so you'll likely need to plant more than one specimen.

As with most things in life, you get what you pay for when you go plant shopping. Vigorous, high-quality plants may be more expensive, but they will establish quickly and reach their potential for size, appearance, and productivity.

Resist the impulse to buy plants you don't need just because they're inexpensive or appealing. Your plant selection should follow the design that you created for your yard.

**The roots of healthy bare-root plants should be firm and fleshy; not dry and brittle or soft and slimy.**

There will always be opportunities to move, divide, and add plants. Crowding plants causes stressful growing conditions that may contribute to insect and disease problems. Buy dwarf forms of desired plants when they are appropriate and available. Carefully measure and mark the area that each plant will occupy. It's relatively easy to divide and move herbaceous perennials.

## WHAT TO LOOK FOR

Take your time when selecting plants for your garden. Bring a checklist to help you choose what plants will best fit into your plan. When you visit the nursery or garden center, look for these characteristics of high-quality specimens:

■ Plants are true to type; they have the correct leaf color, size, shape, and the correct tag.

■ The root system is white to light beige. Roots are growing throughout the container.

■ The size of the fruit tree suits your yard. A range of sizes, from standard to semi-dwarf and dwarf, permit planting in even the smallest yards. If you use training methods, you can grow several varieties of fruit and still have space for vegetables, herbs, and flowers.

### Bare-root plants

Some fruit trees and shrubs, grapevines, brambles, asparagus, strawberries, and others are sold as bare-root plants. Bare-root plants are less expensive than container-grown plants and are available from garden centers and mail-order companies. Bare-root plants are sold in a dormant state without a mass of soil and with no leaves or flowers. A healthy bare-root plant may establish a root system faster than container plants.

## WHAT TO AVOID

Sometimes plants in greenhouses and nurseries appear healthy at first glance but have problems that are revealed upon closer scrutiny. Look carefully at the crown, bark, leaf undersides, and roots (gently remove plants from containers to check roots). Watch out for the following:

■ Off-color or undersize foliage indicates the plant grew under stressful conditions, such as lack of water or nutrients, or root damage.

■ Dead or dying twigs at the ends of branches indicate poor growing conditions, root injury, or even insect or disease problems.

■ Plants that are wilted, have weeds growing around the main stem, or are waterlogged indicate poor care.

■ Dead (brown), overgrown, or circling roots indicate a plant that has been in a container too long. Roots that grow around the crown of the tree can girdle and kill the plant.

■ Plants with obvious signs or symptoms of pests or diseases indicate poor care.

■ Vegetable transplants without blooms are more desirable than blooming ones. Plants that bloom prematurely may be stressed and fail to perform as well in the garden.

**Removing blooms on vegetable plants when transplanting encourages root growth.**

## PLANTING 1-2-3

Vegetables and herbs grow easily from seed. Follow the planting instructions on the back of the seed packet, whether you start seeds indoors to get a jump on the growing season or plant directly in the ground later in the season when soil conditions allow.

If you need to hold young seedlings or other plants that are ready to go into the ground because you don't have time to plant them or the site is not yet prepared, keep the roots moist and cool. Gradually introduce seedlings or plants grown indoors or in a greenhouse to outdoor life. Set them in a protected place, such as under a shrub in the yard, for a few days until they acclimate to the current conditions. Store unused seeds in a

**Plant bush varieties in hilled-up soil, 5 to 7 seeds per hill.**

cool, dry place. Many seeds, such as lettuce, beans, and basil, remain viable for several years or more if stored appropriately. See page 28 for more seed-starting details.

Before planting seeds or seedlings, loosen soil to a depth of 12 inches and amend with organic matter. Begin transplanting by digging a hole suited to the plant. Make a planting hole twice the width of the root ball. The roots at the top of the root ball should be level with the soil surface.

Second, gently tap plants out of their containers. Use your fingers to gently tease apart the roots. If the plants are tightly pot-bound, use a knife or trowel to cut into the root mass and loosen the roots. Spread the roots into the planting hole.

Third, nestle the plant into the hole and scoop amended soil around the root mass, filling the hole. Press the soil around the plant to ensure good contact between roots and soil. Water thoroughly to settle the soil and moisten the root zone. Water new plantings every few days until they're established.

## PLANTING FRUITING TREES AND SHRUBS

The graft or bud union should be planted 2 to 3 inches above the soil line. If the graft union is buried under the soil, the cultivar that was grafted on top will root, and the benefits of the rootstock will be lost. The bud union shows later as a bulge just above the ground line. Some nurseries place the bud of the fruiting variety high on the rootstock, 6 or 8 inches above the roots. Identify where on the tree the union is so that you position it properly when planting.

Be careful not to bury the bud union in soil or mulch at any time during the life of the tree. Check the bud union frequently for signs of rooting and keep mulches a few inches away from it. Another reason to keep mulch from the base of fruit trees is that mice or voles may use the mulch as cover when chewing on the bark of the tree.

## INTERPLANTING

As an efficient planting method, interplanting crops saves space, looks good, and sometimes aids growth. To interplant, imagine what will be going out of season when something else is coming in and consider which plants use different zones of space. For instance you'll harvest lettuce long before the first tomato is ready, but while it grows, lettuce thrives in the shade cast by tomato foliage and controls weeds under the taller plants. As a garden design technique, interplant vegetables, herbs, and flowers, instead of relegating each group to its own separate area. Diverse plantings offer textural interest in the garden as well as more variety in the harvest basket.

Sow the seeds of radishes in between carrots. Although both are early-season crops, the radishes will be ready for harvest first, leaving room for the carrots to develop fully without the need for thinning.

## MATCH CROPS TO SEASONS

Vegetables are usually divided into two categories: warm- and cool-season crops. No matter where you live, you should be able to grow both kinds. The trick is timely planting and succession gardening, both of which allow you to plant cool-season crops early in the year, follow them with warm-season crops during summer, and then replant cool-season crops for fall and winter harvest.

If you live in a northern climate, you don't have to limit your growing season to the months between the last and first frosts. Enjoy year-round harvests by planning ahead.

Some crops benefit from cold weather; their flavor improves after a few fall frosts. Leeks, garlic, parsley, cilantro, carrots, parsnips, parsley, rutabagas, beets, and turnips can be left in the ground under mulch all winter in raised beds or in climates where the ground temperature stays above 30°F. As long as hardy vegetables are protected from wind and cold, harvesting continues.

Salad greens are the most reliable winter producers. Sow arugula, chard, claytonia, mâche, mizuna, sorrel, and spinach in late summer through fall for harvest through the winter. Endive, escarole, sugarloaf chicory, and radicchio also thrive in cold weather; even when their outer leaves are mushy from ice, the tender hearts are still delectable. Kale requires frost to develop its best flavor and easily remains green throughout the winter in a cold frame. To determine when to sow seed for winter-harvest crops, follow the timing instructions on seed packets.

Tomatoes, peppers, corn, and other warm-season vegetables don't germinate or perform well in cool weather.

If they summer outdoors, move lemon and other tender fruit trees indoors for the winter, unless you live in a frost-free area.

## CROP ROTATION

Closely related vegetables tend to attract the same pests and diseases and consume the same nutrients from the soil. To avoid problems, move related plants (tomato, eggplant, pepper, and potato, for instance) to different locations each year. Wait three or four years before returning vegetable relatives to the same spot.

## PLANTING IN RAISED BEDS

Raised beds help plants overcome poor soil and improve growing conditions in small, defined areas. Raised beds offer other benefits as well. Drainage and aeration are improved in raised beds. Raised beds dry out and warm up earlier, so you

**Raised beds with a wide frame provide a place to sit or kneel while tending and harvesting your crops.**

can plant sooner. Weeding is less of a chore than garden beds next to lawn because the raised plot is not open to competition from weeds.

Raised beds are larger in size than containers and sit on the ground, although not necessarily on soil. They are easy to construct, fill, and disassemble if necessary. Raised beds

**Cedar planks painted in cheery colors add to the attractiveness of these raised-bed vegetable gardens.**

are typically enclosed by stones, concrete blocks, bricks, pressure-treated (nontoxic) timbers, or recycled plastic boards. Create a bed without any physical border, if you prefer, by piling soil into a berm.

Design raised beds to fit any size or type of outdoor space. Choose a sunny location and leave enough room in your plan for paths around the bed (large enough to accommodate a garden cart). You'll want to be able to access the bed from any side. Raise your bed 6 to 12 inches above ground level. Fill it with a mix of compost, topsoil, composted manure, and packaged soil, such as Miracle-Gro Enriched Garden Soil. Amend the soil annually.

## PLANTING IN CONTAINERS

Many vegetable plants are well suited for containers, including small carrots, bush tomatoes, peppers, bush beans, herbs, salad greens, and bush cucumbers. Dwarf citrus, fig, or kumquat trees can be grown in containers indoors in winter and moved outside during the summer. Even strawberries can thrive in pots outside the back door.

Choose roomy containers, such as tubs, buckets, lined and half barrels. They retain more soil moisture than smaller ones. Pots at least 10 inches in diameter can hold herbs, green onions, lettuces, and other small crops. Containers holding 5 to 15 gallons or more work best for larger plants and small trees. Grow three pepper plants in a half barrel, or one tomato plant with a few basil plants.

Make sure all containers have drainage holes in the bottom. Cover the holes with fine-mesh screen. Use a high-quality potting soil labeled for food crops, such as Miracle-Gro Enriched Potting Mix, and stir in some well-rotted compost. Position plants' root balls on enough potting mixture so their crowns are slightly below the rim of the container. Fill in around the plants with more potting mix to about an inch below the pot rim. Water thoroughly. For nursery-grown fruits, remove the commercial container and loosen the roots with your fingers or a garden fork. Use a clean knife or scissors to cut away any long roots that have circled the pot. Set the plant in your own container at the same depth as it was in the nursery pot, fill with potting mix to about an inch below the rim, and water thoroughly.

Soil dries out more quickly in containers than in the garden. Water deeply and frequently; water every day in hot weather and whenever the soil just beneath the surface feels dry. Feed twice as often with half as much plant food as you would use for inground plants because container plants are limited to whatever nutrients are in the pots and some may wash out with watering. Potted plants are not as cold tolerant as those in the ground, so protect them or move them indoors when temperatures dip below 40°F.

**Marjoram, mint, and other trailing herbs make attractive hanging gardens.**

# Chapter 4

# POST-PLANTING CARE

**Watering, feeding, mulching, and protecting plants from wildlife are some of the tasks that lie ahead. Taking care of plants in the garden gives you a sense of accomplishment.**

## ENJOY GARDENING MORE

Let your garden do more for you. Before life gets hectic as crops mature, weeds flourish, and insects become more prevalent, employ gardening techniques that will save you time, energy, and resources throughout the rest of the growing season. There are many ways to make less work in the garden, leaving you more time to enjoy it.

When it comes to watering, feeding, and weeding plants, you may have favorite ways to get the job done, but there might be easier ones. Whether an automated inground watering system takes care of watering for you or simpler soaker hoses deliver water to the soil around plant roots, both techniques prove efficient. Neither require you to stand at one end of a hose.

Similarly you'll find continuous-feed foods, all kinds of mulches, and protective devices that make gardening less complicated and more enjoyable. Choose improved varieties that have better fruiting characteristics, disease resistance, and tolerance of special soil and climate conditions. These are some of the secrets to successful gardening.

Of course your success will also be determined by the following: your site; the variety selection appropriate to your climate; the susceptibility of your crops to frost injury; your soil type; your ability to manage diseases, pests, and animal pressures; good cultural practices; and your ability to react and make decisions at the appropriate time. If you learn about your growing conditions, choose varieties that fit them, start small, and give your plants proper attention and care, you're bound to succeed.

# WATERING NEW PLANTS

Supplying water to developing root systems is the single most important thing you can do for new plants. Vegetables, herbs, and flowering annuals have relatively shallow root systems, as do many herbaceous perennials, woody shrubs, and small fruits. Natural rainfall alone will probably not give your new plants adequate water at the right time. New plants require frequent watering to promote root growth. Here are some guidelines to follow when determining when and how much to water.

**Drip irrigation is an efficient method for watering the root zone of perennials.**

■ Water all plants after planting. The amount will depend on the type of soil, the size of the planting area, and the weather conditions at planting time.
■ Water plants growing in sandy soils more frequently. Soils high in clay absorb, release, and drain water slowly. Adding lots of organic matter to soils helps them hold more water for plant growth and drain away excess water.
■ Water before you notice wilting foliage. New plants may require watering two to three times per week in spring if rainfall is lacking.
■ Water plants deeply and thoroughly. Dig down 4 to 6 inches with a screwdriver or finger to test for moisture.
■ Water in the morning if possible. Avoid wetting foliage if watering late in the day. Plants need time to dry off before nightfall to avoid disease.
■ Water spring-planted shrubs and trees throughout the growing season and into the fall. Roots actively grow in fall even though leaf growth has ceased.
■ Once garden and landscape plants are established, water them deeply and less frequently to encourage a more extensive root system and improved plant growth.
■ Avoid applying excessive water where soil drainage is inadequate. Roots die off when the soil's pore spaces are filled with water instead of air for more than 24 hours.

## WATER WISELY

Water is a necessity for a productive garden. For best yields, vegetables need enough water to keep the soil around their roots moist, not drenched. Most vegetable plants require roughly 1 inch of water per week (in arid regions, 2 inches). Larger plants, such as corn and squash, typically need more water than smaller ones, such as salad greens.

Most gardens require supplemental water, especially during hot, dry weather. Soil type partially determines how much additional water is needed. Sandy soils or soils low in organic matter require more frequent irrigation than soils high in clay or organic matter. Heavy clay soils, on the

other hand, can retain too much water. Mulch decreases irrigation needs by reducing evaporation from the soil surface.

When watering, saturate soil to a depth of about 6 inches, then allow it to dry out partially before irrigating again. A thorough weekly watering encourages plants to sink roots deeply into soil, while frequent superficial watering keeps roots close to the soil surface. Shallow-rooted plants succumb to heat and drought more easily than plants with deep roots.

If possible, irrigate early in the morning. Applying water to your garden in the late afternoon or early evening may leave excess moisture on and around your plants, which can promote disease and pest problems.

Garden sprinklers supply water at highly variable rates. You may have to run the sprinkler for several hours to soak soil to 6 inches deep, or cycle-water to avoid runoff.

Drip irrigation consists of perforated hoses capped at one end. Place these hoses directly on the ground beside plants to provide a slow (you have to run them for hours), steady supply of water directly to soil around roots. Drip irrigation systems cost more than hose-end sprinklers but they save as much as 60 percent of the water that would be used by a sprinkler.

## WATERING FRUIT TREES

**Shape a water-holding basin at the base of a newly planted fruit tree and keep the young plant well-watered during its first couple of seasons.**

Standard fruit trees need a lot of water. If this isn't supplied by rain, deep irrigation is necessary. Dwarf trees may not need as much water, but they require a constant supply. At planting time, water each layer of soil in the planting hole. Finish by soaking the soil around the newly planted tree.

Do not water again before new growth begins. The roots are not growing actively at this time, and soggy soil will invite root rot. When new growth begins, let the top inch of soil dry and then soak the plant completely. Be sure to water at the top of the planting mound. Your best bet is to water very thoroughly but less often.

Plants that are actively growing generally need 1 inch of water once a week, or about 2 gallons of water per square foot of root spread. (The roots generally spread out somewhat farther than the top canopy of the tree.) A newly planted tree would have a root spread of up to 2 square feet and, therefore, would need 2 to 4 gallons of water a week. Make adjustments for rainfall and soil type. Heavy rainfalls leach nutrients from soil, while clay soils hold nutrients better than sandy soils.

# FEEDING

## PLANT NUTRIENTS

Plants need certain nutrients to grow and thrive. They absorb most nutrients from the soil through their roots, but plants also take them up through leaves and stems. The three primary nutrients plants require are nitrogen, phosphorous, and potassium.

Plants use nitrogen to develop stocky stems and lush leaves. Nitrogen keeps plants green and flourishing. Leafy vegetables, such as cabbage and spinach, are called heavy feeders and need lots of nitrogen. Tomatoes, peppers, and other plants that produce flowers and fruit, if given too much, may yield huge plants with few flowers and fruit.

Root development, overall plant growth, and fruiting hinge on phosphorous.

Plants require potassium for vigor and strength. It encourages early root development, increases resistance to certain diseases, and helps plants tolerate heat and drought.

Plants also need some micronutrients, such as boron and iron, in tiny amounts. But micronutrient deficiencies are rare in vegetable gardens because most soils contain sufficient amounts in available forms.

## TYPES OF PLANT FOODS

There is a wide range of plant food products available to the home gardener. Products sold as plant foods are regulated by state departments of agriculture and must contain the advertised amounts of nutrients. Most plant foods are balanced; they supply nitrogen, phosphorous, and potassium (the element symbols are N-P-K, respectively). These nutrients are represented by the three numbers on the product label, and are always listed in the order of N-P-K. The numbers indicate the percentage by weight of each nutrient. For example, a 50 pound bag of a 5-10-10 plant food contains 2.5 pounds of nitrogen, 5 pounds of phosphorous, and 5 pounds of potassium. The other 37.5 pounds is a carrier or filler usually made from clay (similar to cat litter).

Plant foods come in a variety of forms—granules, powder, liquid, coated, and pelletized. Granular plant foods are easy to apply and popular with home gardeners.

## ORGANIC PLANT FOODS

Organic plant foods differ from manufactured plant foods in their chemical makeup, nutrient content, release rate of nutrients, and affect on soil structure and biology. However, the nutrient elements released from both types of plant foods and taken up by plant roots are identical. A nitrate molecule (form of nitrogen) from an application of compost is identical to a nitrate molecule from a container of 24-8-16 plant food.

Commercial organic or natural plant foods are made from pelletized fish meal, composted manure, or mixtures of pulverized seed meal. Liquid forms, such as fish emulsion, are mixed with water and poured onto soil. Because nutrients are less concentrated they are less likely to burn plants. Still, don't overapply them, and follow the directions on the product labels.

Over the long term, organic plant foods help build soil and provide a splendid source of nutrients for vegetables. But if a crop shows signs of nutrient deficiency, few organic plant foods provide a quick fix.

**The first number on a bag of plant food refers to the percentage of nitrogen, the second to phosphorus, and the third to potassium.**

## APPLYING PLANT FOOD

The method of plant food application to use depends on the product you select and the type of growing situation plants are in. Use a hose-end feeder or watering can for instant feeding. Spread continuous feeding granules on the soil surface. For containers use a soil that contains nutrients to get plants going, then begin feeding with an instant feeding plant food every two weeks, or a continuous feeding plant food according to label directions. For individual plants sprinkle plant food around the plant according to label directions. For beds broadcast plant food throughout the bed prior to planting according to label directions.

Side-dressing means applying plant food alongside plants at critical times after planting, when additional nutrients are needed. An example is when the first tomato fruits develop.

Continuous-feed plant foods have become increasingly popular with gardeners. By selecting plant foods with a continuous release over two, three, or four months, you can match the feeding you provide your plants with the length of your growing season. Once-per-season feeding is a convenient way to save time yet provide the nutrients plants need.

You can also apply foliar feed by spraying plant leaves with liquid and water-soluble plant foods, or pour the solutions over the roots. Make foliar applications in early morning, early evening, or on a cloudy day. Water evaporates more slowly at these times, so the crop absorbs more nutrients.

## FEEDING FRUITING PLANTS

Like vegetables and herbs, fruits primarily need nitrogen, phosphorous, potassium, and small quantities of other trace elements. Nitrogen is the element most often in short supply, while phosphorous, potassium, and minor nutrients may be available naturally and should be added only when based on a soil test.

Check plants for signs of nutrient deficiency, such as poor fruiting and pale leaf color or shoot growth. Add supplemental food as needed, following product instructions.

Compost and composted manure improve soil texture as well as add nutrients, but they're lower in nitrogen than commercial plant foods. Composted manure and compost may also contain salts, which can be deleterious in dry climates. The full effect of composts and manures on the soil may require two to four years.

**Blueberries require an acidic soil. Take a soil test to determine how much sulfur is necessary to lower pH and which other nutrients may be needed.**

**Most small fruits, such as raspberries (shown), strawberries, and blackberries, grow well with the addition of composted manure every other year.**

## WATERING & FEEDING PLANTS IN CONTAINERS

Container plants have smaller root systems and less room to grow than garden plants, so they require frequent watering and fertilization. Plants grown in full sun often need daily watering in hot summer months. Exposed, windy locations and reflected heat from buildings and hard surfaces increase the need for frequent watering. Soluble plant nutrients quickly leach out of containers and must be replaced.

■ Buy or make self-watering containers that have a reservoir of water at the bottom that plant roots can grow into. Some containers have a capillary mat that wicks water up into the root zone. The drainage holes are on the side of the container, not the bottom. You can leave plants in these containers for a few days without watering.

■ Plastic containers hold water better than porous ones, such as wood or terra-cotta.

■ Use a water breaker on the end of your hose to deliver a soft, steady stream of water that won't damage or dislodge plants and soil mix.

■ Build a simple drip irrigation system for your containers to reduce water use and improve efficiency.

■ Water containers until you see or hear water draining out the bottom.

■ Group container plantings together to reduce the heat gain around plants, increase humidity levels, and make watering more efficient.

■ Use a special soil mix specifically designed for container use. An example is Miracle-Gro Moisture Control Potting Mix. This soil is enriched with plant food and helps protect against overwatering and underwatering.

### Feeding fruit plants in containers

If you use a purely synthetic mix, you must be careful about feeding. The added nutrients often wash right through the soil when you water, so you'll have to feed more often.

One good feeding method is to give each plant about half the recommended quantity of complete fertilizer every two or three weeks. If the label recommends 1 tablespoon per gallon of water each month, use ½ tablespoon per gallon instead and feed every two weeks. A liquid fertilizer is easier to measure in exact proportions and is also less likely to burn plant roots.

Another method is using continuous-feed fertilizers. These pellets release fertilizer with each watering as the plant needs it.

Feed from the beginning of the growing season until the end of summer if the plant is to receive winter protection. Stop about mid-July if the plant will stay outdoors through winter. In both cases, ceasing to fertilize gives any new growth ample time to harden off.

### Watering fruits in containers

If you check the soil occasionally by digging down an inch or two, you'll soon learn when to water. Water whenever the soil just under the surface begins to dry. The top inch may stay moist for a week in fairly cool weather, but in hot, windy weather you'll need to water more often. Water enough each time so a good amount drains from the bottom of the container. Don't count on rain to do all of your watering. The foliage of plants in containers can act as an umbrella, shedding most of the rainfall.

**Strawberries adapt well to container culture, bearing heavy crops of sweet, tasty fruit.**

# WEEDING

**W**eeds compete with vegetables for water, sun, and soil nutrients. If you ignore the weeds, they will reduce your harvest. Attack weeds before they grow large. Don't let them form seed heads and establish a foothold. Use one or a combination of these methods to defeat weeds in your garden.

■ **Mulching:** For most weeds, mulching provides easy, long-term control. Mulch smothers weed seeds, while making them easier to pull if they do germinate and grow.

■ **Tilling:** Rototill to control weeds along garden rows and walkways, but don't till close to vegetables.

■ **Mowing:** Mow around the garden before weeds form seed heads to help keep weeds in check.

■ **Hoeing:** In unmulched soil, hoeing kills weeds and loosens any crust that forms on soil. Crust can prevent water from entering soil. Work only the top inch of soil, hoeing lightly every few days.

■ **Hand weeding:** You can remove weeds with a dandelion fork or trowel. Insert the tool under the roots of the plant and lift up.

Weeds are easier to remove from moist earth, so hand weed after rain or watering. Pull the weed out by the roots; breaking it off at the soil surface is ineffective.

After hoeing or pulling, leave annual weeds to wither and die and serve as a mulch for the garden. Or till them into soil to add organic matter, letting them dry out on the ground for a day beforehand. Do not till under or mulch with weeds that are setting seed.

Compost weeds if your pile heats sufficiently to kill seeds and roots (140°F)—most piles do not get this hot. When in doubt, toss weeds in the trash.

■ **Solarization:** For new planting areas, solarize or cook weed seeds, roots, and pests, such as nematodes. Lay clear plastic on freshly tilled soil. Shovel soil over plastic edges to anchor and seal it; leave it for six weeks. The temperature of soil 10 inches deep should rise at least 10°F, so solarization is effective only in sunny areas.

■ **Herbicides:** Most herbicides are formulated to kill specific types of plants. Apply them with care to avoid damaging your crop or the environment. Always follow label directions.

## TOOLS FOR WEEDING

Weeding is easier when you invest in quality tools. Start with a pair of cotton, latex, or washable leather gloves to protect your hands.

Fishtail weeders, also called dandelion forks, help dig weeds easily. Slip the tool tip under the roots of the weed, then lift up.

Use a hand cultivator to pry up clumps of grass. Slip the prongs under the clump and pull back on the handle like a lever.

Before buying a hoe, try out different models to see which feels most comfortable. Hoes come in various weights and handle lengths, so pick one to match your size and strength.

To keep tools in shape, pour about a quart of used motor oil into a 5-gallon bucket of sand. After removing soil from tools, shove them deeply into the bucket several times, then store. The oil coating prevents rust.

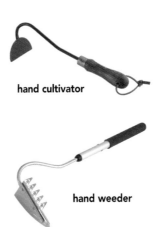

**hand cultivator**

**hand weeder**

**Hoeing weeds in a vegetable bed is easiest when the hoe is sharp.**

## CARING FOR HERBS

Most herbs are adaptable plants and thrive in a range of moisture conditions. They will appreciate occasional deep watering, just like vegetables. Weeding is important, but make sure you're familiar with the appearance of your herbs, especially perennial species, so you remove only weeds and not herbs, too. Mulch enables soil to retain moisture and can also help lower the number of weeds.

Unlike many vegetables, herbs receiving high levels of nutrients produce inferior growth with little flavor or fragrance. For that reason, keep your garden soil in the average-to-fertile range. Organic mulch often provides enough nutrients for herbs.

**Compact varieties of herbs and vegetables grow well in pots and make a handsome display on a patio, deck, or other small space.**

# MULCHING

## THE VIRTUES OF MULCH

**Cedar mulch breaks down more slowly than hardwood mulches.**

**An attractive pine straw mulch works well in annual and perennial flower beds.**

**Hardwood bark mulches decompose slower than other organic mulches.**

**Keep mulch several inches away from plant stems so water can reach roots. Doing so also prevents rot.**

Mulch is an invaluable tool for gardeners. It takes little initial effort to apply, but the benefits are very worthwhile.

Mulch can decrease your workload throughout the growing season and can increase yields by as much as 50 percent. Mulch helps control weeds, reduces erosion, retains moisture in the soil, moderates soil temperature, and by reducing watering, reduces the loss of soil nutrients. Some mulches add organic matter and nutrients to your soil.

A mulch is any material applied around your crop on top of the soil. Organic mulches, such as sawdust, leaves, bark chips, partially rotted hay or straw, or grass clippings will break down during the growing season. They can then be tilled into the soil at the end of the year. (Never apply fresh manure as a mulch because it can burn plants.)

Organic mulch layers should be about 3 to 6 inches deep, depending on the bulk of the mulch. Because they settle and decompose as the season progresses, put down a larger amount initially. As the mulches degrade, add more material to maintain the ideal 3- to 6-inch depth.

Inorganic mulches, such as plastic sheeting (1.5 to 2 mils thick) or fabric weed barrier, cannot be incorporated into the soil at the end of the season. However, many inorganic materials can be reused for several years.

Light-color plastic and aluminum-coated mulches control weeds and help keep soil cool in the heat of the summer because they reflect sunlight. Clear plastic will not control weeds because the sun can shine through it. But it helps retain moisture and nutrients in the soil. Black plastic mulch controls weeds and accelerates your planting season by absorbing sunlight and heating the soil, which may allow you to plant earlier in the spring. However, as summer progresses, dark plastic mulches can overheat the soil. Remedy this problem as temperatures rise by placing a light-color organic mulch on top of the plastic or by removing it altogether.

## OTHER TYPES OF MULCH

**Newspaper:** All pages, except glossy paper, can be used. Most newspaper inks are soy based and contain

no dangerous heavy metals. Overlap the newspaper sections, and cover them with straw or grass clippings.

**Straw, grass clippings, shredded leaves:** These organic mulches are used in vegetable beds. They decay in one season and may be tilled under at the end of the season.

**Shredded bark or woodchip mulches:** These may be used around fruit trees and shrubs; cedar and cypress last the longest. You can freshen these mulches with a new thin layer each year.

**Woven landscape fabrics:** Cut holes into the fabric, then plant fruit trees or non-suckering fruiting shrubs through them. Cover with an organic or natural mulch.

## PLAYING IT COOL

Mulch can be the key to survival for many garden plants. During the growing season, mulch around plants to help conserve moisture in the soil and discourage weeds from growing. Mulch keeps the soil cool so that temperature spikes won't dry out tender roots, and it reduces the amount of moisture lost to evaporation through the soil surface.

## TIMING AND QUANTITY

Timing and quantity are important factors when applying mulch. In autumn or winter wait until air temperatures have been below 32°F for 2 weeks and plants are completely dormant before covering them with 2–4 inches of mulch. Remove the mulch in early spring so that the sun can warm the soil around the plants. When temperatures climb in summer, replace the mulch around the plants to keep the soil cool and moist.

Most garden plants benefit from mulch during the growing season. Even vegetables and herbs growing in partly shaded conditions need protection from soil moisture evaporation caused by wind. As in winter, just a couple of inches of mulch are enough. Too much mulch can provide a safe haven for pests to hide and encourage disease development by trapping too much moisture around plants.

# PROTECTING PLANTS

Freezing temperatures and hungry critters threaten the well-being of plants and prospective harvests. Plants that are marginally hardy in your area are more prone to winter injury caused by extended freezing temperatures, alternating freezes and thaws, and browsing animals.

Protect plants from winter damage and extend the gardening season by using cold frames, row covers, or cloches. These devices also enable you to get a jump on the growing season in early spring before the weather warms.

## SEASON-STRETCHING DEVICES

Many gardeners use special devices to grow plants outside before the weather warms up, including cloches, cold frames, and plastic tunnels. All of these devices protect crops from cold weather and cold soils early in the season.

### Cloches

Cloches fit over plants to form mini-greenhouses. Gallon-size plastic milk jugs work as well as commercial glass or plastic cloches. To make a plastic milk jug cloche, remove the jug's bottom and cut a V-shaped slit in the top of the handle. Place this modified jug over each plant and push a stick through the handle and into the ground deep enough to anchor the jug in the soil. Leave the caps off the jug unless frost is expected. Remove the plastic cloche on warm, sunny days (50°F to 60°F) to prevent excessive heat buildup inside the jug; replace it at night if a cold snap is expected.

### Cold frames

Use a cold frame with a translucent top in or near the garden to shelter young plants, letting the sun in and keeping the wind out. A cold frame allows you to control temperatures to an extent, by ventilating it during warm, sunny days, and closing it at night to protect plants frost. Cold frames are also useful for raising transplants under more-intense light conditions than are ordinarily available indoors. Also use a cold frame to harden off transplants and prepare them for garden life.

Choose a commercially available cold frame or build one using lumber for the sides and corrugated fiberglass for the top. Recycled building materials, such as cement blocks and old windows, make fine, low-cost cold frames. Place blocks (or straw bales) around your crop and set windows on top.

### Tunnels

Plastic tunnels work much like cold frames. Cut support hoops of 10-gauge wire or ½-inch bendable pipe into pieces long enough to arch 14 to 18 inches over beds or rows. Six-foot-long supports fit perfectly over 3-foot-wide beds. Push the hoops 2 inches into the ground on each side of the row. Space them 2 feet apart.

Cover the supports with clear plastic sheeting (at least 2 mils thick) and secure the edges to the ground using

**Slip a length of plastic drainage pipe around the trunk of a young fruit tree to protect it from gnawing rabbits and rodents.**

**Secure rabbit fencing underground to prevent tunneling critters from invading the garden.**

bricks, cement blocks, or landscape timbers. Remove the tunnels when daytime temperatures consistently reach 60°F to 70°F. Remember to water plants growing under cold frames and tunnels regularly so they don't dry out.

## Row covers

Although not as warm as greenhouses, row covers protect vegetables in cool weather, keeping them 2°F to 3°F warmer than the surrounding air. It's a small difference, but often enough to save crops from a late-spring frost.

## PROTECTING PLANTS FROM WILDLIFE

Various animals, from deer to rabbits, squirrels, and chipmunks, may feed on and damage plants. The first step in preventing critters from injuring or destroying your plants is to identify the culprit. Then evaluate how much damage is being done. Do a little research to understand more about the animal's life cycle and habits before you attempt to circumvent them. Consult your county extension service for more suggestions about specific pests in your region.

Spray liquid fencing on and around plants to help repel deer, rabbits, and other animals.

Plastic netting draped over grapevines, berry bushes, or small fruit trees protects ripening fruit from hungry birds.

Protect plants from frost by draping them with a fabric row cover.

Use a hefty rock to hold a lightweight fabric cover in place.

A small cold frame provides a place to nurture plants, such as arugula or other greens.

# PRUNING & TRAINING

**The goal of pruning and training is to open up the plant to light and air, encouraging healthy growth and larger fruits. Pruning is one of the most effective ways to improve plants' performance and keep them in excellent condition.**

## BENEFITS OF PRUNING

Pruning removes part of a plant to benefit the whole. Cutting away any part directly affects the plant's growth. Depending on how and when it is done, use pruning to achieve the following results:

■ Shape a young tree.
■ Produce new growth where desired.
■ Help control and direct overall growth.
■ Correct or repair damage.
■ Help control and prevent insects and diseases.
■ Rejuvenate or reshape an older plant.
■ Bring about earlier blooming and fruiting.
■ Increase the production, size, and quality of fruit.

If you're confused about where to begin, remember that you can't hurt a plant by cutting out dead, diseased, or damaged wood or branches that cross and rub together.

### PRUNING TOOLS

The pruning tool shed should contain hand pruners, a long-handled pruning saw, a folding pruning saw, and loppers. The best-quality pruning tools cost more than others, but they are worth it. They will last longer than inexpensive tools and do a better job in the long run.

Always use sharp tools. Dull blades damage stems and make plants susceptible to disease. Keep a sharpening device handy. Fill a spray bottle with rubbing alcohol and use it to disinfect pruning tools between uses to help prevent the spread of plant diseases. Clean tools before putting them away. Sap, disinfectant, moisture, and plant debris can cause rust to form on tools. Wash tools with a soapy water solution, then rinse and dry them thoroughly.

## PRUNING FRUIT TREES

Pruning and training your fruit trees keeps them healthy and productive for many years. By creating a strong structure to support the weight of the crops and keeping all parts of the trees open to sunlight, you are helping to prevent damage from wind, pests, and diseases. You will also promote the development of high yields, and make it easier to harvest the fruit when the time comes.

Apples, pears, cherries, and plums produce their best fruit on 2- to 3-year-old wood. Almonds and apricots add new fruiting spurs each year, while their oldest spurs should be removed annually. Peaches and nectarines bear their fruit on last year's growth. Pruning each year encourages productive fruiting wood. Unpruned trees quickly lose their productivity and become more susceptible to health problems.

## PRUNING METHODS

Prune mature trees in late winter to early spring in cold-winter climates and when trees are dormant in warm-winter climates (between leaf fall and the start of new bud swell). There are two basic types of pruning cuts: thinning and heading.

**Thinning cuts** remove wood in order to stop growth. These cuts are made at the base of a branch or sucker, leaving no buds to sprout. Use loppers and a long-handled pruning saw to remove any dead or damaged wood.

Make all cuts at an angle and close to nodes where new shoots will grow. The stubs left at the cuts should be no more than ¼ inch long to prevent decay and a possible point of entry for disease.

Next remove any branches that grow toward the trunk or point downward toward the soil. Then remove any branches that cross over one another. To further reduce the

Make thinning cuts to remove buds and stop excess growth.

Cut at an angle, leaving no more than a ¼ inch stub to prevent decay.

Make heading cuts to stimulate new branches. Remove the terminal buds of young saplings to encourage growth.

Cut to buds on the outside of branches so that new branches grow away from the tree's interior.

density of the tree canopy, use hand pruners to snip thin twigs. Remove any water sprouts and suckers.

**Heading cuts** shorten branches to stimulate new growth. Fruit trees vary in the amount and type of heading cuts needed. Young trees—sometimes whips with no branches—are often cut back at the time of planting to remove the terminal bud. The bud at the end of any branch is a terminal bud. Cutting off a terminal bud stimulates the growth of branches to either side. Lateral buds are those spaced along the length of a branch, sometimes in clusters or pairs. Cutting off a branch just above a lateral bud will direct new growth in the direction the bud is pointing. Make pruning cuts to buds on the outside of branches so that new growth will be directed away from the center of the tree.

# TRAINING METHODS

Fruit trees should be trained to one of three forms—vase or open, central leader, or modified central leader—beginning when they are planted. Training creates a structure appropriate for optimum health and productivity. Left untrained, fruit trees become overgrown with weak, twiggy branches and small, sometimes diseased fruit.

The vase or open-training method shapes the tree to a short trunk about 3 feet tall from which rise three or four main limbs, each of which has secondary branches. This method is commonly used for peach and nectarine trees as well as some apples, pears, and cherries.

Central-leader training shapes the tree into one straight trunk with whorls of branches around it spaced 6 to 10 inches apart vertically. This creates a pyramid- or Christmas-tree shape that is strong but difficult to maintain or harvest if the tree is tall. Dwarf apple trees are often trained to this shape.

A tree trained to a modified central leader combines the strength of a central trunk with the open habit of a vase-shape tree. The main trunk is allowed to grow as a central leader but the top of the tree is cut back each year to force growth of lower branches. This method is used for some apple and pear trees.

Training individual branches while trees are young helps to avoid breakage and disease later on. Ideally, branches should be balanced around the trunk, at angles of 45 to 60 degrees. Branches that grow parallel to the ground or slightly upward will be the strongest and most fruitful. If a young branch is in a desirable scaffold position but has a narrower angle, use a wedge of wood between it and the trunk to spread the angle as the branch grows, or tie a bag of sand to the outside end of the branch to weigh it down as it grows. Remove the wedge or weight when the branch can hold the angle on its own.

**Thinning fruit** – After mature trees begin to bear big crops, thinning of large-fruited cultivars, such as apples and peaches, is necessary to achieve maximum production of top-quality, full-size fruits. Trees naturally drop

some fruit in summer but not enough to prevent overcrowding in healthy trees. The best time to thin fruit is just after a tree's natural fruit drop, typically a few weeks after bloom. Start by removing any underdeveloped, infested, and diseased fruits from a cluster. Then remove all but one healthy fruit where there are several in a cluster. Finally, thin the remaining fruits so they are spaced 6 inches apart. If you are skeptical about the value of thinning, leave one branch unthinned and compare the size and

quality of its fruit to those on thinned branches at harvest.

Fruit trees can also be grown as hedges or espaliers, which save space but require routine training and pruning. Espalier training directs the growth of a tree flat against a wall, trellis, or other support. Dwarf apples and pears are best suited to espalier training because they bear on old wood. Peaches, nectarines, apricots, and plums are better sculpted as hedges, where old, nonfruiting wood can be removed without ruining the design.

**Cutting off the terminal bud at the end of the branch will encourage growth at the vegetative lateral buds below.**

**Prune scaffold branches as if they were young trees, heading back or removing any that overtake the leader.**

**Prune out broken or narrow-angled branches. Those that grow at a slightly upward angle are the strongest.**

**Prune out suckers and water sprouts at the base of the branches so that no buds are left to sprout.**

## PRUNING AND TRAINING FRUITING BUSHES

**Brambles** include raspberry, blackberry, and trailing dewberry. Cane growth is a two-year process. The first year, a nonfruiting vegetative cane (primocane) emerges from a root or plant crown. The second year the cane is called a floricane. A floricane flowers and produces fruit; the cane dies a short time later. To prevent crowding, which causes a lack of light and weak growth, and to reduce disease, prune canes at ground level after fruiting.

**Raspberries and blackberries** – There are many types of raspberries: summer-bearing red raspberries, summer-bearing yellow raspberries, fall-bearing red raspberries, fall-bearing yellow raspberries, summer-bearing black raspberries, and summer-bearing purple raspberries. The type of raspberry determines the way it is trained and pruned.

Summer-bearing raspberries produce a primocane the first year, followed by flowers and fruits in early summer of the second year. Fall-bearing raspberries produce flowers and fruits on the top part of the primocane in late summer of the first year, followed by flowering and fruiting on the lower part of the floricane in early summer of the second year of growth.

Raspberries and blackberries have vigorously growing primocanes. Support the canes with a trellis system, either temporary or permanent, to keep the tips from bending over and letting the fruit come in contact with the soil. Many forms of trellising are used; one of the simplest employs 8-foot-long posts set 2 feet in the ground every 15 to 20 feet along the plant row. Attach a set of heavy-gauge wires to the posts, placing one wire 3 feet above the ground and the other 2 feet higher. When the canes reach the wires, tie them loosely in place to maintain upright growth.

Remove fruited tips of fall-bearing raspberry canes after they have finished bearing.

Fall-bearing red raspberries produce a crop in late summer. To simplify pruning, cut off all shoots at ground level after the fruit is picked the first year. A simple method is to mow down the plants with a sharp-bladed lawn mower. The following growing season, new canes emerge and produce fruit at the end of summer. With this method, no pruning is necessary until fall. At that time, remove all the aboveground stems. If first-year shoots are allowed to grow for two years, a crop will be produced on the tips of canes the first year and a second crop on the lower part of the canes the second year. With this method, prune as for summer-bearing red raspberries.

Cut or head back primocanes of erect-growing blackberries to 4 or 5 feet in midsummer. Heading develops a stout cane and promotes lateral branching with more fruit the following year. Less vigorous varieties will not reach the top wire and should be headed at 3 or 4 feet. In early spring, shorten the lateral branches to about 16 inches. After the floricanes have fruited, remove them.

Thin excess raspberry shoots in spring to avoid crowding and to allow light penetration.

Prune summer-bearing red raspberries only in the second spring, removing any winter-killed cane tips while thinning dense growth. Remove old canes at ground level after fruiting. Take care to remove only the floricanes at that time and not the primocanes.

Pinch cane tips of black and purple raspberries to develop stout canes and laterals.

Prune back excessively long purple or black raspberry canes in winter.

## PRUNING & TRAINING FRUITING BUSHES AND VINES

**Grapes** – Because grapevines naturally climb, train them to an arbor or a trellis. A fence also works as long as you can easily reach the vine for pruning and picking. A simple trellis called the Kniffen system is one method of support.

Erect the Kniffen system by placing stout posts at each end of the row where the grapevines are growing. Place the end posts deep enough in the ground (3 feet) so tension on the attached wires from the weight of vines and fruit won't move the posts. Fasten two 10-gauge wires to the end posts, one at 2½ feet and the other at 5 feet above the ground. Place line posts between the end posts at 8-foot intervals as needed.

After planting, select a vigorous shoot (cane) as the main trunk. Train the cane upward until it reaches the bottom wire or support. Select two vigorous shoots at the height of the lowest wire and remove all other shoots. Loosely tie the resulting canes to the wires to maintain upright growth. In March of the second year, prune the canes back to three or four buds at the bottom wire; if a cane has reached the top wire, do the same at that location. Early in the third spring, select two of the most vigorous canes at each wire and prune them back, leaving three or four buds on each.

Remove all other canes on the plant. Spring pruning causes bleeding of sap from pruning cuts, but the bleeding results in little if any damage to the plant.

Through the third year, remove all flower buds or developing fruit clusters to keep energy directed into plant growth. Leave two main canes pointed in opposite directions on each wire in the fourth year of growth. Prune back these canes, leaving a dozen buds on each cane. Abundant fruit should be produced during the fourth growing season. Prune the plants in future years the same as in year four.

**Gooseberries and currants** – Gooseberries and red currants produce fruit on spurs of two- and three-year-old canes; black currants produce fruit on one-year-old shoots. Prune all currants and gooseberries in late winter or early spring before growth begins.

Remove canes of gooseberries and red currants four years old and older, because these canes are past fruit-bearing age. Leave 10 to 12 main canes ranging in age from one to three years. For good sunlight penetration prune so the center of the plant is left open.

## PRUNING & TRAINING HERBS

Pruning shapes herbs and helps them produce growth to harvest. Potted herbs require frequent pruning. Make cuts to shape a plant and keep the foliage mass proportionate to the pot size. The correct pruning times and methods vary from herb to herb.

■ **Spring cleanup:** In general, prune shrubby perennial herbs with woody stems, such as sage, lemon balm, artemisia, tansy, and rosemary, in the spring, removing dead branches and cutting the rest of the stems back by half. This keeps the plants bushy and well shaped.

■ **Summer shortcuts:** Trim several inches off stems in midsummer to initiate fresh, tender growth during the latter half of the growing season. Place these cuts to adjust the plant's overall shape and growth. During the growing season, harvest shoots or leaves as needed.

■ **Woody herb wisdom:** Avoid trimming woody perennial herbs, such as germander, santolina, and lavender. Their new growth develops on the woody stems that matured during the last growing season. Pruning can keep the plants from growing. If you desire a lush lavender planting, don't trim those plants the first three years of growth. It takes that much time for lavender to establish and mature. Remove only dead plant parts—well after the remainder of the plant has greened up.

■ **Prefrost pruning:** Do not prune woody perennial herbs later than eight weeks before the first frost date in fall. If these plants are pruned too late in the season, the new growth won't have enough time to harden before freezing weather arrives.

■ **Standard fare:** Standards, or tree-form herbs, feature a strong center stem and a lollipoplike top of foliage. Begin to train a potted plant by stripping the lower leaves. Rosemary, lavender, and santolina lend themselves to training as standards. Stake the plant. Trim the top growth periodically to promote a lush, rounded shape.

When flowers form on herbs, such as basil, snip them off to encourage plants to continue growing lush foliage.

# TRAINING, STAKING & TRELLISING

## ESPALIERS

An espalier is a plant pruned to grow all in one plane. Supple young branches are fastened to a fence, a wall, or wires with string or rubber bands. Leave at least 6 inches of space between the wall and the plant, allowing for air circulation and room to grow.

For a limited growing space, the espaliered fruit tree offers an artistic way to break up a bleak wall or fence as well as produce edible fruit. The one-dimensional configuration allows the fruit to receive maximum sun, resulting in good color and size.

Dwarf varieties of apples and pears are the preferred fruit trees for espalier, but plums and cherries also work. The main criteria for likely candidates: varieties that produce long, flexible shoots.

The plants must be trained from a very young age. Locate the espalier where direct sun won't shine on it in winter. This can break dormancy and cause freeze damage to the plant at night.

If wire is used to form the framework on a wall or fence, fasten eyebolts to the structure and string heavy-gauge wire between them. Loosely tie the shoots to the framework using twine, string, or strips of rubber. Check the ties for tightness every few weeks during the growing season. If the ties become too tight as the shoots grow in diameter, they can girdle and kill the shoots.

Do most structural pruning during the dormant period. During the growing season, bend shoots to follow the framework.

**Apple and pears are best suited for espaliers. Plant bare-root trees at least an arm's length apart.**

## TRELLISING

Trellising is a form of training in which a plant is fastened to a structure to give support or shape. A structure can be as simple as a wooden stake or as intricate as interwoven lattice. A plant may be trained on a trellis to conserve space, increase light penetration into the plant, display the plant and fruits in an interesting way, improve air circulation, reduce disease, ease harvesting, or give support to a weak trunk.

Tomato plants are usually trained to grow in tomato cages rather than flat against a traditional trellis. These wire mesh cages keep the foliage and fruit from coming into contact with the soil, thus avoiding rotting. Sometimes, tomato plants require heavy stakes and flexible ties to help them remain upright. Plants without support will likely fall over and break when they become heavy with fruit. Tomatoes and other plants can be trained to conform to a two-dimensional trellis that is mounted on a wall or a place where a normally bushy plant would not work.

Grapes, peas, pole beans, and other vining or climbing edibles can be trained on a fence, a wire trellis, a wall, or an arbor. When trained on an A-frame or tepee-type structure, the fruit of peas or beans can be picked from inside as well as outside the support. Some vines have tendrils that cling to a support and help the plants climb and remain upright; others require ties to keep heavy plants from falling over or being whipped by the wind. Use soft fabric or plastic ties that will not damage plants.

Newly transplanted fruit trees and vegetables, such as peppers and eggplant, benefit from staking. Plant a stake at the same time that the plant goes into the ground and loosely tether the plant to the stake with a soft tie to keep it from toppling or being damaged by strong wind.

**Encourage peas to cling to adjacent fencing and keep them growing upright.**

**Training tomatoes to vertical cordons of jute rope takes only a little time each week. The result looks tidy and bears heavily.**

# Chapter 5
# PROPAGATION

**Starting new plants from seeds, cuttings, or divisions is one of the most rewarding aspects of gardening. Multiply your plant collection at little cost and share the bounty with friends.**

## STARTING FROM SEED

**P**lanting a seed is one of the most magical acts in gardening. You plant a tiny seed, water it, and within days a green plant begins to emerge.

When the traditional spring-planting time arrives in your area, you can plant many cool-season seeds and transplants directly into the ground once soil reaches about 40°F and is fairly dry. It's dry enough to plant if you can press a handful of soil in your fist and it readily crumbles apart.

Before planting seeds of vegetables, herbs, or flowers in the garden, loosen the soil by tilling or turning it with a long-handled garden fork. Topsoil should be finely textured and free of large clods. This allows sprouts to push through the soil surface, and water and fertilizer to seep into the root zone. After tilling, shape the soil into rows or beds.

### SOWING SEEDS DIRECTLY

When direct-seeding, dig a shallow furrow in the middle of the row with a hoe or trowel. For straight rows run a plumb line from two stakes located at the end of each row as a guide. Cover small seeds such as lettuce and carrots, with a scant ¼ inch of soil; cover larger seeds such as corn and beans with an inch or more. Check the seed-packet recommendation for planting depth.

Water your garden gently as soon as seeds are planted; soil should be moist but not wet. Watch the garden daily to make sure soil stays moist until seedlings have emerged and look vigorous. Apply a thin layer of light mulch, such as straw, over seeded beds to retain moisture. Remove the mulch gently as soon as seedlings begin to emerge so they can get full sun.

## SOWING SEEDS INDOORS

Most vegetables and herbs can be started from seed. Get the growing season off to an early start by sowing seeds indoors in a soilless starting mix. Some vegetables, such as onions and tomatillos, have a long growing season and should be started early indoors. Follow seed-sowing directions on seed packets.

Containers for growing plants should have drainage holes. Cell packs are good containers for growing young plants from seed until they are ready to be set in the garden. Plastic flats or other containers in which masses of seeds can be sown and later transplanted to individual pots also work well. Recycle common household containers and reuse them for seed-starting. Clear, plastic produce boxes with hinged lids, for example, work well because they have built-in drainage holes.

Scoop seed-germinating soil mix into the container, scrape off any excess, and gently firm the soil mix.

Check the seed packet label to determine whether special germination requirements are necessary. Some seeds, such as yarrow, hollyhock, and alyssum, require light to germinate; once the seeds are sown, they are not covered with soil mix so they receive the required light. Other seeds should be covered to the recommended depth.

When planting a cell pack, use a pencil or chopstick to poke a hole in the soil mix. Place one or two seeds in the hole in each cell. When using a flat or other tray-type container, sow the seeds in rows. Mark shallow rows in the soil mix by pressing a pencil horizontally into the surface. Place the seeds in a vibrating seeder and follow label directions for use of the seeder.

As soon as seeds are planted in packs or flats, place a label on the container. Include the date the seed was sown and the plant name. Place a watertight tray under the container. Gently water the seeds and soil mix with a trigger-type spray bottle.

**Assemble necessary materials on a comfortable work area where spilled soil mix can be easily cleaned up.**

**Fill germination containers with seed-starting mix. Scrape off excess material with a trowel.**

**Use a seeding device for accurate seed placement.**

**Moisten the seeded trays with a gentle shower to prompt germination.**

## GERMINATION REQUIREMENTS

Seeds must have the correct temperature, moisture, and light in order to germinate and grow. In addition, the emerging roots and shoots must have proper growing conditions.

Most vegetable and herb seeds sprout at room temperature, but some, such as peppers and tomatoes, germinate faster in warmer soil. Germination medium placed in a sunny south- or southwest-facing window will be warm enough during the day so another heat source is usually not needed. Raise soil temperature by placing containers on a root zone heating mat. Shut off the heat at night; cool nights make seedlings stocky and robust.

Keep the germinating medium evenly moist, not wet, by adding water to the tray under the container.

Once seedlings emerge, place fluorescent grow lights 2 inches above plants and set the fixture on a timer to provide 14 to 16 hours of light per day.

## TAKING SEEDLINGS TO THE NEXT STAGE

Once seedlings have germinated and developed their first set of true leaves, you'll want to transplant them to individual compartments of cell packs or seedling pots where they can grow on until they're ready for the garden. Alternatively, thin young seedlings by snipping out all but the strongest-looking ones, leaving them room to develop.

Carefully transplant young seedlings by prying them out of the flat with a pencil or a similar tool. Hold the seedling by a leaf and delicately lower its root system into the prepared planting hole of a cell pack filled with moist potting medium. Gently firm the growing medium around the roots and water the cell pack once all the cells are planted. Feed seedlings with a water-soluble formula diluted with twice the amount of water recommended. Transplant to the garden when weather conditions suit the plants and a handful of soil is dry enough to crumble when squeezed.

**M**ultiplying herbs by cuttings, layering, or division is easy and inexpensive. It also affords an opportunity to share favorite plants with friends.

## ROOTING CUTTINGS

Propagate cuttings form new growth in spring or early fall by snipping 3- to 4-inch stems. Pinch off bottom leaves and any flowers or buds.

Dip cut ends in rooting hormone powder to help them grow and stand cuttings 1 inch deep in containers of soilless medium.

Rooting cuttings from the stems of woody herbs is a simple way to get many new plants. There are three main types of woody stem cuttings:

■ Softwood cuttings: Spring and early-summer cuttings from new growth that has not yet hardened.

■ Semihardwood cuttings: Midsummer cuttings from growth that has started to harden at the base.

■ Hardwood cuttings: Late-season cuttings made from fully hardened wood.

For all three types, cut 4- to 6-inch-long sturdy pieces of stem, making the cut just below a leaf. Next, pinch off leaves on the lower third of the stem, taking care not to tear the stem. Dust or dip the cut end in a powder or liquid rooting hormone.

With a pencil, make a hole in a pot of moistened, sterile potting soil, horticultural vermiculite, or perlite. Insert the stem up to the bottom of the leaves and firm the potting medium around it. Add more cuttings to the pot, placing them 2 inches apart.

Insert a label with the plant name and date planted. Cover the pot with a plastic dome or bag, making sure it doesn't touch the leaves. The dome holds in moisture, keeping cuttings from wilting, but it also can cook plants by retaining heat. Keep the pot out of direct sunlight and open the dome a crack to let heat escape.

Set the pot in a spot with bright indirect light. Keep the soil moist. Placing the pot on a heating mat speeds rooting. When cuttings show signs of growth, usually after four to six weeks, remove the dome. If a gentle tug on the cutting yields resistance, the stem is developing roots. How long that takes varies with herb species. At this point, pot the plant and move it outdoors to a location out of direct sunlight for a few days (or weeks) before transplanting it in the garden.

## LAYERING

Layering is a good way to propagate low-growing or creeping plants that are difficult to root from cuttings. With layering, rooting occurs while the stem is still attached to the plant. Bend a shoot to the ground. Scoop out a small hole where the shoot touches the ground, then hold the stem in place with a peg-type clothespin or a hairpin-shape wire. Mound soil over the pegged stem, gently firming it. Keep the area moist until new growth develops. Then cut the newly rooted plant from the main plant. Transplant it immediately.

## DIVISION

Divide plants such as chives in early spring or late fall. Begin by digging up the entire plant.

Divide the plant using a sharp knife or spade, cutting through the root ball. Plant the divisions.

Many perennial herbs, such as oregano and sage, send out an ever-widening circle of growth. These new plants crowd the original plant, which then declines. Dig up an overgrown clump or break it apart. Depending on the plant, an alternative is to dig small plants at the clump edges. Early spring or fall are the best times to divide perennial herbs and vegetables.

## BUDDING AND GRAFTING

Grafting kits contain grafting wax, a knife, budding strips, and budding tape.

A whip and tongue graft is one of the easiest grafts to make on young trees.

### Dwarfing Rootstocks

The easiest and most effective way to produce permanent dwarfing is by grafting fruit cultivars (shoots or buds of a desired cultivar) onto dwarfing rootstocks. This method offers many advantages. Grafting is an easy way to produce large numbers of plants in a relatively short time. It ensures true reproduction of a desired variety, which is important because seed does not always breed true. And grafted dwarf trees remain uniformly smaller and tend to bear fruit at a younger age than standard trees, sometimes as early as their second year of growth.

Plant parts may be spliced onto other plant parts for a variety of reasons, such as creating a dwarf plant, producing a hardier tree or shrub, increasing resistance to disease and insect pests, or creating a novelty form of the plant.

Splicing a standard variety of apple onto a root system that keeps the tree small produces a dwarf apple tree. As long as the plants are closely related and the cambium tissue (green tissue between bark and wood) of the parts align in the splice, the cells will grow together. Almond, apricot, European plum, and Japanese plum may be grafted onto a peach root system.

**Budding and grafting** are two types of tissue splices. Budding uses a bud from the desired variety and unites it with a compatible rootstock. Grafting unites a section of twig from the desired variety with a rootstock. Both budding and grafting require much practice to be successful. Budding and grafting should be done when the air is still, the humidity is high, and temperatures are cool to prevent drying and killing the cambium tissue.

**Chip budding** may be used on grapes, fruit trees, or woody ornamentals such as roses. Remove a chip of wood a few inches above the soil from the plant that will function as the root system. Remove a chip exactly the same size from another plant that will form the plant top. Place the bud chip in the chip void on the rootstock. Be sure the green cambium on each part lines up. Cover the cut surfaces with budding tape or budding strips of rubber to prevent tissue drying. Avoid covering the bud by carefully wrapping above and below it and leaving the bud protruding. Once the bud starts growing into a new shoot, remove the old stem above the bud to allow the new shoot to become the new plant top.

In whip-and-tongue grafting, a 3- to 4-inch-long piece of twig (scion) with one or two buds is spliced onto the root system of another plant. Make the graft in late winter on a dormant, bare-root plant using a dormant scion. Make a 2-inch sloping diagonal cut through the stem of the root system about 6 inches above the soil line. Next make a ½-inch-long vertical cut down the stem starting one-third of the way down the slope from the tip. Prepare the scion with cuts of the same shape. Force the two cut surfaces to slide together. A tonguelike projection from each will fit into the other. Make sure the cambium tissues line up as much as possible between the two parts. Wrap the joined area with twine to hold it together and cover with grafting wax or pruning paint to prevent tissue drying.

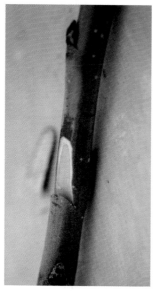

To chip bud, place a bud chip of the desired variety into a chip opening cut into the rootstock.

Use cleft grafting on large diameter trunks or limbs.

Use cleft grafts on large rootstocks. Cut off the top of the plant selected for the rootstock. Using a hatchet or cleft grafting tool, make about a 4-inch-long split (cleft) down the center of the rootstock trunk. Cut wedge-shaped ends on two scions ½ inch in diameter. Force a cleft grafting tool into the cleft to spread it open. Place the wedges of the scions in the cleft with the cambium of the rootstock and scions contacting one another. Remove the spreading device to leave the scions firmly held in place. Cover all of the exposed cut areas with grafting wax or pruning paint.

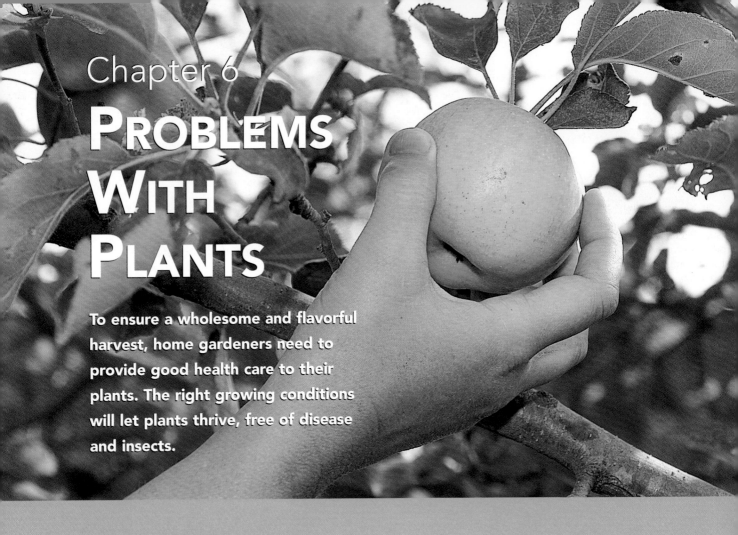

# Chapter 6

# PROBLEMS WITH PLANTS

**To ensure a wholesome and flavorful harvest, home gardeners need to provide good health care to their plants. The right growing conditions will let plants thrive, free of disease and insects.**

# PLANT HEALTH CARE

Plant health care is a holistic approach to gardening. It considers the garden as part of the whole landscape. A homeowner with a lawn, trees, shrubs, perennials, annuals, and a vegetable garden needs an effective garden plan that takes them all into consideration. A plan that focuses on only one or two problem plants does not address the best interests of the entire yard and garden. A garden plan should focus on fixing problems leftover from previous years and preventing problems in the future.

## PREVENTING PROBLEMS

There are five simple things you can do to maintain healthy plants during the growing season.

**1.** Maintain appropriate levels of nutrients.
**2.** Supply plants with adequate moisture, especially during droughts.
**3.** Mulch to conserve moisture and prevent weed growth.
**4.** Harvest fruits, vegetables, and flowers at timely intervals. Overripe produce attracts insects and is susceptible to disease. Unremoved flowers result in seed formation instead of new flower production; they also serve as a site of infection.

**5.** Clean up each fall. Remove spent plants and any diseased plant parts as soon as you have finished harvesting a particular fruit or vegetable. Clean up debris around plants.

Healthy gardens consist of plants as well as bacteria, fungi, insects, and nematodes. Most of these organisms are benign and merely coexist with plants. Some of these organisms, such as fungi that form mycorrhizae, or nitrogen-fixing bacteria, are beneficial and are necessary for healthy plant growth. Other fungi and bacteria are essential for breaking down dead plant material into humus in the compost pile. Beneficial insects and nematodes prey upon and parasitize pests in addition to having important roles in pollination. Although it may not seem like it to an embattled gardener, only a small percentage of insects actually cause damage, and only a few microorganisms are capable of causing disease.

When confronted with a plant problem, most gardeners assume that an insect or a disease is involved, then wonder what pesticide to spray. Most plant problems, however, are not due to disease-causing agents (pathogens) or insects but to environmental conditions and stresses. More often than not, these problems are caused by or due to actions taken—or not taken—by gardeners.

## SCOUTING FOR PROBLEMS

**1** Pick insects off infested plants. Wear gloves, if you prefer

**2** After removing insects from a plant, drop them into soapy water to kill them.

## WEEDS

Weeds compete with more desirable plants in the lawn and garden. The pernicious ones vie for light, water, food, and space. Once weeds are identified, they are usually removed easily without much thought. However, identifying the weed and determining why it has invaded is the first step in managing garden weeds.

Traditional weed control consists primarily of hand pulling and mulching. When properly timed, this two-pronged approach is usually effective. Weeds are easiest to control when the seeds are germinating, to prevent them from becoming established. They are more easily removed when the soil is moist, though not excessively wet. Once the weeds are established, control often requires hard work, herbicides, or both. For this reason, prevent weeds from going to seed.

After identifying the weeds, review your garden and lawn care practices. Carefully consider what adjustments are needed to maintain a healthy weed-free garden.

## INSECTS

Scouting for insects is more challenging than scouting for weeds. In a matter of days, insects can arrive, damage your plants, and then seemingly disappear. Monitoring your plants routinely will help you keep on top of the insect population and prevent infestations. Biweekly scouting of plants enables you to make some control choices before the damage reaches destructive levels. You can remove some pests physically from the plants by handpicking them, by using a garden hose to wash them from the plants, or by spraying them with insecticidal soap or horticultural oil. These approaches are the least toxic way to control insect problems. For them to be effective, you must be vigilant to make sure the problem insect doesn't become established.

When scouting your yard or garden, include all plant groups (lawn, trees, shrubs, fruits, vegetables, annuals, and perennials), and inspect several plants within each group. Be sure to choose several plants at random. Inspect the tops and undersides of several leaves or leaflets per plant. Determine how much damage is acceptable to you. If damage is minimal, you may choose to handpick pests, avoiding the need for chemical control. If the infestation is severe, you may need to spray to prevent the problem from

increasing, or to reduce insect populations to a level that becomes pickable.

Anyone who gardens will inevitably confront an infestation of something. Before reaching for a pesticide to spray, carefully examine the problem. Sometimes, it will take care of itself. Insects are susceptible to disease and predation too. Large populations of aphids are a food source for adult and immature lady beetles (ladybugs). These beetles are voracious. One can eat several hundred aphids. Praying mantis prey upon smaller insects, as do spiders. Remember that your garden and yard are part of the larger environment. When spraying to control an insect pest problem, consider that you may unintentionally kill beneficial insects as well.

Aphids are a favorite food of lady beetles (ladybugs). Here an adult lady beetle is feasting on rose aphids.

## DISEASE

Leaf spots, discoloration, and wilting are indications of plant distress. Early detection, accurate diagnosis, and understanding how pesticides and herbicides work are essential for plant disease management. By scouting regularly, you can quickly discover problems, correctly diagnose them, and prevent further spread of a pathogen before the disease reaches epidemic proportions.

The next step is accurately identifying the disease. Most disease diagnoses are not easily made in the home garden, so harvest a characteristic sample of the affected plant, wrap it in newspaper or paper towel (plastic causes samples to rot) and take it to the horticulture clinic of your cooperative extension service for identification.

## DIAGNOSING PLANT DAMAGE

Diagnosing plant problems takes an investigative approach, like a criminologist working on a case. The key difference is that your victim and all the witnesses don't talk. You need to reconstruct the event and the factors that contributed to the problem. There can be numerous causes for any given symptom, not all of them related to insects or diseases. Soil nutrition and texture, weather conditions, quantity of light, and other environmental and cultural conditions influence the health of a plant. An accurate diagnosis helps ensure the success of your management strategy.

If the infection is not severe, you may be able to keep it under control by removing infected leaves.

### STEP ONE: **KNOW YOUR HOST**

Correctly identifying the affected plant is the first step to successful diagnosis. Using the plant's botanical (Latin) name is more helpful than using its common name.

### STEP TWO: **DETERMINE IF A PROBLEM EXISTS**

Knowing what is normal and when it occurs allows you to recognize abnormalities. Keep in mind that many ornamentals have variegated leaves, brightly colored new growth, or double flowers.

Use a reliable reference book, such as Ortho's *Home Gardener's Problem Solver,* to correctly identify the problem and determine possible control measures.

### STEP THREE: **DECREASE THE SUSPECT LIST**

After identifying the host, look in books or log on to a web site to research what insects and diseases affect that plant. Many beginning gardeners confronted with their first garden problem, look at pictures of problems in gardening books and attempt to match the problem with the picture. Outstanding books, such as Ortho's *Home Gardener's Problem Solver,* have useful photos to aid you in your diagnosis. However it is easy to make a simple, but incorrect diagnosis instead of determining the cause of more complex problems. Like any skill, diagnosing plant problems requires practice. The more you garden, the more practice you will get.

### STEP FOUR: **DEVELOP AN INVESTIGATIVE APPROACH**

Diagnose plant problems on the basis of symptoms and signs. Symptoms, such as wilting, leaf spotting, and discoloration, describe how a plant responds to damage. Signs, such as the webbing of insects, are the direct evidence of an organism causing damage that creates characteristic symptoms.

Wilting is a symptom with many possible underlying causes.

### STEP FIVE: **DETERMINE THE CAUSE OF THE PROBLEM**

Plants require the appropriate light, temperature, humidity, nutrients, and water. Plants undergo stress when they receive too much or too little of these basic necessities. Stress predisposes plants to attack by insects and disease. Damage may be caused by these sources: environmental (weather or site), mechanical (foot traffic or wind), chemical (pesticides or herbicides), animals, insects, and diseases.

### STEP SIX: **DEFINE THE PROBLEM**

Closely examine the entire plant and others around it. Know how normal appears so you can define what is abnormal about the plant. In defining the problem, determine exactly what is going on. For example, if the plant's leaves have insects on them, can you observe the insects actually causing damage? What kind of damage do you perceive? Do you see holes in the leaves? Do the holes appear in patterns or randomly? Is there any discoloration of the plant parts or other symptoms?

Irregular holes chewed in leaves are evidence of grasshopper feeding even though they may no longer be present.

### STEP SEVEN: **LOOK FOR PATTERNS**

To find patterns, examine nearby plants to see whether they have the same problem. Consider whether the problem is seasonal. Evergreens do lose their needles in fall and throughout the winter. Check to see whether the affected plant(s) are all the same type. Pathogens are host specific; insects are less so. Are the affected plants in the same place or in different locations? Damage to a few species of plants or only to plants of the same species may indicate the presence of living factors.

### STEP EIGHT: **EXAMINE THE PROBLEM'S DEVELOPMENT**

Living factors tend to multiply over time, resulting in a problem that spreads from one plant to the next. Note whether the problem is increasing on a single plant or multiple plants within a planting. This can indicate living factors. Many people mistakenly believe that a problem suddenly developed overnight. In most instances problems were present at very low levels, and environmental conditions changed to favor the growth of the living factor.

Symptoms that develop suddenly (within three days) or remain in a particular spot or on a particular plant are usually due to nonliving factors.

### STEP NINE: **IDENTIFY THE SPECIFIC CAUSE**

Uniform, unusual, distinct, or repeated patterns indicate damage caused by nonliving factors, including chemicals, nutrient disorders, mechanical damage, environmental factors, and animal damage. Insect damage is caused by chewing, piercing, or rasping. The presence of an insect is additional evidence that may support your diagnosis. Make sure that the damage you find is the type caused by the insect you suspect. Use a hand lens to identify the causal agents of plant disease. Pathogens include fungi, bacteria, viruses, nematodes, and even other plants.

### STEP TEN: **BE PATIENT**

Experience with plant problem diagnosis is born of practice. There is no better teacher than to diagnose the plant problems outside your door. Know the host and its interactions with the factors that cause plant damage, both living and nonliving. Keep a balanced approach in managing problems rather than relying on any one strategy. Seek professional diagnostic help when in doubt.

Cedar apple rust on crab apple shows up as circular orange spots with yellow edges.

Fire blight on a pear tree is caused by a bacterium. Leaves appear scorched.

## FRUIT GROWER'S REALITY CHECK

When it comes to fruit growing and pests, you may want to give your approach a reality check with respect to the time, money, and energy you're willing to devote to scouting for pests, spraying, and most important, carrying out all the cultural practices that will help you avoid spraying in the first place.

Home gardeners may find it more difficult and expensive to grow high-quality tree fruit than small-fruit plants, such as strawberries, grapes, blueberries, and brambles. One reason is that many different pests and diseases plague tree fruits. Summer rainfall and high humidity favor the growth and spread of disease-causing organisms. Insects are also challenging.

Power spray equipment isn't practical for a small planting, yet getting spray into the canopy of a large fruit tree is a challenge. Dwarf fruit trees offer one solution for the home gardener because pesticides can be applied with hand-operated spray equipment.

But you'll still need to be on your toes, scouting faithfully for insect presence, noting changes that occur on the leaves and the growing fruits, and keeping track of the weather so you're able to time your sprayings accordingly. Most cooperative extension services have home fruit production guides and Web sites that provide the specific information home gardeners need to grow fruit crops successfully.

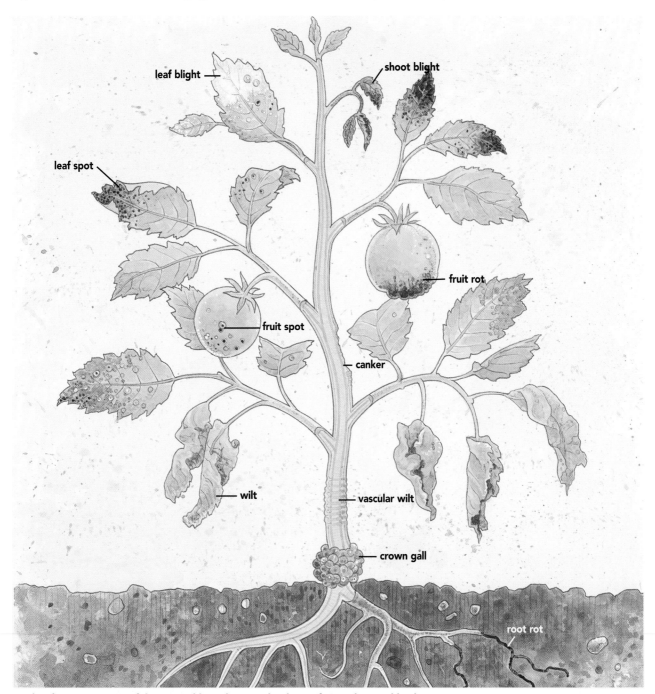

**Be alert for various types of disease problems that may develop on fruit and vegetable plants.**

## SPRAYING FRUIT TREES

Fruit trees offer ornamental beauty as well as delicious harvests year after year if they are carefully managed. Obtaining picture-perfect fruit in a home garden requires special attention to pruning, fruit thinning, and controlling pests and diseases. Careful planning begins with the correct choice of cultivar for your climate and site. Choose from the variety of fruit trees available and find cultivars bred for resistance to the diseases common in your growing area. Check with your local extension agent to find out which types are best.

Few fruit trees perform reliably year after year without the use of pesticides. Help to prevent pests and diseases by keeping the ground around your trees free of dropped fruit and other vegetative debris. For guaranteed pest-free harvests, however, you will need to learn the basics of how and when to spray your trees.

For home-garden spraying of just a few trees, a conventional pump sprayer may be sufficient, although a motorized sprayer is easier on your hands. Wear long pants, a long-sleeved shirt, protective eyewear, and rubber gloves while mixing and spraying chemicals. Read and follow the label instructions completely, measure carefully, and do not exceed the recommended application. Keep children and pets away from the area while you are working. Mix only what you need for one application; a small amount of excess can be rinsed onto the ground underneath the trees. No amount should ever be stored.

Apply dormant oil before buds swell, when the tree is dormant and the temperature is above 40°F, to smother insects that have overwintered on the tree. Dormant oil or horticultural oil applied a little later, when green leaves on apples and pears are ¼ inch to ½ inch long, may be even more effective. Bordeaux mixture, used to prevent fire blight, can also be applied at this stage. Pesticides to control mites, aphids, leaf miners, scale, and psylla should also be used at this green-tip stage but should not be applied at the same time as, or directly after, the oils.

Spray pesticides when buds are fully formed and showing color but aren't open. Fungicides for control of scab, rust, and powdery mildew are also applied at this stage and again on open blossoms. Avoid spraying pesticides when flowers are in bloom to avoid killing pollinators such as honeybees. Spray pesticides and fungicides again to apples, pears, and cherries when nearly all of the flower petals have fallen—a good time to prevent plum curculio, leaf rollers, stinkbugs, and other pests, as well as diseases encouraged by hot, humid weather. (Wait for 10 days after petal fall on other fruit trees before spraying to control various types of rot.) Use either or both again at 10-day intervals until fruit sets. Fall-fruiting trees can be sprayed again with insecticidal soap or pesticide at 14-day intervals throughout the summer as long as the temperature is not above 90°F. Stop spraying fruit trees 3 weeks before harvest.

**1** Follow label directions carefully to measure the correct amount for one application only.

**2** Fill the sprayer with the correct amount of water for the amount of pesticide added to the sprayer.

**3** A conventional pump sprayer is sufficient for home-garden treatment of just a few trees.

**4** Adjust the nozzle for accurate spraying and to avoid drift onto nontarget areas.

**5** Spray fall-fruiting trees with pesticide through summer but stop applications 3 weeks before harvest.

# GALLERY OF
# VEGETABLE, FRUIT
# & HERB CARE

Grow your own vegetables, fruits, and herbs for a flavorful gardening experience. With proper care of your kitchen garden and home orchard you'll reap a bounty of fresh produce.

'Gala' apple, *Malus sylvestrus ×domestrus*

**Asparagus, Asparagus officinalis**

'Blue Lake' bush bean, *Phaseolus vulgaris*

'Purple Cape' cauliflower, *Brassica oleracea* Botrytis group

CHAPTER **7**

GALLERY OF VEGETABLE, FRUIT & HERB CARE

# COMMON NAME INDEX VEGETABLES, FRUITS & HERBS *continued*

**Grape, *Vitis vinifera***

**Red 'Mars' and yellow 'Candy' onions, *Allium cepa***

**Heirloom peppers, *Capsicum annuum***

**Potatoes, *Solanum tuberosum***

| COMMON NAME | BOTANICAL NAME | SEE PAGE |
|---|---|---|
| Garden pea | *Pisum sativum* | 110 |
| Garden sage | *Salvia officinalis* | 124 |
| Garlic | *Allium sativum* | 45 |
| German celery | *Apium graveolens var. rapaceum* | 49 |
| Ginger | *Zingiber officinale* | 135 |
| Globe artichoke | *Cynara scolymus* | 79 |
| Gooseberry | *Ribes uva-crispa* | 121 |
| Grape | *Vitis spp.* | 132–133 |
| Grapefruit | *Citrus ×paradisi* | 67–70 |
| Greek oregano | *Origanum vulgare hirtum* | 104 |
| Green bean | *Phaseolus vulgaris* | 107 |
| Green onion | *Allium cepa* | 44 |
| Green pea | *Pisum sativum* | 110 |
| Green pepper | *Capsicum annuum* | 60–62 |
| Groundnut | *Arachis hypogaea* | 49 |
| Guava | *Psidium guajava* | 118 |
| Gumbo | *Abelmoschus esculentus* | 42 |
| Hawaiian papaya | *Carica papaya* | 63 |
| Hazelnut | *Corylus spp.* | 71 |
| Highbush blueberry | *Vaccinium corymbosum* | 128–129 |
| Honeydew melon | *Cucumis melo melo* | 72–73 |
| Horse bean | *Vicia faba* | 130 |
| Horseradish | *Armoracia rusticana* | 50 |
| Hot pepper | *Capsicum annuum* | 60–62 |
| Husk tomato | *Physalis ixocarpa* | 109 |
| Irish potato | *Solanum tuberosum* | 126 |
| Italian parsley | *Petroselinum crispum* | 106 |
| Japanese medlar | *Eriobotrya japonica* | 81 |
| Japanese persimmon | *Diospyros kaki* | 81 |
| Japanese plum | *Prunus salicina* | 116–117 |
| Jerusalem artichoke | *Helianthus tuberosus* | 87 |
| Jostaberry | *Ribes nidigrolaria* | 121 |
| Kale | *Brassica oleracea Acephala group* | 55 |
| Kiwifruit | *Actinidia deliciosa* | 43 |
| Kohlrabi | *Brassica oleracea Gongylodes group* | 57 |
| Kumquat | *Fortunella margarita* | 84 |
| Ladies' fingers | *Abelmoschus esculentus* | 42 |
| Lamb's lettuce | *Valerianella locusta* | 130 |
| Leek | *Allium porrum* | 44 |
| Lemon | *Citrus limon* | 67–70 |
| Lemongrass | *Cymbopogon citratus* | 79 |
| Lettuce | *Lactuca sativa* | 89 |
| Lima bean | *Phaseolus lunatus* | 107 |
| Lime | *Citrus aurantiifolia* | 68 |
| Litchi | *Litchi chinensis* | 91 |
| Loganberry | *Rubus spp.* | 123 |
| Loquat | *Eriobotrya japonica* | 81 |

| COMMON NAME | BOTANICAL NAME | SEE PAGE |
|---|---|---|
| Lovage | *Levisticum officinale* | 90 |
| Low-bush blueberry | *Vaccinium angustifolium* | 128–129 |
| Lychee | *Litchi chinensis* | 91 |
| Macadamia | *Macadamia integrifolia* | 95 |
| Mâche | *Valerianella locusta* | 130 |
| Mandarin orange | *Citrus reticulata* | 69 |
| Mango | *Mangifera indica* | 99 |
| Marionberry | *Rubus spp.* | 123 |
| Melon | *Cucumis melo melo* | 72–73 |
| Michigan banana | *Asimina triloba* | 51 |
| Mint | *Mentha spp.* | 100 |
| Muscadine grape | *Vitis rotundifolia* | 133 |
| Mushroom | *Agaricus bisporus* | 43 |
| Muskmelon | *Cucumis melo melo* | 72–73 |
| Nectarine | *Prunus persica* | 115 |
| Okra | *Abelmoschus esculentus* | 42 |
| Olive | *Olea europaea* | 103 |
| Onion | *Allium cepa* | 44 |
| Orange | *Citrus sinensis* | 69 |
| Orange mint | *Mentha ×piperata 'Citrata'* | 100 |
| Oregano | *Origanum vulgare hirtum* | 104 |
| Oriental persimmon | *Diospyros kaki* | 81 |
| Pak choi | *Brassica rapa* Chinensis group | 58 |
| Papaya | *Carica papaya* | 63 |
| Parsley | *Petroselinum crispum* | 106 |
| Parsnip | *Pastinaca sativa* | 105 |
| Passionfruit | *Passiflora edulis* | 104 |
| Pawpaw | *Asimina triloba* | 51 |
| Pawpaw | *Carica papaya* | 63 |
| Pea | *Pisum sativum* | 110 |
| Peach | *Prunus persica* | 115 |
| Peanut | *Arachis hypogaea* | 49 |
| Pear | *Pyrus communis* | 119 |
| Pecan | *Carya illinoinensis* | 63 |
| Pennyroyal | *Mentha pulegium* | 100 |
| Pepper | *Capsicum annuum* | 60–62 |
| Peppergrass | *Lepidium sativum* | 90 |
| Peppermint | *Mentha piperata* | 100 |
| Persimmon | *Diospyros spp.* | 81 |
| Pie cherry | *Prunus cerasus* | 112 |
| Pie plant | *Rheum ×cultorum* | 120 |
| Pigweed | *Amaranthus tricolor* | 46 |
| Pimpernel | *Sanguisorba minor* | 124 |
| Pineapple | *Ananas comosus* | 46 |
| Pineapple guava | *Feijoa sellowiana* | 82 |
| Pineapple mint | *Mentha suaveolens 'Variegata'* | 100 |
| Plantain | *Musa ×paradisiaca* | 101 |
| Plum | *Prunus spp.* | 116–117 |
| Pole bean | *Phaseolus vulgaris* | 107–108 |
| Pomegranate | *Punica granatum* | 118 |

| COMMON NAME | BOTANICAL NAME | SEE PAGE |
|---|---|---|
| Popcorn | Zea mays | 134–135 |
| Potato | Solanum tuberosum | 126 |
| Pot marigold | Calendula officinalis | 59 |
| Pummelo | Citrus maxima | 70 |
| Pumpkin | Cucurbita spp. | 75–78 |
| Purple granadilla | Passiflora edulis | 104 |
| Rabbit-eye blueberry | Vaccinium ashei | 128 |
| Radish | Raphanus sativus | 120 |
| Raspberry | Rubus spp. | 122–123 |
| Rhubarb | Rheum ×cultorum | 120 |
| Red beet | Beta vulgaris | 53 |
| Red currant | Ribes silvestre | 121 |
| Red raspberry | Rubus idaeus | 122–123 |
| Roquette | Eruca sativa | 82 |
| Rosemary | Rosmarinus officinalis | 122 |
| Rutabaga | Brassica napus | 54 |
| Sage | Salvia officinalis | 124 |
| Salad burnet | Sanguisorba minor | 124 |
| Savory | Satureja spp. | 125 |
| Scallion | Allium cepa | 44 |
| Scarlet runner bean | Phaseolus coccineus | 107 |
| Scotch kale | Brassica oleracea Acephala group | 55 |
| Shallot | Allium cepa | 44 |
| Siberian kale | Brassica oleracea Acephala group | 55 |
| Snap bean | Phaseolus vulgaris | 107–108 |
| Snap pea | Pisum sativum | 110 |
| Snow pea | Pisum sativum | 110 |
| Sour cherry | Prunus cerasus | 112–113 |
| Southern pea | Vigna unguiculata | 131 |
| Soybean | Glycine max | 87 |
| Spearmint | Mentha spicata | 100 |
| Spinach | Spinacia oleracea | 127 |
| Squash | Cucurbita spp. | 75–78 |
| Strawberry | Fragaria spp. | 84–86 |
| Strawberry guava | Psidium littorale var. longipes | 118 |

| COMMON NAME | BOTANICAL NAME | SEE PAGE |
|---|---|---|
| String bean | Phaseolus vulgaris | 107–108 |
| Striped cushaw | Cucurbita mixta | 76 |
| Sugar pea | Pisum sativum | 110 |
| Summer savory | Satureja hortensis | 125 |
| Summer squash | Cucurbita spp. | 75–78 |
| Sunchoke | Helianthus tuberosus | 87 |
| Swede | Brassica napus | 54 |
| Sweet cherry | Prunus avium | 112–113 |
| Sweet corn | Zea mays | 134–135 |
| Sweet marjoram | Origanum majorana | 103 |
| Sweet pepper | Capsicum annuum | 60–62 |
| Sweet potato | Ipomoea batatas | 88 |
| Swiss chard | Beta vulgaris cicla | 53 |
| Tampala | Amaranthus tricolor | 46 |
| Tangelo | Citrus ×tangelo | 69 |
| Tangerine | Citrus reticulata | 69 |
| Tart cherry | Prunus cerasus | 112–113 |
| Thyme | Thymus vulgaris | 127 |
| Tomatillo | Physalis ixocarpa | 109 |
| Tomato | Lycopersicon esculentum | 91–94 |
| Tropical guava | Psidium guajava | 118 |
| Turnip | Brassica rapa Rapifera group | 58 |
| Turnip-rooted celery | Apium graveolens var. rapaceum | 49 |
| Ugli fruit | (Citrus ×paradisi × Citrus reticulata) | 69 |
| Vegetable amaranth | Amaranthus tricolor | 46 |
| Walnut | Juglans spp. | 88 |
| Watermelon | Citrullus lanatus | 66 |
| Wax bean | Phaseolus vulgaris | 107 |
| White currant | Ribes rubrum | 121 |
| White sapote | Casimiroa edulis | 64 |
| Winter savory | Satureja montana | 125 |
| Winter squash | Cucurbita spp. | 75–78 |
| Yard-long bean | Vigna unguiculata ssp. sesquipedalis | 131 |
| Zucchini | Cucurbita pepo | 77–79 |

**Radish, *Raphanus sativus***

**'Painted Lady' scarlet runner bean, *Phaseolus coccineus***

**Tomatoes, *Lycopersicon esculentum***

**'Delicata' winter squash, *Cucurbita* spp.**

Fresh fruits, vegetables, and herbs, carried the short path from garden to kitchen, taste better and have more nutritional value than those grown far away and shipped long distances. Homegrown produce has an intrinsically healthy value just as tangible as its flavors: Your own work in the garden makes it possible and particularly satisfying.

You're the one who studies the catalogs each winter and chooses plant varieties that will thrive in your climate and growing space. You survey your plot and design a planting scheme to take advantage of sun, site, and water availability. You build the beds and prepare the soil; hoe weeds, rake rocks, and dig in compost and manure. You sow seeds and plant seedlings that you've started indoors or selected from your favorite source. You water and feed the growing plants, weeding between the rows and pinching back the herbs, training a vine up a fence and pruning suckers from a tree. You research the best ways to keep insects and infections from undermining your efforts.

When harvest time comes—when you savor the first sweet strawberry right off the vine, slice into a warm, juicy tomato, make the extra zucchinis into pickles for winter, or take a basket of just-ripe peaches to a friend—you know that what you have grown is the best it can be. The care you give your garden and the plants growing in it results in healthy, delicious food and an easily sustainable source of more to come. What could possibly be more gratifying?

# OKRA

*Abelmoschus esculentus* ah-bel-MOS-kus es-kyoo-LEN-tus

Pick red okra pods at 2–4" long. Okra is also known as gumbo or ladies' fingers.

**ZONES:** NA
**SIZE:** 2–8'h × 1–1½'w
**TYPE:** Tropical annual
**GROWTH:** Fast

**LIGHT:** Full sun
**MOISTURE:** Average
**FEATURES:** Hibiscus-type flowers, edible seedpods

**SITING:** Direct-seed ½" deep after danger of frost is past and soil temperature is at least 60°F. Seeds will germinate in 1–2 weeks. Or plant transplants 1–2' apart in rows 2' apart in fertile, loamy, neutral or slightly alkaline soil after the ground has been above 60°F for at least two weeks. Use black plastic to warm the soil in cooler zones. Okra does best if the soil dries between waterings; it can tolerate short periods of drought but will not thrive in wet conditions. Transplants are sun sensitive; keep the roots moist until the plants are established.

**CARE:** Okra is a member of the mallow family, related to hibiscus and hollyhock. Its large pale yellow flowers attract pollinating insects. Broad leaves shade the soil below, so mulch may not be needed. Low-growing, shade-tolerant herbs such as summer savory can be planted between the rows. Use starter solution, such as Miracle-Gro Liquid Quick Start Plant Food, to prevent transplant shock. Use water-soluble plant food, such as Miracle-Gro Water Soluble All Purpose, every 2–4 weeks when plants are in flower. Wear gloves when handling varieties with spiny hairs, which can irritate skin.

**PROPAGATION:** Soak seeds overnight to speed germination. Or start plants indoors 6–8 weeks before the last frost date; thin seedlings to one per pot by snipping weak ones instead of pulling them out, to avoid disturbing the roots.

**HARVEST:** Pods mature about 60 days after flowering. They can quickly become tough, so harvest frequently from the plant when 2–4" long. Store unwashed pods in the refrigerator for use within a few days; pressure-can or blanch and freeze pods for longer storage. Store away from fruits and vegetables that give off ethylene gas. The pods are high in calcium and fiber and can be boiled, fried, sautéed, dried, pickled, or added to soups, stews, and gumbos. Pods release a mucilaginous compound; to minimize it cook pods whole with the caps still attached. The sticky substance is a thickening agent that may be desired in some dishes. Mature pods add interest to dried flower arrangements. Okra is related to cotton; its long stem fibers can be used to make paper and rope. Oil extracted from the seeds is commonly used for cooking in Mediterranean countries. Dry and grind the ripe seeds for a caffeine-free coffee substitute.

**PESTS AND DISEASES:** Okra is susceptible to root knot nematode and fusarium wilt, and to southern blight in hot, humid zones. Blights and wilt are best controlled through crop rotation. Green stinkbugs, Japanese beetles, and leaf miners may feed on the leaves but generally are not a serious problem. Severely curled pods and pods with warty bumps indicate earlier feeding by stinkbugs or leaf-footed bugs. Damage to leaves does not affect harvest.

**RECOMMENDED CULTIVARS:** 'Clemson Spineless' grows well north and south. 'Red Velvet' has wine-red pods and stems. Early-yielding 'Cajun Delight' is good in northern gardens. Dwarf 'Baby Bubba' works well in containers and small spaces.

Cook pods whole to minimize the sticky substance they release.

Gently pull the pods away from the stem and clip free with sharp scissors.

# KIWIFRUIT
### *Actinidia deliciosa*  ak-tih-NID-ee-uh deh-lih-see-OH-suh

**Taste one fruit to test for ripeness before picking others. Kiwifruit is also known as Chinese gooseberry.**

**ZONES:** 8–11
**SIZE:** 9–12'h × 18–30'w
**TYPE:** Woody perennial vine
**GROWTH:** Fast

**LIGHT:** Full sun to part shade
**MOISTURE:** High
**FEATURES:** Attractive ornamental plant, edible fruits

**SITING:** Kiwis do best in deep, well-drained loam that is mildly acid and low in sodium. Plants are susceptible to damage from frost and wind, so locate them in a protected area. Space plants 15–20' apart, leaving room to erect a trellis. Water deeply and often when vines are blooming or fruiting, less often in dormancy.

**CARE:** Kiwifruit vines are fast growing but take 8 years to fruit. Work slow-release plant food into the soil around young vines. Older vines are heavy feeders; use water-soluble plant food every 2 weeks during the growing season. Train the vines up strong posts. Pinch off suckers, but wait to prune until after the male vines have flowered and females have set fruit. Prune again when the plants are dormant.

**PROPAGATION:** Grow from hardwood cuttings ½" in diameter with several nodes.

**Feed often at the base of vines and pinch off any suckers.**

Vines are male or female; use one male per one to eight females. Choose cultivars with the same chilling requirements so they flower at the same time.

**HARVEST:** The fruit takes about 5 months after achieving full size to develop the desired taste and texture. Test for maturity by picking one and allowing it to soften at room temperature for a few days before eating it. If it tastes sweet, pick all the fruits and keep them refrigerated. Fruits can stay on the vine as long as there is no threat of frost.

**PESTS AND DISEASES:** Treat leaf-rolling caterpillars with *Bt.* Treat scales with neem oil. Careful preparation and proper watering of a well-drained planting site is the best way to avoid root rot and other stress-related diseases.

**RECOMMENDED CULTIVARS:** 'Hayward' is the most common kiwi in North America and is easy to grow except in areas with very warm winters. *A. arguta* has smaller red or green fruits the size of large grapes; the skin is edible. *A. kolomikta* has very small fruit but is an especially cold-hardy species. *A. chinensis* 'Zespri™ Gold' has bright yellow flesh sweeter than 'Hayward'.

# MUSHROOM
### *Agaricus bisporus*  uh-GAIR-ih-kuhs by-SPOR-us

**Mushrooms grow in little or no light.**

**ZONES:** NA
**SIZE:** ½–8"h × ¼–8"w
**TYPE:** Fungi
**GROWTH:** Rapid to average

**LIGHT:** Low to none
**MOISTURE:** High
**FEATURES:** Edible stems

**SITING:** Plant button mushroom spawn in trays filled with a manure-based soil mix of compost mixed with straw. Plug shiitake (*Lentinus edodes*) spores into specially prepared hardwood logs, usually oak. The growing area must be 55–70°F with high humidity, even moisture, good air circulation, and little or no light.

**CARE:** Mushrooms require decaying organic matter to grow. Some species develop quickly and are easy to cultivate; others require considerable attention over a period of months. All require constant high humidity (80–85 percent) and misting. When flushes (groups of mature heads) stop appearing, compost the exhausted soil mix and logs.

**PROPAGATION:** Grow from spores, called spawn, available from commercial growers.

**Cut or twist mature mushroom stems close to the growing surface.**

**HARVEST:** Pinheads develop into flushes every week or two until the nutrients in the soil mix are exhausted. The first flush of button mushrooms occurs 30–60 days from spawning; shiitakes take 6–9 months; oyster mushrooms (*Pleurotus*) take 3 weeks. Pick mushrooms by cutting or twisting the stems near the medium surface, then cut the stem stumps below the surface to prevent disease. Common white and brown button mushrooms are eaten raw in salads and can be dried, pickled, sautéed, grilled, fried, or added to soups and stews. Large brown *cremini* (portobello) mushrooms are often used as meat substitutes. Shiitake, enoki, oyster, chanterelle, and other exotic types add an earthy, nutty flavor to dishes.

**PESTS AND DISEASES:** Slugs love mushrooms, so elevate and enclose outdoor growing areas. Cleanliness and moisture control prevent problems caused by competing molds. Properly prepared compost eliminates insect larvae.

**RECOMMENDED SPECIES:** *Volvariella volvacea* (straw mushroom), and *Morchella esculenta* (morel, which requires sunlight) are additional edible types of mushrooms.

# ONION
*Allium cepa* *AL-lee-um SEE-puh*

Harvest green shallots when the bulbs begin to swell.

**ZONES:** NA
**SIZE:** 4–8"h × ¼–5"w
**TYPE:** Herbaceous perennial usually grown as annual

**GROWTH:** Average
**LIGHT:** Full sun
**MOISTURE:** High
**FEATURES:** Edible bulbs and stems

**SITING:** Plant in well-drained soil rich in organic matter. The soil should be consistently moist but never waterlogged.
**CARE:** Cultivate onions for their immature green stems, called scallions; for their immature bulbs, called green onions; or for their mature, storable bulbs. Shallots are grown for use as dried bulbs and have a more delicate flavor than onions. A month before the first frost-free date, direct-sow seed ½" deep in rows 12–18" apart, thinning throughout the season. In early spring in northern zones and in autumn in warmer climates, plant bulbs or transplants 4–6" apart in rows 1' apart (or 6" apart for shallots in raised beds), with the pointed end just showing above ground. Weed frequently to reduce competition for nutrients. Remove seed heads. Mulch lightly to prevent sunscald. Use water-soluble plant food twice a month during the growing season. Shallots can be left in the ground from year to year but grow and taste better if lifted and stored each fall.
**PROPAGATION:** Onions grown from seed need 90 to 120 days to mature, so plant sets or transplants in northern zones.

'White Lisbon' scallions are immature onions.

Shallots are grown from individual bulbs or sets available commercially.
**HARVEST:** Dig or pull scallions and green shallots when the tops are 4–8" tall and green onions when the tops are 6–8" tall and bulbs have begun to swell. To use as dried bulbs, wait until the green tops have withered and browned, then stop watering. Lift shallots after a week; let onions cure in the ground for 2 weeks before digging. Store for 1 week in a dry, shady spot. When they are completely dry, remove any remaining stalks and trim the roots, then hang the bulbs in mesh onion bags in a cool (35–55°F), dry location.
**PESTS AND DISEASES:** Onions are susceptible to thrips, maggots, and soilborne diseases, all best avoided by crop rotation. Shallots are susceptible to pink rot, particularly in the South; treat garden soil with fungicide.
**RECOMMENDED CULTIVARS:** Choose onions based on their day-length requirements. Bermuda and Spanish onions do best in warm climates; 'White Lisbon' (often harvested for green onions) and 'Yellow Globe' grow well in cooler areas. *A. fistulosum* (Japanese bunching onion) is the common commercial green onion. 'Yellow Multiplier' and 'French Red' shallots thrive in all zones and keep well.

# LEEK
*Allium porrum* *AL-lee-um POR-rum*

Mound soil on leek stalks to blanch the lower part of the stems.

**ZONES:** NA
**SIZE:** 8–18"h × ½–2"w
**TYPE:** Biennial grown as annual

**GROWTH:** Average
**LIGHT:** Full sun
**MOISTURE:** High
**FEATURES:** Edible shanks, frost tolerant

**SITING:** Plant in well-drained soil rich in organic matter. In clay soil areas, plant bulbs in a raised bed amended with humus. The soil should be consistently moist but not waterlogged.
**CARE:** Leeks mature in 70–150 days but grow rapidly in cool weather. To increase the amount of white shank on the stalk, blanch the stems by mounding soil around them, or plant the leeks in the bottom of trenches, gradually filling in with soil as the stems grow. Weed around plants frequently to discourage competition. Use water-soluble plant food, such as Miracle-Gro Water Soluble All Purpose, twice a month. In cool zones, dig plants and store in a cool location before the first frost date, or leave them in the garden under heavy mulch and harvest as needed. Dig any remaining leeks in spring.
**PROPAGATION:** Seed germinates best in soil temperatures from 70–75°F but can be sown a month before the last frost date. Seedlings started indoors can be transplanted around the last frost date and anytime up to a month before the first frost.
**HARVEST:** Dig or pull leeks any time after the shanks are ½" or more in diameter.

Leeks are famous in potato-leek soup (vichyssoise) but can be eaten raw in salads and baked, broiled, or sautéed like root crops.
**PESTS AND DISEASES:** None are significant.
**RECOMMENDED CULTIVARS:** 'American Flag' and 'Giant Musselburgh' are good choices .

Leeks can be left in the garden all winter and harvested as needed. Mulch them well for protection.

# GARLIC

*Allium sativum* AL-lee-um sub-TEE-vum

Save some garlic cloves to start next year's crop. Store the rest in a cool, dry location.

**ZONES:** NA
**SIZE:** 8–24"h × 1–4"w
**TYPE:** Herbaceous perennial usually grown as an annual

**GROWTH:** Average
**LIGHT:** Full sun
**MOISTURE:** Average
**FEATURES:** Edible bulb

**SITING:** Plant the cloves pointed end up in well-drained, fertile, friable loam. Plant 2–3" deep and 6" apart in midautumn or early spring in northern zones and in late autumn or early winter in the South.

**CARE:** Garlic needs regular moisture but will rot in soil that stays wet all the time. Keep weeds removed and cut off flower heads to encourage bulb production. Use water-soluble plant food, such as Miracle-Gro Water Soluble All Purpose, once a week until summer. Mulch well around plants to retain moisture.

**PROPAGATION:** Grow from individual cloves split from a bulb.

**HARVEST:** Hard-neck garlics produce a coiled seed stalk in summer and white, red, or purple-striped bulbs with large cloves. Soft-neck garlics are tan, white, or purple-tinged and do not produce seed stalks. Mature bulbs are ready to dry in 90–110 days. Push the tops over to the ground and stop watering when about half the lower leaves begin to wither and turn brown. Let the bulbs cure for a week in the garden, then lift them and hang them for a week in a dry, shady location with good air circulation. Trim off any leaf stalks and cut the roots close to the base of each bulb. Store the bulbs in mesh bags in a cool (35–55°F), dry location. Save the largest cloves for planting next season—they'll produce the largest bulbs.

**PESTS AND DISEASES:** Avoid soilborne diseases and insects by crop rotation and clean planting practices. Pink rot and mildew can be problems in warm, humid climates; treat garden soil with fungicide.

**RECOMMENDED CULTIVARS:** 'German Porcelain' is a popular hard-neck garlic with white-wrapped cloves. 'Killarney Red' is a hard-neck with large pink-skinned cloves. Soft-neck 'Silverskin' types are well suited to cooler climates and store well. 'Red Toch' is a large Russian soft-neck type that grows well in warm climates. Elephant garlic (*A. scorodoprasum*) is more closely related to leeks but produces huge, garlic-type bulbs with a mild flavor.

**1** To plant garlic, separate the cloves.

**2** Plant the pointed ends up.

**3** Mulch with straw over winter.

Harvest and hang bulbs to dry.

# CHIVES

*Allium schoenoprasum* AL-lee-um skee-noh-PRAY-zum

Chive flowers are edible garnishes. Stems can be used to flavor foods as well.

**ZONES:** 3–10
**SIZE:** 8–12"h × 8–12"w
**TYPE:** Herbaceous perennial
**GROWTH:** Fast

**LIGHT:** Full sun to part shade
**MOISTURE:** Average
**FEATURES:** Edible leaves and flowers

**SITING:** Plant in average, well-drained soil in beds or pots. Chives are evergreen in warm climates but die back to the ground in cooler zones in winter.

**CARE:** Chives are somewhat drought tolerant and don't require plant food or much attention besides regular cutting. They eventually become overcrowded, so dig and divide clumps every few years and plant the divisions in new locations.

**PROPAGATION:** Grow from seed in early spring or by division in spring or fall.

Harvest a few stems as needed from container-grown plants.

**HARVEST:** These tiny onions are grown for their hollow leaf stems, not their bulbs. Chives are ready to cut in 75–85 days when grown from seed. Snip chives as needed by cutting through them just above the ground with scissors or a sharp knife. Chives can be dried but retain their color and flavor better when frozen. Snip a few leaves in salads, sauces, and quiches; add to baked potatoes and egg dishes at the end of cooking to preserve the onion flavor. The small, fragrant pinkish-purple flowers are also edible and can be used as a garnish.

**PESTS AND DISEASES:** Chives are seldom bothered by pests and may even repel Japanese beetles.

**RECOMMENDED CULTIVARS:** 'Forescate' has rose-red flowers. 'Ruby Gem' has gray-green foliage and red flowers. Chinese or garlic chives (*A. tuberosum*) grow taller than common chives and have flat leaves and white flowers. They can be invasive.

# VEGETABLE AMARANTH
*Amaranthus tricolor* am-uh-RAN-thus TRY-kuh-lor

**Chinese spinach or tampala tolerates hot weather. It is also known as pigweed.**

**ZONES:** NA
**SIZE:** 1–3'h × 1'w
**TYPE:** Annual
**GROWTH:** Fast

**LIGHT:** Full sun
**MOISTURE:** Average
**FEATURES:** Edible leaves

**SITING:** Broadcast seed in loose, fertile, well-drained soil and cover with a fine layer of sifted soil or compost. Amaranth is adaptable but grows best in consistently moist soil. It is an excellent substitute for spinach and lettuces that bolt in hot summers. Because it is quick to mature, it can also be grown in temperate zones in midsummer.

**CARE:** Thin seedlings to 6" apart in rows 12" apart. Keep young plants watered well and feed them two or three times a month with high-nitrogen, water-soluble plant food. Pinch off terminal buds to promote branching. Keep the soil evenly moist around the roots and pull any weeds. Mulch during periods of prolonged drought. Cut the entire plant at ground level before the first frost.

**PROPAGATION:** Grow from seed.

**HARVEST:** Unlike ornamental and grain amaranths, vegetable amaranth—also called Chinese spinach, tampala, and pigweed—is grown for its edible leaves, which are high in vitamins A and C and rich in minerals. Amaranth is commonly used in Asian, African, and West Indian cuisines. Young leaves and thinnings are used raw in salads; older leaves are steamed like spinach or added to soups and stews. Leaves are ready to pick in about 50 days when grown from seed. Pinch out new leaf rosettes and cut individual leaves at least once a week to encourage plants to produce new leaves. Freeze some leaves for winter use.

**PESTS AND DISEASES:** Chewing insects, such as Japanese and cucumber beetles, may damage the leaves. Use floating row covers to discourage them.

**RECOMMENDED CULTIVARS:** 'Green Leaf' is the most common; 'Calaloo' has purple-veined dark green leaves; 'Garnet Red' has ruby leaves; 'White Leaf' is a dwarf type with light green leaves and tender stems.

# PINEAPPLE
*Ananas comosus* uh-NAN-us koh-MOH-sus

**Locate the spiny-leaved plants away from people and pets.**

**ZONES:** 9–11
**SIZE:** 3–5'h × 4–5'w
**TYPE:** Herbaceous perennial
**GROWTH:** Slow

**LIGHT:** Full sun
**MOISTURE:** High
**FEATURES:** Attractive plant, edible fruits

**SITING:** Plant crowns or offsets 4–6" deep and 12–18" apart in acid, well-drained sandy loam. The leaves are sometimes spiny, so locate plants away from the outside edges of garden plots.

**CARE:** Water and weed often, especially while plants are becoming established. Use Miracle-Gro Fruit & Citrus Fertilizer Spikes between rows, and side-dress plants with compost or seaweed once a month before fruiting. Mulch to discourage weeds.

**PROPAGATION:** Grow from offsets or crowns. Cross-pollination is required.

**HARVEST:** Growing pineapple is a slow and often high-maintenance process with a tremendous reward. Plants bloom after a year or so, in knobs of reddish flower clusters over a period of 2–3 weeks. Each flower produces one fruitlet; the fruitlets eventually merge into a single fruit, the pineapple. Mature pineapples give off a strong fragrance. Test for ripeness by pulling on leaves near the crown; they will be loose on mature fruit. Cut the stalk with a sharp knife a couple of inches below the fruit. Store the fruit whole until ready to eat or cook. Pineapples are sweetest near the base, so the day before using one, cut off the top and turn the fruit upside down in a shallow bowl in the refrigerator to let the juice filter down through the whole fruit. Add fresh pineapple to salads and desserts or use it in jams, preserves, syrups, and juices.

**PESTS AND DISEASES:** Mealybugs, scales, and mites are the most common pests. Remove them by washing the leaves in a mild soap solution and rinsing well. Hot sun will usually kill nematodes. Treat rots with a fungicide labeled for pineapple.

**RECOMMENDED CULTIVARS:** 'Smooth Cayenne' is among the most common types, with sweet, highly acidic bright yellow flesh that keeps well. 'Red Spanish' has pale yellow to white flesh and is best eaten fresh.

**Leaves near the crown will be loose on mature pineapples.**

# DILL
*Anethum graveolens* *ub-NEE-thum grub-VEE-ob-lenz*

**Dill tolerates cool temperatures and is not bothered by pests.**

**ZONES:** NA
**SIZE:** 12–36"h × 6–24"w
**TYPE:** Annual
**GROWTH:** Very fast
**LIGHT:** Full sun
**MOISTURE:** Average
**FEATURES:** Edible leaves and seeds

**SITING:** Broadcast seed in nutrient-rich, moist, well-drained soil and cover with a fine layer of sifted compost. Dill grows well interplanted with almost anything but other carrot family members. It is tolerant of cool weather; it is often the last herb standing in a late-autumn garden.
**CARE:** Thin plants when they are large enough to use in the kitchen. Sow seed once a month for a continuous supply of ferny new growth. Hand-weed around young plants. Remove flowers to encourage foliage and prevent self-sowing, or let some plants flower and go to seed for new crops. Feed monthly with high-nitrogen, water-soluble plant food. Dill is adaptable but does best in consistently moist soil.
**PROPAGATION:** Grow from seed. Established plants will self-sow.
**HARVEST:** Dill is ready for leaf harvest 30–55 days after seeding. It goes to seed in 75–100 days. Snip leaves as needed or pull whole stems for thinning. To save seeds, cut 4" below the flower heads when the seeds are turning brown, and hang the heads upside down inside paper bags to catch the seeds as they ripen. Leaves can be air-dried or frozen for long-term storage. Fresh leaves add flavor and visual interest in salads, sauces, soups, breads, pesto, potato salad, and egg dishes. Use the dried seeds in pickling brine.
**PESTS AND DISEASES:** Dill is sometimes attacked by parsleyworm. Handpick them to control.
**RECOMMENDED CULTIVARS:** 'Bouquet' is the most commonly grown. 'Fernleaf' is a dwarf blue-green variety with high leaf yield, excellent for kitchen gardens or containers. 'Superdukat' is high in essential oils and thus intense flavor.

**Interplant dill with anything but carrots.**

**Harvest the ripened brown seeds of dill for cooking or planting.**

# CHERIMOYA
*Annona cherimola* *ub-NOH-nub chair-ib-MOH-la*

**Eat cherimoyas fresh off the tree but avoid the toxic seeds.**

**ZONES:** 10 and 11
**SIZE:** 15–25'h × 15–25'w
**TYPE:** Subtropical briefly deciduous tree or shrub
**GROWTH:** Slow
**LIGHT:** Full sun
**MOISTURE:** Average
**FEATURES:** Edible fruits

**SITING:** Plant young trees 25–30' apart in 2'-wide pits enriched with compost. Cherimoya grows best in medium soil of moderate fertility kept consistently moist except during dormancy.
**CARE:** Seeds may take up to 2 months to germinate. Use plant food, such as Miracle-Gro Fruit & Citrus Fertilizer Spikes, twice a year on young trees during the first and second years. In the third year switch to 10-15-15 fruit tree spikes. Prune lower branches during dormancy to improve tree form and allow sunlight to penetrate the canopy. Irrigate two or three times a month except when the trees are dormant. Sweetly fragrant flowers bloom from late winter through early summer. Hand-pollinate by gathering pollen from blossoms in the male stage, storing it for 36 hours in a plastic bag, then applying it when the blossoms are in the female stage.
**PROPAGATION:** Grow from seed, air layering, or by grafting.
**HARVEST:** Trees grown from seed will fruit in 3–4 years. Fruits on most cultivars ripen from October to May. Ripe fruits look a bit like upside-down artichokes; they are heavy, pale green to yellow, and firm but may give just a little. Fruit deteriorates rapidly off the tree, so use it immediately or freeze it to eat like ice cream later. Cut the fruit in half and scoop out the flesh with a spoon. Remove the seeds—which are toxic—from the pulp before using it in salads, beverages, and sherbets. Because it is almost always consumed fresh off the tree, cherimoya makes a perfect choice for the home garden in areas where winter temperatures do not dip below freezing but do fall below 45°F for a few weeks.
**PESTS AND DISEASES:** Few problems affect cherimoya. Knock off mealybugs with a sharp stream from a garden hose.
**RECOMMENDED CULTIVARS:** 'Bays' is a favorite for superior flavor. 'Chaffey' bears well even without hand pollination. 'Booth' is more cold tolerant than most other types. 'Ott' ships better than some other types. *A. cherimola ×squamosa* (atemoya), a hybrid of cherimoya and custard apple *(A. reticulata)*, is even sweeter tasting.

# CHERVIL
*Anthriscus cereifolium* an-THRIS-kus ser-ee-ib-FOH-lee-um

**Chervil needs full sun to germinate but light shade for best flavor.**

**ZONES:** NA
**SIZE:** About 20"h × 8"w
**TYPE:** Annual
**GROWTH:** Very fast

**LIGHT:** Part shade
**MOISTURE:** Average
**FEATURES:** Edible leaves

**SITING:** Chervil does not transplant well, so broadcast seed directly into the garden several times throughout the spring and summer for a continuous supply. The seeds need sunlight to germinate, but plants grow best in light shade. Interplant it among taller crops to provide the shade it needs. Keep the soil continuously moist.

**CARE:** Thin seedlings for kitchen use. Pinch out flower stalks to promote foliage growth. Mulch around plants to keep roots cool and moist. Overwinter in a cold frame or grow in a pot indoors for year-round use.

**Pinch out the flower stalks to promote growth of new leafy stems.**

**PROPAGATION:** Grow from seed.
**HARVEST:** Plants are ready for kitchen use in 30–40 days. Snip bits of chervil from the outside edges of a plant as needed and use immediately. The leaves lose their flavor rapidly and should not be cooked.

A relative of carrots and parsley, chervil is an essential ingredient, along with parsley, thyme, chives, and tarragon, in the French fines herbes. It is rich in vitamin C, beta carotene, iron, and magnesium. Chervil's faintly aniselike flavor is excellent paired with salmon, asparagus, eggs, cream soups, cottage cheese, butter, mayonnaise, carrots, peas, or potatoes.

**PESTS AND DISEASES:** Chervil has no significant pest problems. Chervil may repel slugs and aphids.

**RECOMMENDED CULTIVARS:** Chervil comes in flat and curly-leaf types. Some growers think that curly chervil has a slightly bitter taste. 'Brussels Winter' is larger and slower to bolt than standard varieties.

# CELERY
*Apium graveolens* AY-pee-um gruh-VEE-oh-lenz

**Keep the soil consistently moist to avoid black heart of celery.**

**ZONES:** NA
**SIZE:** 2'h × 1'w
**TYPE:** Biennial grown as an annual
**GROWTH:** Slow

**LIGHT:** Full sun to part shade
**MOISTURE:** High
**FEATURES:** Edible leaf stalks (petioles) and leaves

**SITING:** Plant in muck or in deep, fertile, well-drained soil that holds moisture well. Direct-sow in Zones 8–10; sow indoors in Zones 4–7 and transplant when the soil temperature is above 55°F.

**CARE:** Sow seeds for transplanting in individual pots, just a few seeds to each pot. Thin seedlings several times until there is just one plant per pot. Transplant outdoors after the last frost date, 1' apart in rows 2' apart, using water-soluble transplant-starter solution. Thin direct-sown seedlings to the same spacing. Side dress with compost and seaweed or bone meal for added calcium every few weeks. Add mulch around the plants as often as needed to retain moisture. Irrigate frequently; too little moisture or dry weather will cause the stalks to crack and be underdeveloped, which invites disease. Use a water-soluble plant food, such as Miracle-Gro All Purpose, twice a month. Wrap cardboard, brown paper bags, newspapers, or drainage tiles around Pascal-type celery stalks, leaving the top few inches of leaf exposed, to blanch them. Cover plants if frost is possible.

**PROPAGATION:** Grow from seed.

**Blanch tall cultivars with newspaper or another method of sun protection.**

**HARVEST:** Stalks are ready to eat 3–5 months from transplanting. Cut the entire plant at ground level with a sharp knife when stalks are about 1' tall. Use the outermost stalks for cooking only (not eating raw), or compost them, especially if they have insect damage. Chill the cut plant quickly to preserve its crispness. Store at 32°F in high humidity, such as in the refrigerator crisper drawer.

**PESTS AND DISEASES:** Slugs, aphids, leafhoppers, and caterpillars are attracted to celery. Use slug traps and floating row covers; knock insects off with a strong stream of water from the garden hose every few days or spray plants with insecticidal soap or neem. Treat blights and leaf spot with fungicide labeled for celery. If rot develops, destroy infected plants and rotate crops elsewhere for at least 4 years. Black heart, the most common malady, is caused by uneven soil moisture.

**RECOMMENDED CULTIVARS:** Pascal (green) cultivars are most popular in the United States. 'Ventura' and 'Comet' are tall cultivars ready to harvest in 90–100 days. Yellow cultivars are more common in Europe. The stalks are broader and more tender. Try 'Golden Self-Blanching', which matures in about 100 days.

# CELERIAC

*Apium graveolens* var. *rapaceum*  *AY-pee-um gruh-VEE-o-lenz ruh-PAY-see-um*

Celeriac needs a long, cool growing season. It is also known as German celery, celery root, or turnip-rooted celery.

**ZONES:** NA
**SIZE:** 1'h × 1'w
**TYPE:** Herbaceous perennial grown as an annual
**GROWTH:** Average

**LIGHT:** Full sun to part shade
**MOISTURE:** High
**FEATURES:** Edible roots

**SITING:** Direct-sow in Zones 8–11; sow indoors in Zones 4–7 and transplant when the soil temperature is above 55°F. Transplant or thin seedlings 4–6" apart in rows 18–24" apart in fertile, well-drained soil that holds moisture well.

**CARE:** Like celery, celeriac needs a long, cool growing season. Irrigate frequently and mulch to keep roots cool. Use a balanced, water-soluble plant food twice a month. After harvesting, compost the stalks, which are usually too bitter to eat.

**PROPAGATION:** Grow from seed.

Use a garden fork to dig celeriac when roots are large enough.

**HARVEST:** Celeriac is easier to grow than celery but adds the same flavor and crunch to foods. Dig roots when they reach several inches in diameter, approximately 100–150 days from sowing. Dig any remaining roots; store for the winter at 32°F in buckets or boxes filled with moist soil or sand. Celeriac stores well for up to 4 months. It can also be frozen but is suitable only for cooking once thawed. Peel and dice the thick, tuberous roots into salads or use as a cooked vegetable just like carrots or potatoes.

**PESTS AND DISEASES:** Use bait or traps if slugs are a problem. Carrot rust flies are best controlled through crop rotation, although drenching the soil with parasitic nematodes may control damage for the current season. Control leaf spot with clean cultural practices and crop rotation.

**RECOMMENDED CULTIVARS:** 'Diamant' and 'Giant Prague' are vigorous growers.

# PEANUT

*Arachis hypogaea*  *AR-uh-kis hy-poh-JEE-uh*

Ripe peanut seeds fill the pods, which are light-colored inside. Peanut is also known as groundnut.

**ZONES:** NA
**SIZE:** 1–2'h × 1–3'w
**TYPE:** Annual
**GROWTH:** Average

**LIGHT:** Full sun
**MOISTURE:** Average
**FEATURES:** Edible seeds (nuts)

**SITING:** Plant 2" deep and 4" apart in rows 20" apart, or in hills a bit closer together, in deep, highly fertile, loose, well-drained soil. Add gypsum if the soil is low in calcium. Rotate peanuts to a new location each year.

**CARE:** Mix slow-release plant food, such as Miracle-Gro Shake 'n Feed All Purpose, into the soil before planting. In summer peanuts send up short stems, each bearing a yellow pea-type flower. The mature heads form "pegs" that gradually bend over and plant themselves into the soil to form new nuts. Mulch lightly around plants to maintain soil moisture and control weeds. Keep the soil consistently moist until a week before harvest. Discard any moldy peanuts.

**PROPAGATION:** Direct-sow raw, shelled seed with the skins intact as early as possible in spring, or start indoors in northern climates a month before the

Once peanut flowers are pollinated, they produce "pegs" that burrow into the soil.

last frost date. Use seed inoculated with rhizobium if the site has not been previously planted with legumes.

**HARVEST:** Each plant produces 25 to 50 peanuts 90–120 days from sowing. Dig or pull peanuts when the kernels fill the pods but the pod interiors are still light in color. Dry the pods outside in full sun or indoors in a warm, ventilated area for 4–7 days before separating the pods from the plants and storing them. The nuts, which are actually seeds, are high in protein, unsaturated oil, and vitamins E and B. Peanuts can be eaten raw or roasted, salted or not; ground into peanut butter; chopped into desserts and baked goods; or processed for cooking oil. Remove the skins by blanching the nuts in boiling water. Roast in a single layer in a 325°F oven for 20 minutes.

**PESTS AND DISEASES:** Hungry animals sometimes dig up peanuts. Rot is caused by overly wet or heavy soil. Healthy plants and timely irrigation are the best defenses against insect pests. To control leaf spot, avoid wetting the foliage.

**RECOMMENDED CULTIVARS:** Virginia types, such as 'Virginia Jumbo', are the best choice for boiling or roasting. 'Early Spanish' is good in northern climates.

# HORSERADISH

*Armoracia rusticana* arm-or-AY-see-a rus-tih-KAY-na

**Isolate horseradish to prevent it from spreading too far.**

**ZONES:** 3–9
**SIZE:** 1–4'h × 1–2'w
**TYPE:** Herbaceous perennial; can be grown as an annual
**GROWTH:** Slow
**LIGHT:** Full sun to shade
**MOISTURE:** Average
**FEATURES:** Edible roots

**SITING:** Although horseradish thrives in cool climates, it is not fussy about location and grows so vigorously that it can become invasive if left unattended. Choose a spot where the soil can be prepared a foot deep or more. A raised or otherwise isolated bed helps to keep horseradish from spreading too far. It is grown for its roots but has large dark green leaves that provide vertical interest at the back of an herb bed. It is highly adaptable but does best in soil that can be kept consistently moist.

**CARE:** Plant root cuttings 3" deep and 12" apart. Thin overcrowded plants in autumn by harvesting. If the roots seem small and underdeveloped, add potassium to the soil, working it in as deeply as possible. To encourage large taproots, remove a few inches of topsoil in midsummer and trim the fine lateral roots off the main root, then replace the soil.

**Cut away the lateral roots to promote growth of the long taproot.**

**PROPAGATION:** Start from lateral root cuttings from near the top of the taproot.

**HARVEST:** Cuttings planted in spring will be mature roots in 180–240 days but have the best flavor if left in the ground until after a few frosts have sweetened them. Loosen the soil with a pitchfork and pull up the roots by hand, using those that are 6–12" long and replanting the smaller ones. Save some cuttings for next year's crop, or simply leave the plants in the ground and mulch them for winter protection. Store unwashed harvested roots in plastic bags in the refrigerator as you would carrots. Horseradish root is ground and used as a condiment with meat. The flesh smells and tastes quite sharp—often too piquant for some palates. Grate washed and peeled roots with a ginger grater or in a food processor and serve fresh, or mix with a small amount of vinegar and store in the refrigerator for up to 6 months.

**PESTS AND DISEASES:** None are serious.

**RECOMMENDED CULTIVARS:** 'Bohemian' is popular because of its hardiness and high-quality roots. A distant relative used in Asian foods, wasabe (*Wasabia japonica*), is grown in streams in mild climates for its highly aromatic, spicy rhizomes.

# FRENCH TARRAGON

*Artemisia dracunculus sativa* ar-tih-MIZ-ee-uh druh-KUN-kyoo-lus sub-TY-vuh

**Tarragon's lance-shape leaves are ornamental as well as edible.**

**ZONES:** 3–9
**SIZE:** 12–24"h × 12–18"w
**TYPE:** Herbaceous perennial often grown as an annual
**GROWTH:** Fast
**LIGHT:** Full sun to part shade
**MOISTURE:** Average
**FEATURES:** Edible leaves

**SITING:** Plant cuttings 18–24" apart in fertile, well-drained soil in a location with good air circulation. Allow the soil to dry between waterings. Tarragon can be grown indoors or outside in containers.

**CARE:** An attractive ornamental, tarragon has glossy, lance-shape leaves on slender stems. Remove flowers to encourage foliage growth. Plants will grow vigorously if cut regularly. Cut them back in fall and

**Cut back the plants and pinch out the flowers to promote new growth.**

mulch for winter protection or take cuttings in late summer for overwintering indoors in containers. Divide plants in spring or take cuttings in spring or late summer.

**PROPAGATION:** Grow from rooted cuttings or divisions. Plants rarely produce seed and must be replaced every few years.

**HARVEST:** French tarragon's anise-flavored leaves are used to season a wide variety of salads, soups, and fish and poultry dishes—and are the key to a perfect béarnaise sauce. Snip leaves as needed from the tops of stems. Add leaves just before hot foods are served to enjoy the most flavor. Store in vinegar or freeze. Essential oil of tarragon is used commercially in mustards, vinegars, and other foods, as well as in some cosmetic products.

**PESTS AND DISEASES:** None are serious.

**RECOMMENDED CULTIVARS:** Although Russian tarragon (*A. dracunculoides*) can be sown from seed and is hardier than French cultivars, it does not have the flavor desired for culinary uses. Mexican mint marigold (*Tagetes lucida*) has similar flavor but is more heat tolerant than tarragon.

# PAWPAW
*Asimina triloba* ab-sib-MY-nub try-LOH-bub

The sweet fruit of pawpaw can be eaten fresh, but the seeds are toxic. It is also known as Michigan banana.

**ZONES:** 5–8
**SIZE:** 10–20'h × 6–10'w
**TYPE:** Deciduous tree
**GROWTH:** Slow

**LIGHT:** Part sun to shade
**MOISTURE:** Average
**FEATURES:** Attractive ornamental tree, edible fruits

**SITING:** Pawpaw is a small, shade-tolerant ornamental tree native to North America. Mature trees will flower in sun or shade. Although not as well known as other indigenous fruit, pawpaw is easy to grow. Basically unchanged from trees grown hundreds of years ago, they are often found growing wild in hardwood understories or along the shady, protected edges of old-growth forests. They grow well in urban settings, providing tropical-tasting fruit in climates where true tropicals do not grow, and have unusual and attractive foliage and flowers. The open branches droop. Exotic dark red to purple blossoms hang upside down among the long dark green leaves in early spring. Choose a shady, fertile, well-drained location—protected from wind—where the soil can be prepared deeply. Plant seeds 1' apart and 1" deep; thin seedlings to the healthiest specimens. Or plant young trees 8' apart. Keep consistently moist but not wet or waterlogged.

**CARE:** Protect transplants and young seedlings from the sun until they are 3 years old. Provide water-soluble plant food, such as Miracle-Gro Water Soluble All Purpose, until roots are established, then feed with fruit tree spikes, such as Miracle-Gro Fruit & Citrus Fertilizer Spikes. Flower stigmas ripen before the pollen, and the trees often bloom before flies and bees are active, so hand pollinate with a small brush or swab to ensure fruit formation. Prune out dead or damaged limbs and remove suckers.

**PROPAGATION:** Grow from seed or by grafting or budding, although transplanting can be difficult. Seedlings are not identical to the parents. Because of pawpaw's long taproot, container-grown trees have the best survival rate. Almost all types are self-incompatible, so plant more than one cultivar for successful pollination. Grafted trees may bear fruit in as few as 3 years.

**HARVEST:** Trees fruit in 5–8 years when grown from seed. Fruit ripens approximately 180 days after flowering—in late summer to early autumn, depending on cultivar and zone. Ripe fruit is noticeably fragrant and comes off easily by hand or by shaking the tree gently—don't stand under it! Check the ground beneath trees for ripe fruit that has already fallen. Ripe skin is medium to dark green, often mottled with dark brown or purple streaks like a banana; it becomes darker if stored after picking. The large, heavy, distinctive butter yellow fruits are extremely high in vitamin C, potassium, iron, calcium, and magnesium. They taste like banana and caramel with a hint of citrus or berry and have a custardlike texture and large, dark seeds. Eat fresh out of hand or in ice cream, or process the pulp for use in pies and other baked goods (it can be used in place of persimmon pulp). Pawpaw seeds are toxic; neither seeds nor skin should be consumed. Pawpaws can be stored for a week in the refrigerator. Store seeds in a plastic bag on an open shelf in the refrigerator for planting in spring; they should not freeze or dry out.

**PESTS AND DISEASES:** Pawpaws have few significant pests. Natural compounds in the leaves, bark, and tissue have insecticidal properties. Peduncle borers (moth caterpillars) may cause the flowers to drop before fruit sets. Be careful when removing caterpillars; the larvae of zebra swallowtails also like pawpaws, so sharing may be in order. Raccoons and squirrels eat the fruit as it ripens.

**RECOMMENDED CULTIVARS:** 'Davis' has large, fragrant fruit and refrigerates well. 'Duckworth', a shrub form, and 'White', a white-fleshed variety, can be grown in the Deep South. 'Susquehanna' is less fragile than older cultivars but just as sweet.

Trees bloom early and so may need assistance with pollination.

Pawpaws will flower and set fruit in sun or part shade.

The large, heavy fruits will fall to the ground when completely ripe.

# ASPARAGUS

*Asparagus officinalis* *uh-SPAIR-uh-gus ob-FISH-ib-nal-is*

**Let some asparagus spears grow into ferns to produce energy for next year's crop.**

**ZONES:** 4–9
**SIZE:** 7–10"h ×
12–24"w
**TYPE:** Herbaceous
perennial
**GROWTH:** Slow

**LIGHT:** Full to part
sun
**MOISTURE:** High
**FEATURES:** Edible
stems (spears)

**SITING:** Choose a level, well-drained location with light, friable, fertile soil where asparagus has not been grown previously and where supplemental irrigation can be provided. Plan on future space needs because mature crowns may grow up to 24" wide and unharvested spears grow into ferns more than 6' tall. Although the plants take time to establish, they may produce spears for up to 20 years. Transplant seedlings at 90 days in mounds 3" tall in the middle of furrows 6" deep and 4' apart. Or plant crowns with the buds up 12" apart in furrows 4' apart and 6" deep and covered with 2" of soil, gradually filling in the furrows as the spears grow.

**CARE:** Amend the soil annually with well-composted horse or cow manure. Asparagus prefers a soil pH slightly greater than 7.0; have a soil sample analyzed to be sure. If the test shows low availability of phosphorus or potassium, use appropriate plant food to correct that, being careful not to add much nitrogen. Water frequently until the plants are well established; watering during hot summer weather and post-harvest drought for maximum fern production. Control weeds in the first year with a hand cultivator or hoe. In subsequent years, lightly till large beds as soon as the soil dries out in spring but before spears emerge. To avoid damage to spears underground, control weeds by shallow hoeing, or use an asparagus herbicide labeled for the specific weed to be eradicated. After 4–6 weeks of harvesting, allow spears to grow into ferns, which produce food for next year's crop. Let them remain standing for as long as any green shows, even through the winter. Check them routinely for signs of pests or

disease, which will reduce the following year's yield.

**PROPAGATION:** Transplanting year-old dormant roots (crowns) saves a year in production time. Choose male hybrids to avoid unwanted seedlings.

**HARVEST:** Begin harvesting when spears are at least 5" tall, ½" in diameter, and have closed tips. Pick for just 2 weeks during the first harvest season, increasing to 4 weeks the second season and 6 weeks in years thereafter or for as long as the spear size is normal. Break or cut spears off at or near ground level. Cool spears immediately to preserve their nutritional content and crisp texture. Store the spears for several days in the refrigerator upright in a jar holding an inch of water, or wrapped in moist paper toweling inside a plastic bag in the crisper drawer.

**PESTS AND DISEASES:** Soilborne pathogens cause fusarium stem and crown rot and fusarium wilt and root rot. Disinfect seeds

and roots with fungicide before planting and plant in an area where asparagus has not been grown for at least 8 years. Control asparagus rust with fungicide; begin regular applications at the first sign of infection. Asparagus beetles and aphids are the most damaging pests; control them with specifically labeled insecticides. Follow label instructions carefully so that beneficial bees are not harmed.

**RECOMMENDED CULTIVARS:** 'Washington' varieties are still the most popular although all-male hybrids such as 'Greenwich', 'Jersey Knight' and 'Jersey Giant' may have greater disease resistance and higher yields. 'Jersey Centennial' is reported to be more vigorous, productive, and rust resistant. Spears of 'Viola' or 'Purple Passion' have a deep-purple color when raw; when cooked, the color dissapates to green, but the flavor is sweeter than many green varieties.

**1** Use a spade or shovel to dig trenches 6" deep and 4' apart.

**2** Plant crowns 12" apart in the trenches with the buds pointed up.

**3** Lightly cover the crowns with soil. Fill in the trenches as the spears grow.

**4** Begin harvesting spears when they are about ½" in diameter.

# BEET

*Beta vulgaris* BAY-tuh vul-GAIR-is

**Leave an inch of foliage on beets to be cooked to prevent color bleeding. Beets are also known as red beets.**

**ZONES:** NA
**SIZE:** 2–12"h × 2–12"w
**TYPE:** Annual
**GROWTH:** Fast

**LIGHT:** Full sun to part shade
**MOISTURE:** Average
**FEATURES:** Edible roots and leaves

**SITING:** Beets grow best in loose, fertile, slightly alkaline soil cleared of rocks and amended with well-rotted compost. Plant seeds ½" deep and 1" apart in rows 12" apart. Keep the soil uniformly moist.
**CARE:** Gradually thin beets to 4" apart for best root development, eating the thinnings as greens. Mulch the plants to keep them cool and moist, and weed around them carefully by hand. In cool climates, sow beet seed at 3-week intervals for an all-season supply. In warmer zones, plant seeds in late summer and early autumn.
**PROPAGATION:** Grow from seed.
**HARVEST:** Beets are often the first and last vegetables harvested from the garden, providing both tender greens for salads and crisp roots for cooking, pickling, and canning. Dig or pull small globe varieties when the roots are 1" in diameter; dig large and cylindrical types when they reach 2",

**Thin young beets and use the thinnings as fresh salad greens.**

about 45–55 days from seeding. Leave an inch of foliage on roots to prevent bleeding of the strong colors, which permanently stain porous cookware and serving dishes. Harvest beets for greens at any time, but smaller leaves up to 4" have better flavor. Store unwashed beets as you would carrots, at 32–40°F in high humidity. Leave fall crops in the ground until needed or until the soil begins to freeze.
**PESTS AND DISEASES:** Leaf miners may overwinter in the soil. Aphids, flea beetles, and other insects may do minor damage to the leaves or roots. Use floating row covers to protect seedbeds from egg-laying adults. Control leaf spot with fungicide. Sugar-beet cyst nematodes may be a problem in cool climates and are best controlled through crop rotation.
**RECOMMENDED CULTIVARS:** 'Red Ace' is highly adaptable to a variety of soil and weather conditions. 'Big Top' has the largest, most prolific greens. 'Golden' has yellow flesh. 'Forono' has long, smooth deep purple roots that are prized for canning. 'Chioggia' is an heirloom variety with pink and white rings. 'Lutz Green Leaf' provides a winter crop of greens.

# SWISS CHARD

*Beta vulgaris cicla* BAY-tuh vul-GAIR-is SIH-kluh

**Cut chard back in late summer for a new flush of leaves in autumn.**

**ZONES:** NA
**SIZE:** 6–20"h × 10–30"w
**TYPE:** Annual
**GROWTH:** Fast

**LIGHT:** Full sun to part shade
**MOISTURE:** Average
**FEATURES:** Edible leaves and stalks

**SITING:** Plant seeds ½" deep and 1" apart in rich, slightly alkaline soil.
**CARE:** Plants tolerate summer heat and light frost. Keep the soil constantly moist until seedlings are established, then mulch with straw to keep roots cool and moist. Thin young plants to 2" apart, using the thinnings in salads. Use balanced water-soluble plant food twice a month. Cut plants back in late summer to rejuvenate them for fall production.
**PROPAGATION:** Grow from seed soaked overnight to speed germination.
**HARVEST:** Begin harvesting when leaves are about 5" tall. Break off only one or two outer leaves from each plant, leaving the inner leaves to develop. Eat young leaves raw in salads and cook mature ones like spinach or other greens. Mature ribs (stalks) are often used as a cooked vegetable in Asian cuisine.

**PESTS AND DISEASES:** Aphids and leaf miners sometimes bother chard. Remove and destroy affected leaves. Pick off corn borer larvae by hand. Young leaves may show evidence of flea beetle feeding; dust with rotenone. Use bait or traps for slugs and snails. Choose varieties resistant to downy mildew.
**RECOMMENDED CULTIVARS:** 'Fordhook Giant' is a dependable, hardy dark green chard with white ribs. 'Rhubarb' has red ribs. 'Bright Lights' and 'Rainbow' ribs are vivid reds and yellows.

**Harvest a few outer leaves and petioles (stalks) as needed.**

**Some cultivars have ribs in bright colors. This is 'Bright Lights'.**

# RUTABAGA
## *Brassica napus* BRASS-ih-kuh NAP-us

**Rutabaga, also known as Swede, tastes sweeter if harvested after a few frosts.**

**ZONES:** NA
**SIZE:** 12–18"h × 8–12"w
**TYPE:** Biennial grown as annual
**GROWTH:** Average

**LIGHT:** Full sun to part shade
**MOISTURE:** Average
**FEATURES:** Edible roots

**SITING:** Plant seeds ½" deep and 2" apart in rows 18" apart in deep, fertile, loose, well-drained soil enriched with humus and cleared of stones and other debris. Amend the soil if it is low in potassium, but do not add nitrogen. Keep the soil consistently moist; choose a planting location where you can provide supplemental irrigation during hot or dry periods.

**CARE:** Gradually thin seedlings to 8" apart; pull weeds by hand. Mulch rows to keep roots cool and moist. Overwinter autumn-grown roots in the ground under heavy mulch.

**PROPAGATION:** Grow from seed planted 4–6 weeks before the last frost in spring

**Mulch rutabagas to keep them cool in summer and for winter protection.**

and 90 days before the first autumn frost date.

**HARVEST:** Easy to grow, rutabagas are larger and hardier than turnips but the leaves are bitter. The roots have a slightly sweet, nutty flavor between turnip and cabbage. Dig rutabagas about 90 days after seeding, or anytime after they are 3–5" in diameter. Pull only what you need and leave the rest in the ground. Autumn-grown rutabagas taste sweeter if harvested after a few frosts. Cook rutabagas as you would turnips or potatoes—steamed and mashed, baked as a side dish, or diced and added to soups and stews. Small roots can be eaten raw in salads or served as crudités. Store harvested rutabagas like other root crops, in cool but not freezing temperatures and high humidity.

**PESTS AND DISEASES:** Knock aphids off with a strong stream from the garden hose. Dust with rotenone to combat flea beetles if they are present in significant numbers. Control clubroot through clean gardening practices and crop rotation.

**RECOMMENDED CULTIVARS:** 'American Purple Top' and 'Laurentian' are dependable and sweet.

# COLLARDS
## *Brassica oleracea* Acephala group  BRASS-ih-kuh oh-leh-RAY-see-uh ay-SEF-uh-luh

**Collards are adapted to most climates but grow best in cool weather.**

**ZONES:** NA
**SIZE:** 24–36"h × 18–36"w
**TYPE:** Biennial grown as an annual
**GROWTH:** Average

**LIGHT:** Full sun to light shade
**MOISTURE:** Average
**FEATURES:** Edible leaves

**SITING:** Plant seeds ½" deep and 1" apart, or transplant 3" seedlings 6" apart in rows 24–36" apart, 30 days before the last frost date in the spring and 90 days before the first autumn frost date, in well-drained sandy soil or loam amended with organic matter. Collards tolerate periods of drought but do best in consistently moist soil.

**CARE:** Although collards are typically associated with Southern cooking, they are adaptable to a wide range of climates and taste best when they mature during cool weather. They are more heat tolerant than other cole crops and slower to bolt. Thin seedlings to 8" apart when they are 4" tall. Sidedress with well-rotted manure or compost, hand-weed carefully, and mulch well during warm weather. Use water-soluble plant food, such as Miracle-Gro Water Soluble All Purpose, every 2 weeks. Mulch to overwinter.

**Leave the topmost bud on the plant to encourage new leaf growth.**

**PROPAGATION:** Grow from direct-sown seed or from transplants started indoors.

**HARVEST:** Leaves will be ready to pick 70–85 days after seeding. Pick leaves from the top of the plants. The topmost bud is a delicacy, but leave it if you want the plant to produce more leaves. Or cut the entire plant at the ground. Collards can be stored for several weeks in the crisper drawer of the refrigerator. The curly blue-green leaves are high in vitamins C and A and rich in potassium and calcium. Steam or braise them and season like cabbage.

**PESTS AND DISEASES:** Knock off aphids with a strong stream from the garden hose. Remove cabbage worms and loopers by hand, or use Bt for serious infestations. Handpick harlequin bugs or control with pyrethrum. Control clubroot through clean gardening practices and crop rotation.

**RECOMMENDED CULTIVARS:** 'Georgia Southern' is the most common variety and is well known for tolerance of heat and poor soil. 'Champion' and 'Flash' are fast, vigorous, cold-tolerant choices. The heirloom variety 'Green Glaze' is pest resistant.

# KALE

*Brassica oleracea* Acephala group *BRASS-ih-kuh oh-leh-RAY-see-uh ay-SEF-uh-luh*

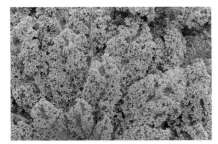

**'Dwarf Blue' is a tightly curled Scotch kale, sometimes called borekole.**

**ZONES:** NA
**SIZE:** 12–18"h ×
12–36"w
**TYPE:** Biennial
grown as an annual
**GROWTH:** Average

**LIGHT:** Full sun to
light shade
**MOISTURE:** Average
**FEATURES:** Edible,
sometimes
ornamental, leaves

**SITING:** Plant seeds ½" deep and 1" apart, or transplant 3" seedlings 6" apart, in rows 24–36" apart, 30 days before the last frost date in spring and 70 days before the first autumn frost date, in well-drained, fertile loam amended with organic matter. Keep the soil consistently moist.

**CARE:** Kale is a nonheading cross between cabbage and greens. Scotch kale is the type most often grown for commercial sale. It has tightly curled grayish-green leaves. The leaves of Siberian kale are smoother but have frilly edges. Ornamental kales are also edible but not as tasty. All varieties taste best when planted so they mature during cool weather. Gradually thin seedlings to 1' apart. When plants are about 4" tall, side dress with slow-release plant food and mulch well to conserve moisture and control weeds.

**Kale's flavor is improved by frost.**

**PROPAGATION:** Grow from direct-sown seed or transplants started indoors.
**HARVEST:** Leaves are ready to pick 55–75 days from seeding. Pick the large basal leaves, or cut the entire plant at ground level. The central rosette is the most delicious part of the plant, but leave it growing if you want the plant to produce more leaves. Tender young leaves harvested in cool weather are delicious in salads. More mature leaves are used like cabbage.
**PESTS AND DISEASES:** Knock off aphids with a strong stream from the garden hose. Remove cabbage worms and loopers by hand or use *Bt* for serious infestations. Handpick harlequin bugs or control with pyrethrum. Kale is somewhat resistant to clubroot.
**RECOMMENDED CULTIVARS:** 'Winterbor' (green) and 'Redbor' (purple) are frilly types used for garnishes. 'White Peacock' and 'Red Peacock' have finely cut edges; young leaves are good in salads. Blue Siberian types grow well in warm climates; 'Dwarf Blue Curled' is a good choice for harvesting even in snow.

# CAULIFLOWER

*Brassica oleracea* Botrytis group *BRASS-ih-kuh oh-leh-RAY-see-uh boh-TRY-tis*

**The leaves of self-blanching cauliflower curl up to protect the heads from sun.**

**ZONES:** NA
**SIZE:** 8–12"h ×
18–36"w
**TYPE:** Annual
**GROWTH:** Average

**LIGHT:** Full sun to
light shade
**MOISTURE:** Average
**FEATURES:** Edible
heads

**SITING:** Sow seed 90 days before the first frost date ½" deep and 24" apart in rows 3' apart in rich, well-drained soil. Or transplant seedlings that have at least three true leaves.
**CARE:** Thin seedlings when they are about 1" tall. Mulch and water regularly to keep the soil cool and moist. Weed carefully by hand, taking care not to damage the

leaves, which can lead to buttoning (underdeveloped heads). To protect standard white-head varieties from sunscald, blanch by pulling the longest leaves up and over the head and holding them in place with twine or strips of soft nylon. Begin blanching as soon as you can see the head; make sure it's dry before you wrap it with leaves. Purple and green heads do not need to be blanched.
**PROPAGATION:** Grow from transplants for spring crops and from seed or transplants for fall crops.

**Purple-head types need extra space.**

**Tie the longest leaves together over the heads to blanch them.**

**HARVEST:** Cut the heads below the inner leaves when the heads are 6–8" in diameter. Heads past their peak will show curds that have begun to separate. To store whole heads for 2–3 weeks, cut them below the outer leaves and wrap those leaves around the heads. Uncooked cauliflower is more nutritious and has a stronger flavor than cooked. Purple- and green-headed types are the most nutritious.
**PESTS AND DISEASES:** Knock off aphids with a strong stream from the garden hose. Remove cabbage worms and loopers by hand or use *Bt* for serious infestations. Hand-pick harlequin bugs or control with pyrethrum. Control clubroot through clean gardening practices and crop rotation.
**RECOMMENDED CULTIVARS:** 'Early Snowball' matures quickly on small plants that fit well in a garden with limited space. 'Snow Crown' is a standard white type that matures before the weather turns hot. Purple-head types need a lot of space but are heat and cold tolerant and freeze well. 'Chartreuse' is a tasty bright green head that's a good choice for warm climates or for fall crops in cold regions.

# CABBAGE

*Brassica oleracea* Capitata group *BRASS-ih-kuh oh-leh-RAY-see-uh kap-ih-TAY-ta*

Keep the soil consistently moist to prevent cabbage heads from cracking.

**ZONES:** NA
**SIZE:** 6–12"h × 10–30"w
**TYPE:** Biennial grown as an annual
**GROWTH:** Average
**LIGHT:** Full sun to light shade
**MOISTURE:** Average
**FEATURES:** Edible leaves

**SITING:** Plant in deep, well-drained loam. Sow seeds ½" deep and 1" apart, or plant 4" seedlings in rows 18–24" apart. Interplant cabbage with earlier crops in small gardens.

**CARE:** Maintain consistent soil moisture to prevent the heads from cracking. Water from the sides to avoid wetting any part of the plants and weed carefully to avoid damaging the roots. Use mulch to conserve moisture and discourage weeds. Use water-soluble plant food twice a month until harvest. Some types may sprout new, smaller heads after the first harvest.

**PROPAGATION:** Grow from seeds sown indoors and transplanted 3–5 weeks after the last frost date for spring crops; direct sow for summer and fall crops.

**HARVEST:** Cut heads with a sharp knife at ground level when they are firm and 4–10" in diameter. Discard outer leaves and inspect the heads for insects before storing. Cracked heads indicate cabbages past their peak. Flavor is best right after harvest, but cabbage stores well in cool, humid conditions for several months. Common green cabbage has smooth leaves and compact heads; Savoy types have flat or semiflat heads of curly leaves. Some midseason cultivars have red leaves.

**PESTS AND DISEASES:** Use a cutworm collar around seedlings. Knock off aphids with a stream from the garden hose. Remove cabbage worms and loopers by hand or use *Bt*. Control harlequin bugs and flea beetles with labelled insecticides. Dust plant bases with diatomaceous earth to prevent cabbage maggots. Control clubroot and black rot through clean cultivation and crop rotation. Choose varieties with good resistance to yellows.

**RECOMMENDED CULTIVARS:** Early types include 'Farao' (green), 'Red Express', and 'Gonzales' (a green, dwarf variety good for small gardens). Midseason types, including 'Tendersweet' (green) and 'Regal Red'. Savoy types, 'Drumhead', or 'Red Perfection', grow well late in the season.

Savoy types have crinkly leaves.

Mulch with straw to conserve moisture.

Water heads from the sides.

Test for firmness before harvesting.

# BRUSSELS SPROUTS

*Brassica oleracea* Gemmifera group *BRASS-ih-kuh oh-leh-RAY-see-uh jem-MIF-er-uh*

A space-efficient plant for small gardens, each tall stalk bears dozens of heads.

**ZONES:** NA
**SIZE:** 12–36"h × 8–18"w
**TYPE:** Biennial grown as annual
**GROWTH:** Average
**LIGHT:** Full sun to light shade
**MOISTURE:** Average
**FEATURES:** Edible heads (sprouts)

**SITING:** Plant seeds ½" deep and 2" apart in an outdoor seedbed about 90 days before the first frost date; transplant 5" seedlings into deep, friable soil rich with added compost or composted manure. Choose a location where you can water during high heat or drought.

**CARE:** Each stalk may bear 50 to 100 sprouts at the points where the leaves join the stalk. Brussels sprouts are a good cool-weather crop for small gardens, where they can be interplanted with lettuces or other quick-maturing crops. Use plant food, such as Miracle-Gro Liquid Quick Start, and shade seedlings from direct sun until they are established. Use a cutworm collar around seedlings. Water frequently during dry or hot spells. Mulch well to conserve moisture and prevent weeds. Weed carefully to avoid damaging shallow roots. Use water-soluble plant food, such as Miracle-Gro Water Soluble All Purpose, twice a month while sprouts are developing. Stake stems to prevent wind damage. Break off yellowing leaves as sprouts grow.

**PROPAGATION:** Grow from seeds or transplants. In cold climates seeds can be started indoors 125–135 days before the first frost date.

**HARVEST:** Begin cutting sprouts from the bottom of the stalks when they are ¾–1½" in diameter. Frost improves their flavor.

**PESTS AND DISEASES:** The same pests that affect cabbage attack Brussels sprouts.

**RECOMMENDED CULTIVARS:** 'Long Island Improved' and 'Catskill' (a dwarf variety) are heat sensitive and best grown as fall crops. 'Jade Cross' and 'Oliver' mature in 90 days and are more heat tolerant than other types.

**1** Pinch out the growing tip when bottom sprouts are ½" wide.

**2** Begin cutting the bottom sprouts when they are ¾" or larger.

# KOHLRABI

*Brassica oleracea* Gongylodes group *BRASS-ih-kuh oh-leh-RAY-see-uh gon-gy-LOH-deez*

**Kohlrabi's rounded stems taste similar to turnips but milder.**

**ZONES:** NA
**SIZE:** : 9–12"h × 9–12"w
**TYPE:** Biennial grown as annual
**GROWTH:** Fast

**LIGHT:** Full sun to light shade
**MOISTURE:** Average
**FEATURES:** Edible stems

**SITING:** Kohlrabi thrives in any medium-textured, nutrient-rich soil that is free of rocks and holds moisture well. Sow seeds ¼" deep and 1" apart in rows 18" apart (10" in raised beds). Space transplants 10" apart.

**CARE:** Thin seedlings to 10" apart. Mulch to conserve soil moisture and prevent weeds. Water during hot or dry periods. Weed by hand to avoid disturbing the roots. Use a soluble plant food twice a month.
**PROPAGATION:** Grow from seed. Direct-sow 4–6 weeks before the last frost date, or transplant 4 weeks before to 2 weeks after the last frost date. Sow again

**Slice off the bulb at the base when the stem is 2–3" in diameter.**

about 10 weeks before the first autumn frost date for a fall harvest.
**HARVEST:** Kohlrabi is a fast-growing cabbage family member with stems that swell into rounded bulb shapes just above the soil. The flavor is similar to turnip but milder. Slice through the roots below the bulbs when they are at least 1½" but no more than 3" in diameter, approximately 50–70 days from seeding. Remove the leaves and store bulbs up to 3 weeks in a root cellar or the refrigerator crisper drawer. Peel and eat kohlrabi raw in salads or with dips or cooked like turnips. Dice, blanch, and freeze pieces for later use.
**PESTS AND DISEASES** Remove cabbage worms by hand or use *Bt* for serious infestations. Handpick harlequin bugs or control with pyrethrum or other labelled insecticide. Dust with rotenone or spray with an appropriate insecticide to control flea beetles. Control clubroot through clean cultivation and crop rotation.
**RECOMMENDED CULTIVARS:** 'Grand Duke' matures quickly. 'Early Purple Vienna' is a good choice for late-season crops.

# BROCCOLI

*Brassica oleracea* Italica group *BRASS-ih-kuh oh-leh-RAY-see-uh ih-TAL-ih-kuh*

**Broccoli thrives with consistent moisture in cool weather.**

**ZONES:** NA
**SIZE:** About 2'h × 2'w
**TYPE:** Annual
**GROWTH:** Fast

**LIGHT:** Full sun to part shade
**MOISTURE:** Average
**FEATURES:** Edible heads (florets)

**SITING:** Broccoli needs rich soil with plenty of nitrogen and calcium. Work in several inches of well-rotted manure or compost before planting. Plant three seeds together ½" deep every 18" in rows 36" apart, thinning 1" seedlings to the most vigorous one in each group. Or transplant seedlings in the same row spacing.
**CARE:** Broccoli grows quickly and vigorously in cool weather; in cool climates with a long growing season, two plantings

are possible. Sprouting plants produce side shoots after the main heads are harvested. Use a collar around seedlings to discourage cutworms. Maintain consistent moisture to prevent slowed growth. Buttons indicate lack of water or plant food or both. Weed carefully to avoid damaging the roots. Use mulch to conserve moisture and discourage weeds. Use balanced water-soluble plant food twice a month until harvest.
**PROPAGATION:** Grow from seed when the soil is 40°F or above, or from transplants when the soil reaches 60°F.

**Side shoots may grow larger after the main head is harvested.**

**HARVEST:** Cut heads with a sharp knife when they are tight and firm, about 55–85 days after seeding. Heads with buds beginning to separate into yellow flowers indicate broccoli past its peak, although it is still edible. Discard any outer leaves and inspect the heads for insects before storing. Flavor is best right after harvest, but broccoli stores well in cool, humid conditions for a week or more.
**PESTS AND DISEASES:** Knock off aphids with a strong stream from the garden hose. Remove cabbage worms and loopers by hand or use *Bt* for serious infestations. Handpick harlequin bugs or spray with an appropriate insecticide to control them. Dust plant bases with diatomaceous earth to control cabbage maggots. Control clubroot through clean gardening practices and crop rotation.
**RECOMMENDED CULTIVARS:** 'Green Comet' and 'Spartan Early' have dark green heads 7" across. 'Gypsy' and 'Arcadia' mature early and are disease resistant. 'DeCicco' and all other varieties produce side shoots for an extended period after the main harvest. Broccoli raab (*B. rapa ruvo*) is a related species grown for its turniplike greens and immature flower buds; try 'Super Rapini'.

# BOK CHOY

*Brassica rapa* Chinensis group *BRASS-ih-kuh RAY-puh chi-NEN-sis*

**Bok choy, or pak choi, forms an upright bunch similar to chard. It is also known as celery mustard.**

**ZONES:** NA
**SIZE:** 9–20"h ×
6–9"w
**TYPE:** Annual
**GROWTH:** Fast to
average

**LIGHT:** Full sun to
part shade
**MOISTURE:** Average
**FEATURES:** Edible
leaves

**SITING:** Chinese cabbage (*B. r.* Pekinensis group) and bok choy are highly adaptable to all soils but will grow largest in fertile loam amended with several inches of well-rotted compost or manure. Grow from seed direct-sown ½" deep and 2" apart in rows 18–24" apart. Thin seedlings or space transplants 10–18" apart. Keep the soil continuously moist.

**CARE:** Chinese cabbage forms heads of crinkly leaves; bok choy forms loose bunches of thick-ribbed leaves similar to chard. They are grown similarly to most cole crops. Protect seedlings from sunscald and cold temperatures. Mulch around plants to conserve soil moisture and deter weeds. Water during dry periods. Water from underneath or to the sides of plants rather than from above, which can invite disease problems. Use water soluble plant food twice a month.

**Some Chinese cabbages form rounded heads. This is 'Kasumi'.**

**PROPAGATION:** Grow from seed started indoors 4–6 weeks before the last frost date. Direct-seed fall crops about 90 days before the first frost date.

**HARVEST:** Plants are ready to harvest in 21–75 days, depending on type. Pull out whole plants as needed when they have reached mature size, or pick outer leaves and leave the plant to produce new ones for later harvest. Chinese cabbage and bok choy are easier to digest than standard cabbage but just as nutritious. Both species can be eaten raw in salads or steamed, stir-fried, or added to soups. Store plants for up to a month in a refrigerator crisper drawer.

**PESTS AND DISEASES:** Use a cutworm collar around seedlings. Knock off aphids with a strong stream from the garden hose. Remove cabbage worms and loopers by hand or use *Bt* for serious infestations. Handpick harlequin bugs or control with pyrethrum. Dust with rotenone to control flea beetles.

**RECOMMENDED CULTIVARS:** 'Joi Choi' bok choy is tolerant of heat and cold and is slow to bolt. 'Greenwich' Chinese cabbage is large and disease resistant. 'Minuet' is also disease-resistant, and is a good choice for small gardens.

# TURNIP

*Brassica rapa* Rapifera group *BRASS-ih-kuh RAY-puh ray-pih-FAIR-uh*

**Use the young tops as greens but leave some to feed the roots.**

**ZONES:** NA
**SIZE:** 6–12"h ×
4–6"w
**TYPE:** Biennial
grown as annual
**GROWTH:** Fast to
average

**LIGHT:** Full sun to
part shade
**MOISTURE:** Average
**FEATURES:** Edible
leaves and roots

**SITING:** Sow seeds in groups of three about ½" deep and 2" apart in rows 12" apart in rich, friable soil 4–6 weeks before the last frost date in spring and 70 days before the first autumn frost date.

Keep the soil consistently moist.
**CARE:** Thin seedlings (and enjoy them in salads) when the first true leaves appear and again if any plants touch one another until they are 6" apart. Cut (rather than pull) the seedlings to avoid damaging the roots of those that remain. Mulch to conserve soil moisture and deter weeds. Water during dry periods.
**PROPAGATION:** Grow from seed.

**Dig turnip roots in cool weather while they are still tender.**

**HARVEST:** Like beets, turnips are an important early crop, bearing greens and edible roots. The roots are nutritious and the greens are extremely high in vitamins and minerals. Pick or cut leaves as needed about 40–80 days after seeding. Dig roots while they are young and tender, no more than 3" in diameter. If the weather turns hot, dig the whole crop and store the turnips unwashed in the refrigerator crisper drawer for up to several weeks, or slice, blanch, and freeze them for cooking later. Cook the spicy leaves like greens or use them raw in salads; leave some if you want to harvest roots later.

**PESTS AND DISEASES:** Most cultivars are disease resistant. Pick off harlequin bugs and cabbage worms by hand, or use *Bt* for serious infestations. Remove and destroy leaves infested with leaf miners and use floating row covers to discourage them.

**RECOMMENDED CULTIVARS:** Grow 'Just Right' for greens. For early-season turnips, grow fast-maturing 'Tokyo' cultivars. For fall crops, plant 'Purple-Top White Globe' or 'Aberdeen', a yellow variety.

# POT MARIGOLD

*Calendula officinalis* *kuh-LEN-dyoo-luh uh-fish-ih-NAL-iss*

**Pot marigold produces bright yellow or orange flowers during cooler summer temperatures.**

**ZONES:** NA
**SIZE:** 12–30"h × 12–18"w
**TYPE:** Annual
**GROWTH:** Fast
**LIGHT:** Full sun

**MOISTURE:** Medium to high
**FEATURES:** Flowers, foliage
**FLOWERS:** ■ ■

**SITING:** Calendula prefers full sun and moderately fertile soil with a pH of 5.5–7.0 and good drainage. The bright orange, yellow, gold, or cream blooms provide long-season color from summer into fall. In hot climates use calendula as a cool-season annual. Place groups in the front of the border, in containers, or as bedding plants covering a large area. Pot marigold makes an excellent fresh cut flower. Container companions include 'Brilliant' and 'Autumn Joy' sedums, cockscomb, and white-flowered 'Miss Wilmott' pincushion flower.

**CARE:** Plant 12" apart in late spring or early summer after the last frost. Water deeply when the soil is dry. Deadhead the blooms to encourage reblooming. Remove the plants just prior to or after the first frost.

**PROPAGATION:** Sprinkle seeds over the soil mix and cover lightly. Thoroughly moisten and keep moist but not soggy. Germination will occur in 10–14 days at 70°F.

**HARVEST:** Gather flowers; use fresh petals as a colorful addition to salads; dried and powdered as a substitute for saffron in rice. The petals have little flavor.

**PESTS AND DISEASES:** Diseases include aster yellows, powdery mildew, and fungal leaf spots. Slugs feed on the foliage.

**RELATED CULTIVARS:** 'Art Shades' (24" tall with orange and cream flowers), 'Fiesta Giant' (a dwarf that reaches 12" tall and has double flowers in light orange and yellow), 'Indian Prince' (dark orange flowers with a reddish tint), and Pacific Beauty Series (double flowers that include interesting bicolors with a mahogany-colored center).

**Harvest flowers just as they open for use in salads.**

**Sprinkle flower petals over salad for a festive look.**

# CAPER

*Capparis spinosa* *kap-PAR-is spin-OH-suh*

**Caper blooms are fragrant; the immature buds are a delicacy.**

**ZONES:** 8–11
**SIZE:** 3'–5'h × 5'–10'w
**TYPE:** Deciduous perennial shrub
**GROWTH:** Slow
**LIGHT:** Full sun

**MOISTURE:** Low
**FEATURES:** Ornamental plant, edible immature flower buds and berries

**SITING:** Capers thrive in dry, rocky, poor soils and along sandy shorelines where temperatures do not fall below 20°F. Choose a location where you can water transplants easily.

**CARE:** Capers are the immature flower buds of a spiny shrub. The flowers are fragrant and attractive, resembling cleome. Space transplants 10' apart and mulch heavily to conserve soil moisture. (Remove the mulch as soon as the plants are well rooted.) Keep transplants moist until they are established; cover them with clear plastic and provide shade from direct sun so they don't wilt. Use balanced water-soluble plant food during the first 3 years. Avoid pruning plants until the third year, then cut them to the ground late in the year.

**Collect the buds by hand when they are swollen but not yet open.**

**PROPAGATION:** Caper is slow to germinate from presoaked seed; it is best established from stem cuttings taken in late winter or early spring.

**HARVEST:** The caper bush buds in the fourth year in U.S. coastal zones and lives 20–30 years. Pick flower buds early in the morning just before they are about to flower. They should be about ⅛–¼" in diameter. Soak the buds in a brine solution for 30 days, then pickle them in salted vinegar and store in glass jars for up to 6 months. Pickling brings out their peppery flavor, which comes from a type of mustard oil contained in the plant tissues. The smallest buds are considered the most desirable.

**PESTS AND DISEASES:** Viruses may be introduced when cuttings are taken or plants are grafted. Clean cultural practices help to avoid such problems. Pick off weevils and cabbage worms by hand or treat serious infestations with Bt or labeled insecticide. Water plants from underneath to avoid mold and botrytis.

**RECOMMENDED CULTIVARS:** 'Josephine' and 'Nocellana' are bred to be spineless. Spineless types may be more pest resistant.

# PEPPER
*Capsicum annuum* KAP-sib-kum AN-yoo-um

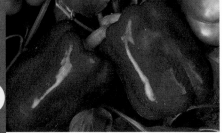

**Green bell peppers grow sweeter when ripened to red on the plant.**

ZONES: NA
SIZE: 6–30"h ×
6–24"w
TYPE: Annual
GROWTH: Average

LIGHT: Full sun
MOISTURE: Average
FEATURES: Edible
fruits; some plants
are ornamental

SITING: Pepper seeds require a high soil temperature to germinate, so in all but the hottest climates start them indoors 40–60 days before transplanting time. Choose a location where the temperature is 70–75°F in the daytime and no lower than 60°F at night. When the soil temperature is consistently 60°F or more, set transplants 12–24" apart in rows 24–36" apart in well-drained loam amended with

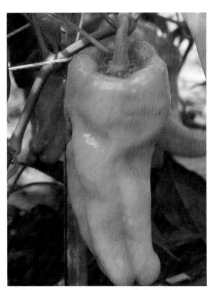

**Lobed Cubanelle sweet peppers come in a variety of colors and are good fresh, fried, stuffed, or roasted.**

rotted manure or compost. If the soil is low in magnesium, dig in a dusting of Epsom salts. Plant sweet and hot varieties as far apart as possible in the garden to avoid cross-pollination. (In small gardens, expect sweet peppers to have a mildly tangy flavor from cross-pollination.)

**Medium-hot Hungarian wax peppers can be used at any stage of maturity.**

CARE: Use starter solution, such as Miracle-Gro Liquid Quick Start, to prevent transplant shock. Keep the soil weed free and consistently and thoroughly moist. Use a soaker hose if necessary during periods of drought or high heat. Feed with Miracle-Gro Water Soluble All Purpose Plant Food twice a month while plants are in flower. Peppers usually don't need staking, but large cultivars planted where they are exposed to strong winds will benefit from tomato cages. Prolonged temperatures below 60°F or above 90°F cause blossom drop, so be prepared to protect plants from such extremes with row covers, cloches, or a cold frame to conserve warmth in cool weather, and shade cloth and mulch when it's hot. Lush plants with

**Mildly hot poblanos, also called ancho peppers, ripen from green to red.**

**'Jimmy Nardello' is a sweet nonbell cultivar good in salads and stir-fries.**

no peppers can also be a sign of excess nitrogen or low humidity. Caution: Wear rubber gloves when handling hot peppers and keep your hands away from your face.
PROPAGATION: Grow from seeds or set out transplants in the garden.
HARVEST: Pick sweet peppers at any color. Pick hot peppers anytime for fresh use, but leave them on the plants until fully ripe if you want to dry them. Pick often so the plants continue to produce new fruits. Use garden scissors to cut the stems and avoid damaging the plants. Peppers are high in fiber, beta-carotene, and vitamins A and C. A red bell pepper contains more vitamin C than an orange. Although people with a preexisting gastrointestinal disorder may find peppers hard to digest,

**Habaneros come in a rainbow of hues but all are blistering hot.**

# PEPPER
*continued*

Capsaicin, a compound suppressed in sweet peppers, is the source of heat in hot varieties but does not cause ulcers.

hot peppers do not cause ulcers. The heat comes from capsaicin, a naturally occurring compound that is suppressed in sweet peppers. Use sweet peppers raw in salads, on sandwiches, and as crudités. Roast, grill, or stir-fry hot peppers and add them judiciously to any dish that calls for a little zing. Poke small holes into a few small hot peppers and drop them into a bottle of olive or other vegetable oil. Within days you'll have a zesty cooking oil worthy of any Asian cuisine. Store unwashed fresh peppers in the refrigerator for up to a week. To dry hot peppers, string them together by running needle and thread through the tops near the caps and hang them in a cool, dry location with good air circulation. Store dried ground peppers in a tightly sealed glass jar in a cool location away from sunlight. Peppers freeze well and do not need to be blanched first. Wash and dry them well, slice or chop, and place in thin layers in plastic freezer bags. **PESTS AND DISEASES:** Knock off aphids with a strong spray from the garden hose; use a mild soap solution for heavy infestations. Handpick and destroy any beetles and caterpillars. If whole peppers rot, check for pepper maggots or corn

earworms and destroy the entire plant if it is infested. Discourage tarnished plant bugs through clean cultivation practices. Choose cultivars with resistance to viruses. Avoid bacterial problems through clean cultivation and crop rotation. Control blossom-end rot by providing consistent moisture throughout the growing season.

**RECOMMENDED CULTIVARS:**
**SWEET PEPPERS:** 'California Wonder' and 'Whopper Improved' are among the most popular green bell peppers because of high yields over a long period and virus resistance (70–80 days to maturity, based on the time transplants are set out). 'Labrador' bell ripens to a bright yellow (60–80 days). 'Ariane' is a large orange bell resistant to mosaic virus (60–75 days). 'Big Early' produces enormous bells up to 8" long and 4" in diameter that can be picked green or left to ripen to red (65–75 days). 'Ace' red bells are smaller but more prolific and resistant to blossom drop. 'Lipstick' is an early, short, lobeless, tapering bell that ripens to an extremely sweet red (55–75 days). 'Blushing Beauty' bells start out ivory and blush from yellow to light orange-red to deep scarlet, never showing any green. The plant is resistant to bacterial leaf spots and many viruses (65–75 days). 'Tequila' bells start out purple and fade to red as they mature (65–75 days). 'Hershey' bells mature from green to chocolate-brown (70–80 days). For a sweet pepper that is ornamental as well as tasty, try 'Roumainian Rainbow'. The fruits turn from ivory to orange to red; plants often have peppers in all stages of coloration simultaneously (60–70 days). **SWEET NONBELL PEPPERS:** 'Banana Supreme' is an 8" early banana pepper that ripens to red (60–75 days). For frying peppers that are also good in salads, try 'Cubanelle' (yellow-green) or 'Corno di Toro', available in red or yellow varieties (65–70 days). 'Giant Marconi', an early, hardy, highly disease-resistant grilling pepper, is sweetest when left to turn red on the vine. 'Cherry Pick', 1½" round

Mulch plants to conserve moisture and control weeds.

Water with a soaker hose during drought or high heat.

# PEPPER
*continued*

cherry peppers can be pickled green or red (65–75 days). 'Pimento L' bears 4"-long heart-shaped fruit that can be eaten fresh or processed as traditional pimientos (90–100 days). 'Sweet Cayenne' (up to 12") and 'Jimmy Nardello' (6–8") look like long, hot cayenne peppers *(C. frutenscens)* but actually are among the sweetest nonbell peppers available (75–85 days). For container growing, try 'Sweet Pickle', an edible ornamental plant that holds its 2" yellow, orange, red, and purple peppers upright on compact plants (75 days). 'Chilly Chili' peppers look like little cayennes but are not hot. The compact, colorful, and extremely heat-tolerant plants are perfect for patio containers (70–80 days).

**HOT PEPPERS:** 'Robustini' is a mildly hot pepperoncini good for salads or for pickling (62 days). 'Paprika Supreme' has 6–8" tapered, sweet red fruits with just a hint of warmth. Remove the ribs to eliminate the heat. Use fresh, or dry them for grinding into paprika powder (55–80 days). 'Hungarian Hot Wax' has 5–6" fruits that ripen from pale yellow to bright red and are good for frying and

**Always wear gloves when handling hot peppers to avoid transferring the heat-bearing capsaicin to your skin.**

**Cut the peppers off with scissors or pruning shears to avoid tearing the stems.**

pickling (55–85 days). 'Big Chili' is a mildly hot 8–10" Anaheim cultivar good fresh or cooked (75–85 days). 'Cherry Bomb' is a small, medium-hot, high-yielding round cherry pepper that ripens from green to red (65–85 days). Use 'Ancho 101' in chile

rellenos recipes (75–85 days). It is a prolific producer over a long season. 'Jaloro' is an unusual yellow jalapeno that ripens to orange and then red, and is especially virus resistant (70 days). 'Mucho Nacho' is a traditional green-to-red jalapeno that is larger and hotter than the standard varieties (70–80 days). 'Serrano' is a hot chile good for salsa or salads, if you dare (75–85 days). 'Serranno del Sol' is a hybrid with longer fruits that mature earlier (65 days).

**EXTREMELY HOT PEPPERS:** 'Super Cayenne II' is prolific and especially disease resistant, with 5–6" peppers (70 days). 'Habanero' *(C. chinense)* is a small but extremely hot pepper that ripens from green to orange. Remove the ribs and seeds to reduce the heat (75–100 days). For high yields try its relatives 'Congo Trinidad' (red), 'Jamaican Hot' (yellow and red), or 'Yellow Mushroom', also available in a red cultivar (75–95 days). 'Jamaican Hot Chocolate' is a reddish-brown habanero-type pepper with a smoky flavor (85 days). 'Scotch Bonnet' is similar to habanero but grows well only in long-season areas (120 days). 'Tabasco' *(C. frutescens)* is a small chile that packs the punch its namesake sauce made famous (80 days). 'Thai Hot' holds its peppers up above the leaves and thus makes an attractive ornamental, but keep it away from children (90 days). Beware the tiny 'Chiltepin', a blistering hybrid of the bird pepper plants that grow wild in the southeastern United States (90–100 days).

**Congo peppers are hot at any stage of development.**

# PAPAYA

*Carica papaya* KAIR-ib-kuh pub-PY-uh

Hand-pollinate papaya flowers to ensure high fruit yields. It is also known as pawpaw.

**ZONES:** 10 and 11
**SIZE:** Up to 30'h × 6'w
**TYPE:** Perennial grown as a tree
**GROWTH:** Fast
**LIGHT:** Full sun
**MOISTURE:** Average
**FEATURES:** Edible fruits

**SITING:** Plant 8–10' apart in light, well-drained soil not overly rich in organic matter. Although papaya needs consistent moisture, it does not tolerate even brief periods of standing water. Provide a windbreak if planting in an open area.
**CARE:** One male plant can pollinate up to 25 females. Cover unopened female flowers with paper bags; after blossoms open use a small brush to dust pollen onto pistils. Bagging bisexual flowers in the same way helps to guarantee self-pollination. Water plants at least once a week during dry weather. Use plant food, such as Miracle-Gro Water Soluble All Purpose, according to label directions. Plants produce well for 3–4 years before weakening. Start a few new plants each year to replace those you must retire and plant them in a different location. Remove and compost any plant debris to avoid soilborne diseases.

Save germination time by washing the seeds before planting them.

**PROPAGATION:** Grow from seed. Germination takes 3–5 weeks; washing the seeds in water to remove the gelatinous membrane before planting saves a week or two.
**HARVEST:** Spring transplants are ready for harvest by November.

Each plant produces two to four fruits per week. Cut the short stalks with a clean knife. Fruits will ripen off the tree but are not as sweet as those picked ripe. Gardeners who are allergic to papain or latex should not touch any part of the papaya plant.
**PESTS AND DISEASES:** Use sulfur to combat powdery mildew and fungicides for ring spot, black spot, blights, anthracnose, and other diseases. Control mosaic virus with clean cultural practices and pesticides labeled for green citrus aphids. Spray whiteflies with insecticidal soap. Spray *Btk* on webworm larvae; knock caterpillars into a bucket of soapy water to kill them. Remove and destroy any branches infested with scales, then wipe off any scales on the trunk with an insecticidal soap solution.
**RECOMMENDED CULTIVARS:** 'Solo' cultivars bear the small, hermaphroditic papayas often sold commercially. 'Blue Solo' is a low-growing hybrid that does well in Florida. 'Solo Sunrise' has larger than average red-flesh fruits that keep well. 'Red Thai' has sweet reddish-orange flesh.

# PECAN

*Carya illinoinensis* KAR-ee-uh ill-ih-NO-een-en-sis

Shake or knock ripe nuts from the tree onto the ground for easy gathering.

**ZONES:** 5–9
**SIZE:** 60–150'h × 60–100'w
**TYPE:** Deciduous tree
**GROWTH:** Slow
**LIGHT:** Full sun
**MOISTURE:** High
**FEATURES:** Edible seeds (nuts)

**SITING:** Plant bare-root trees in deep, well-drained, acid soil in an elevated area to avoid frost damage. Pecans do not tolerate salinity.
**CARE:** Use a balanced plant food once in early spring at a rate of 1 pound per year of age for immature trees and 4 pounds per inch of trunk diameter just below the scaffold branches for bearing trees. Water newly planted trees thoroughly and maintain consistent moisture. Water mature trees during dry spells. Train each tree to a central leader with lateral branches 8–18" apart.
**PROPAGATION:** Grow pecans from grafted rootstock. Plant at least two different varieties to ensure cross pollination.
**HARVEST:** Trees start to bear 5–8 years after planting but have a productive life of at least 50 years. Nuts ripen from late summer to autumn; gather by knocking them from the tree with a long pole or mechanical

Choose cultivars resistant to pecan scab disease and bred for your climate.

shaker onto a sheet spread below. Dry the nuts in burlap bags hung in a warm, dry area with good air circulation. Freeze nutmeats for best long-term storage.
**PESTS AND DISEASES:** Pecan scab disease can be a problem in high heat and humidity. Use a fungicide labeled for pecans early in the season on susceptible cultivars. Use insecticides labeled for yellow and black pecan aphids. Twig girdlers, pecan weevils, and stink bugs attack nuts late in the season. Gather and destroy infested nuts and fallen twigs, and remove other vegetative debris from the area that can harbor insects. Deer eat young shoots and rub their antlers on the bark; squirrels and birds eat the nuts.
**RECOMMENDED CULTIVARS:** Eastern varieties, such as 'Desirable', have large nuts and are resistant to pecan scab disease; western cultivars, such as 'Wichita', have medium-size nuts and are susceptible to pecan scab, so they are suitable only for desert and dry southwestern areas. Both can be pollinated with 'Western Schley' or 'Cheyenne'. 'Kanza' and 'Pawnee' are disease-resistant cultivars developed for Zones 6 and 7.

# WHITE SAPOTE
### *Casimiroa edulis*  kah-see-mi-ROH-uh ED-yoo-lis

**Grafted white sapotes can be grown in containers if pruned regularly.**

**ZONES:** 9 and 10
**SIZE:** 15–50'h × 15–50'w
**TYPE:** Evergreen tree

**GROWTH:** Slow
**LIGHT:** Full sun
**MOISTURE:** Average
**FEATURES:** Edible fruits

**SITING:** White sapote grows anywhere where oranges grow successfully. Plant in any well-drained soil away from patios or other areas where visiting bees, flies, and ants would be a nuisance and where fallen twigs and fruit make a mess.

**CARE:** White sapote is drought tolerant but does best with regular deep watering to discourage surface roots that ruin lawns or break through pavement. Established trees tolerate wet roots and some frost to 25°F. Feed with plant food, such as Miracle-Gro Water Soluble All Purpose. Pinch out the terminal bud to encourage branching, then prune for compact growth.

**PROPAGATION:** Grow from grafted rootstock; seedlings produce inferior fruit.

**HARVEST:** Grafted trees bear fruit in 3–4 years. The apple-size fruit ripens 6–9 months after flowers bloom, from midsummer to February depending on

**Locate the tree away from areas where fallen fruit will make a mess.**

the cultivar and locale. Tree-ripened fruit has the best flavor but is likely to fall first; the fruit bruises easily, and the flesh beneath bruises turns bitter. Handle fruits gently and as little as possible. Clip mature fruits with short stems attached; the stems will fall off when the fruit is ready to eat. Store ripe fruits in the refrigerator for up to 2 weeks. The flesh is creamy white to yellow and tastes like custard. Avoid eating the peel and seeds. Eat fresh fruit out of hand or in salads, or mash and freeze the pulp to use in ice cream or baked goods.

**PESTS AND DISEASES:** Temperature extremes cause temporary defoliation, and harsh winds can cause fruit drop. Control weeds and use traps against snails. Discourage fruit flies by keeping fallen fruit and other vegetative debris collected and destroyed. Prune and destroy branches infested with black scale. Spray mealybugs with insecticidal soap. Control aphids with a sharp spray from the garden hose; use insecticidal soap for heavy infestations. Birds eat the fruit; be prepared to share.

**RECOMMENDED CULTIVARS:** 'Louise', 'Suebelle', and 'Michele' are nearly everbearing small to medium-size trees.

# CHESTNUT
### *Castanea* spp.  kas-TAY-nee-uh

**Squirrels avoid the spiny pods only until the pods split and release the nuts.**

**ZONES:** 4–9
**SIZE:** 40–100'h × 40–100'w
**TYPE:** Deciduous tree

**GROWTH:** Fast
**LIGHT:** Full sun
**MOISTURE:** Average
**FEATURES:** Edible seeds (nuts)

**SITING:** Plant 20–40' apart in deep, acid, fertile, well-drained soil.

**CARE:** Chestnuts bear on new wood, so pruning isn't necessary for good fruit set. Train young trees to a central leader. Water in hot or dry periods, especially in late summer when the pods are filling out. Mulch to keep the soil moist, but keep it away from the trunks. Use a balanced plant food once a year, in spring, at a rate of 1 pound per year of tree age or per inch of trunk diameter.

**PROPAGATION:** Grow from grafted cultivars. Chestnuts are self-infertile, so plant more than one type to ensure pollination.

**HARVEST:** Chestnuts begin bearing 3–6 years after planting. The spiny pods split open in early autumn, releasing one to three nuts. Gather the nuts daily and dry them in the sun for a few days to bring out their sweetness. Store them in a cool, dry location.

**Dry harvested nuts in the sun to bring out their natural sweetness.**

**PESTS AND DISEASES:** Chestnut weevils lay their eggs in ripening nuts; larvae emerge from fallen nuts and burrow into the ground. Control adult weevils with insecticides labeled for chestnuts. Chinese cultivars are susceptible to blight, especially in eastern regions; prune out infected branches or replace trees with resistant types. The spiny pods are squirrelproof until they split open, so harvest daily to avoid loss. Use a tree shelter to protect the trunk from deer, but remove it in autumn to allow the tree to harden off.

**RECOMMENDED CULTIVARS:** 'Revival' is a Chinese chestnut (*C. mollissima*) that grows well in the South and is hardy to 15°F. 'Grimo' cultivars of 'Layeroka' (*C. sativa* ×*mollissima*) are crosses between European and Chinese chestnuts resulting in large, blight-resistant, early-bearing trees hardy to −25°F. 'American Hybrid' (*C. dentata* ×*mollissima*) is a cross of American and Chinese types resulting in an upright growth habit and blight resistance. It is hardy to Zone 4. For small spaces, try 'Chinquapin' (*C. pumila*), a dwarf shrub, 6–10' tall and hardy to −30°F.

# CHAMOMILE
### *Chamaemelum nobile* *KAM-oh-meel-um no-BEEL-ay*

**With blossoms like daisies and a fresh apple scent, Roman chamomile enjoys wide popularity.**

**ZONES:** 5–9
**SIZE:** 8–10"h × 12"w
**TYPE:** Perennial herb
**GROWTH:** Rapid

**LIGHT:** Full sun to partial shade
**MOISTURE:** Moist
**FEATURES:** Fragrant flowers for tea

**SITING:** Sow seeds in a well-prepared area of the garden in easily-draining soil, enriched with compost annually, once soil has warmed in spring.

**CARE:** In a lawn, space chamomile plants 4 inches apart and weed plantings regularly until they're established. When the first flowers appear, snip them off using hand shears; mow plants after

that. In the garden, mulch chamomile plants heavily to protect them from winter extremes.

**PROPAGATION:** Divide offshoots of a mother plant in early spring. Space plants 18" apart.

**HARVEST:** Pinch off the flowers when they have fully developed and the petals begin

**Air-dry chamomile flowers by spreading them on a rack or screen until they're crispy.**

to turn up. Air-dry the flowers and store them in a cool, dark place until used. People with ragweed or other pollen sensitivities may have an allergic reaction to chamomile.

**PESTS AND DISEASES:** Chamomile is typically free of pests and diseases.

**RECOMMENDED CULTIVARS:** German chamomile (*Matricaria recutita*), an annual that grows easily from seed, is often mistaken for the perennial look-alike, Roman chamomile. Sprawling German chamomile reaches 2 to 3'. It also makes delicious tea. *C. nobile* 'Treneague,' a nonflowering variety, forms a soft carpet and needs no mowing. *C. nobile* 'Flore Pleno' displays shaggy, white double blooms.

# ENDIVE
### *Cichorium endivia* *sih-KOR-ee-um en-DY-vee-uh*

**Curly-leaf endive cultivars are also called frisée or Belgian endive. Light frost improves the flavor.**

**ZONES:** NA
**SIZE:** 3–9"h × 6–18"w
**TYPE:** Herbaceous annual
**GROWTH:** Average

**LIGHT:** Full sun to part shade
**MOISTURE:** Average
**FEATURES:** Edible leaves

**SITING:** Sow seeds 4 weeks before the last frost date, and again in mid- to late-summer for a fall crop, ¼" deep in rows 12–18" apart, in well-drained soil to which rotted compost has been added.

**CARE:** Thin seedlings to 8" apart when they are about 3" tall and then to 18" apart

as you begin harvesting (use thinnings in salads). Use water-soluble plant food, such as Miracle-Gro Water Soluble All Purpose, once a month, watering to the sides of each row and not directly on the leaves themselves. Remove any flower stalks as soon as they appear. Water frequently

**Broadleaf endive, or escarole, forms a loose bunch.**

during periods of high heat or drought, because both will cause endive to bolt and taste bitter. To prevent bitterness in warm weather, blanch the leaves: Pull the outer leaves together over the smaller, inner leaves (hearts) and hold them loosely in place with string or a rubber band. An easier method is to invert empty pots over the heads to block out the light for 2 weeks before harvest, being sure to cover the drainage hole with a rock or wood chip.

**HARVEST:** Leaves are ready to harvest in 65–100 days. Pick outer leaves as needed, or wait until a head is fully developed and cut it at the base. Store unwashed leaves and heads for up to 1 week in the refrigerator. Plants can be mulched and protected in a cold frame for winter harvest. Light frost improves the flavor.

**PESTS AND DISEASES:** Use bait or traps for snails and slugs. Handpick caterpillars.

**RECOMMENDED CULTIVARS:** 'Green Curled Ruffec' is a curly-leaf type sometimes called frisée. 'Batavian Full-Heart' is a broad-leaf escarole that almost forms a head at maturity.

# WATERMELON
*Citrullus lanatus* sib-TRULL-us lub-NAY-tus

**Choose watermelon cultivars resistant to fusarium wilt and anthracnose.**

**ZONES:** NA
**SIZE:** 1'h × 6'w
**TYPE:** Annual vine
**LIGHT:** Full sun
**MOISTURE:** High
**FEATURES:** Edible fruits

**SITING:** Watermelons require a lot of space in a sunny location with highly fertile, slightly acid, well-drained soil. Amend clay soil with organic matter sand. Tender vines do best in a site protected from strong winds. Direct-sow seed in southern climates after the last frost date in soil hilled 3" deep and 12" in diameter, six seeds to a hill, with hills at least 6' apart. In the North, start seeds in peat pots indoors 3 weeks before the last frost date, then transplant them into the garden with the pot tops level with the soil at least 2 weeks after the last frost date.

**CARE:** Thin direct-sown seedlings to a few plants per hill after the first set of true leaves appears, then thin again to one or two vines when they are 12–24" long. Remove weeds by hand to avoid damaging the fragile vines. Watermelons are heavy feeders; use plant food, such as Miracle-Gro Water Soluble All Purpose, throughout the growing season, and add potassium or phosphorus if a soil sample analysis indicates the need for it. Mulch only during the hottest part of summer to avoid lowering the soil temperature. Place squares of cardboard under ripening fruits to protect them from rot and insects. Some types can be trained up a fence or trellis, but fruits must be supported. Make slings from bird netting or mesh bags and tie to the support. When nights grow cool in northern areas, pinch out the tips of the vines and remove new flowers as they appear to encourage existing fruits to ripen before frost occurs.

**PROPAGATION:** Grow from seed or transplants. Seedless varieties require pollination by another cultivar planted nearby. Saved seed usually does not breed true.

**HARVEST:** Depending on the variety, melons ripen 70–90 days after planting. They don't ripen off the vine, but you can tell when they are ready to pick. The tendril near the top of the melon will dry out and turn brown when the melon is ripe. The underside of some cultivars turns from white to yellow when the fruit is ripe. Some gardeners rap melons with their knuckles to listen for a telltale hollow "thunk" of ripeness. Watermelon tastes best chilled. Enjoy it as is or blend it into smoothies and fruit juices. Toss chunks or slices in lemon juice and freeze for later use. The rind can be pickled and pressure canned.

**PESTS AND DISEASES:** Discourage cucumber beetles and aphids with floating row covers (but remove the fabric when the flowers bloom). Wash off aphids with a mild soap solution. Red dots on the underside of leaves are squash bugs. Scrape them off; spray rotenone late in the day if the infestation is heavy. Watermelons are susceptible to fusarium wilt and mildews. Ask your county extension agent which diseases affect watermelons in your area and choose cultivars resistant to those problems. Watermelon fruit blotch is a common bacterial rot in hot, humid climates. Cultivars with a lighter green rind may be more susceptible. Purchase only inspected seeds or transplants, use clean cultural practices, avoid wetting the leaves and handling wet plants, and rotate crops to avoid infection.

**RECOMMENDED CULTIVARS:** 'Crimson Sweet' is a round light green melon with dark green stripes and mild dark red flesh. Fruits reach 25 pounds even in northern areas; plants are resistant to fusarium wilt and anthracnose. 'Fiesta', 'Regency', and 'Sangria' are traditional striped dark green melons, 20–25 pounds, resistant to fusarium wilt. 'Orangeglo' has extrasweet flesh with a tropical flavor and is resistant to pests and wilt. For small gardens, grow 'Sugar Bush', 'Sugar Baby', or yellow-fleshed 'Yellow Doll'—all compact vines with smaller melons that fit in the refrigerator. Another small cultivar, 'Golden Midget', turns yellow when ripe but has sweet brilliant pink flesh. It weighs just a few pounds but ripens in 70 days. For a state fair competitor, try 'Mountain Hoosier', which develops melons up to 80 pounds in 85 days. Seedless varieties take the longest to ripen and thus do best in southern climates and drier conditions. They are not truly seedless but contain less conspicuous, edible pips. 'Tri-X-313' and 'SummerSweet' produce melons 15–20 pounds in 90 days. Germination of seedless types is most successful indoors.

**The stem end tendrils of a ripe melon are brown and dry.**

**Small-fruited watermelons grow on compact vines.**

# GRAPEFRUIT, LEMON, LIME, ORANGE

*Citrus* spp. *SIH-trus*

**Limes (*C. aurantiifolia*) thrive in hot, humid areas in soil that drains well.**

**ZONES:** 8–11
**SIZE:** 10–40'h × 10–40'w
**TYPE:** Evergreen shrub or tree

**GROWTH:** Slow
**LIGHT:** Full sun
**MOISTURE:** Average
**FEATURES:** Edible fruits

**SITING:** Grow in deep, well-drained, acid silty soil in a sunny area protected from strong winds and located where you can water easily in dry weather. In hot climates

**Pummelo (*C. maxima*) is grapefruit's tropical ancestor but not as sweet.**

choose a site protected from midday sun. In cooler zones choose early-maturing varieties and plant in the warmest microclimate possible. All citrus plants do best in light soils, but sour orange rootstock will grow in heavier soils. Add sulfur if necessary to increase acidity or lime to increase alkalinity. Space most citrus plants 25' apart in both directions. Mandarins and limes can be planted as close as 15'.

**CARE:** Successful growth requires a long growing season with temperatures between 65–90°F. Lemons, limes, and oranges need the most heat; grapefruits and mandarins are the most cold tolerant, but mandarins suffer the most frost damage. Most trees need no pruning the first several years.

Painting a commercial sprout inhibitor on the trunks of young trees is preferable to using protective wraps, which can encourage insects and diseases. Prune dead and damaged wood and any branch that interferes with the growth of scaffold limbs from mature trees. Remove extremely low limbs to provide better access for irrigation and air circulation and to prevent brown rot of low-hanging fruit. Hedge pruning may be necessary on tightly spaced trees to maintain a manageable shape for harvesting, but it will reduce yields. Top pruning controls tree size and encourages fruit growth but may not be necessary in home gardens with just a few specimens. Remove sprouts flush with the trunk and prune any suckers from the rootstock before the thorns harden. Pull weeds manually or by light tilling; citrus is highly sensitive to herbicides. Feed several times a year from late autumn to midspring, increasing the amount of plant food as trees mature. Monitor nitrogen carefully; it increases yield but also increases the likelihood of scab. Use foliar sprays to add needed minerals such as copper, zinc, manganese, and boron so that excess salts do not accumulate in the soil. Moisture stress harms the fruit; water

**'Improved Meyer' lemon has disease-resistance and few thorns.**

during dry periods but do not allow the trees to stand in water. Excessive moisture promotes the fungus that causes scab.

**PROPAGATION:** Grow from seed, bud grafting, air layering, or cuttings, depending on the variety. Plants grown from root cuttings may fruit several years earlier than budded trees.

**HARVEST:** Lemons and limes are ready to pick 5–9 months after flowering; oranges and grapefruits need 8–12 months. Some varieties, such as 'Valencia' oranges, hold well on the tree for up to several months; others need to be picked regularly to encourage the next crop. Fruits are easily damaged, so handpick dry fruit whenever possible, wearing gloves to protect against contact dermatitis from the peel oils. Move harvested fruits out of the sun as quickly as possible to prevent stylar-end rot. Store in cool but not cold temperatures and very high humidity, or cure for long-term storage. Use lemons and limes as garnishes, for juice, and to remove stains. Flavor baked goods with Key limes. Eat oranges and mandarins fresh or cut the sections into salads. Halve and sweeten grapefruits and pummelos to eat fresh for breakfast or broiled and served as an appetizer at dinner. Drink citrus juice fresh or use it as a flavoring in sauces, desserts, and beverages. Make marmalade from sour oranges. Make candied peel from various citrus rinds.

**PESTS AND DISEASES:** Citrus plants are sensitive to a variety of environmental problems, the most serious of which are wind and water damage. Proper

**Citron (*C. medica*) is typically grown for its rind, used in candy and cooking.**

# GRAPEFRUIT, LEMON, LIME, ORANGE
*continued*

siting and consistent but not too much moisture are key to their survival. They are susceptible to leaf miners, aphids, scales, and other pests as well as to a host of diseases, including viruses, rots, molds, spots, and anthracnose. Cultivars sold for use in your geographic area are bred and grafted to reduce the likelihood of infestation or infection. Ask your extension agent or a nursery owner for spraying guidelines specific to the plants you choose and follow directions carefully when using pesticides.

**RECOMMENDED CULTIVARS:** Citrus plants propagated by bud grafting to a specific

**Grapefruit is among the largest and most cold-hardy of the citrus trees.**

rootstock are the most reliable. They begin fruiting sooner and have increased resistance to cold, wind, pests, and diseases. Choose plants according to rootstock selected for its compatibility with your particular soil type.

**CITRON:** *C. medica* is a small, spiny, evergreen shrub or tree 8–15' tall. Its flowers are fragrant and its leaves smell like lemon. The rough, bumpy rind is lemon yellow when ripe; the pulp is not juicy and has many seeds. It will not tolerate temperature extremes and is highly sensitive to heat, drought, and frost but adaptable to many soils. It is often bud grafted onto lemon, grapefruit, or orange to improve adaptability. 'Etrog' is the most commonly grown cultivar but only the rind is used in candy and marmalades. It begins to bear in 3 years and lives as long as 25 years.

**GRAPEFRUIT:** This popular citrus fruit is not related to grapes. *C. ×paradisi* is a cross of sweet orange with pummelo (*C. maxima*), a grapefruit ancestor, and is larger and somewhat more cold hardy than other citrus plants. The thorny, evergreen trees can grow 30–35' feet tall or more and often have trunks several feet in diameter, so they should be spaced

**Tangerine is a type of mandarin orange with a thin, loose peel.**

farther apart than other citrus trees. The 3½–5"-diameter fruits have few or no seeds and tart, juicy pale yellow, pink, or red pulp. Most types stay on the tree for several months, although red-fleshed fruits fade as the season progresses and late harvests reduce the next year's crop. High soil salinity reduces yields, and excess nitrogen causes malformed fruits. Use nutritional sprays to add copper and zinc as needed. Grapefruit attracts fruitflies and is susceptible to anthracnose, root rots, leaf spots, and molds. Choose cultivars bred for resistance to citrus canker and viruses. 'Redblush' and 'Ray Ruby' are popular red-fleshed grapefruits. Common white-fleshed types are 'Marsh' or 'Duncan'.

**LEMON:** True lemon (*C. limon*) bears fragrant flowers and sharp thorns on trees 10–20' tall. Most types have seeds and

some have variegated flowers and fruits. Lemon is more sensitive to cold than orange; sudden temperature drops below 30°F will kill flowers and fruit; below 25°F can damage the wood. The most flavorful fruits are grown in coastal areas too cool for oranges and grapefruit. 'Eureka' is an early-bearing, almost thornless, disease-resistant cultivar suitable for hot, dry climates. Meyer lemon (*C. meyeri*) is a cross with mandarin orange (*C. reticulata*) and thus better suited to coastal areas and container growing. 'Improved Meyer' is resistant to citrus viruses and is less thorny. Rough lemon (*C. ponderosa*) is a cross of lemon and citron (*C. medica*). It is more sensitive to cold than true lemons but produces large fruit on compact trees. If the soil is alkaline, choose a cultivar grafted onto sour orange stock or alemow (*×C. macrophylla*), a hybrid of lemon and pummelo. Use labeled pesticide sprays for infestations of mites and scales. A copper fungicide will control red algae in summer. *C. meyeri* and *C. ponderosa* are small, shrubby cultivars good for container growing. If you keep container citrus plants outdoors in summer, move them to a somewhat shady spot for a couple of weeks before bringing them indoors to help them acclimate to lower light.

**LIME:** *C. aurantiifolia* grows well in hot climates that are also humid, although it is more drought tolerant and also more sensitive to cold than lemon. It will not

**Japanese Satsuma mandarin cultivars are more cold-hardy than others.**

# GRAPEFRUIT, LEMON, LIME, ORANGE
*continued*

All citrus trees require a long growing season with warm temperatures.

thrive in heavy soils but can be grown in porous lava or other gravelly soils. If soil nitrogen is too low, mulch with cured seaweed or plant leguminous cover crops between rows. Mexican or Key limes are small, often shrubby evergreen trees 6–13' tall with aromatic leaves and sharp spines. The flowers are not fragrant. Seedlings fruit in 3–6 years. Although the trees are everbearing, the best harvests are in late spring and late autumn. Resist the urge to pick fruits until they have ripened from dark green to light greenish yellow and are slightly soft to the touch. Tahitian or Persian limes are larger and hardier than Mexican limes and also usually seedless and free of thorns. The trees grow to 20' tall in sandy soil or even in crushed limestone. They are sensitive to excess water, so in low-lying areas plant them in raised beds. Hand-harvest the fruits from spring through fall, with best yields during the summer months. For containers grow dwarf 'Thornless Key Lime', which is less productive but tasty and thorn free. Kaffir lime (*C. hystrix*) is grown for its aromatic leaves, which are popular in Asian cuisine.

Round or common oranges, like 'Valencia', are grown for juicing.

'Minneola' is a cold-tolerant hybrid of tangerine and grapefruit.

**MANDARIN:** A catchall name for oranges with a thin, loose peel, mandarin includes traditional Willowleaf or Chinese cultivars, such as 'Ledar' and 'Changsha'; tangerines, such as 'Clementine', which have a weeping habit, and 'Murcott Honey', prized for their extrasweet fruit; Japanese Satsuma cultivars, such as the extremely cold-hardy 'Kara'; as well as light-skinned hybrids, such as the large-fruited 'Ugli', a cross of mandarin orange and grapefruit that has few or no seeds and better flavor than some grapefruits. *C. reticulata* Blanco trees are evergreen and often smaller than other oranges. Although mandarins are more cold hardy and drought tolerant than some other citrus species, the fruits are easily damaged by frost. *C. ×tangelo* is a cross of tangerine and grapefruit (or pommelo), *C. paradisi × C. reticulata*, producing such cultivars as 'Minneola' and 'Orlando', which are more cold tolerant than grapefruit. Tangelo fruits are the size of oranges or larger and extremely easy to peel. Tangors are the result of crossing mandarin and sweet orange (*C. reticulata* with *C. sinensis*). 'Temple' is a popular cultivar and often used as a pollinator for other citrus trees. For container growing, try everbearing calamondin (×*Citrofortunella microcarpa*),

a cross between mandarin orange and kumquat (*Fortunella*), often called miniature orange. It is compact and bears fragrant flowers and small and sweet, juicy fruit. Mandarin or Rangpur lime (*C. ×limonia*), sometimes also called miniature orange, is not a true lime but a cross of lemon and mandarin orange suitable for indoor growing. It has fragrant flowers and no thorns. The edible fruit has dark orange pulp that smells somewhat like lime and is sour but makes good marmalade.

**ORANGE:** Sour or bitter orange was the original species introduced to Native Americans and early settlers in Florida. Although its oil has value and its pulp and rind can be used in marmalade, *C. aurantium* is too sour to be eaten fresh. It is highly susceptible to tristeza and other citrus viruses as well as to fungal problems. It can tolerate light frosts for short periods and is adaptable to most soil conditions, including clay, so it is used principally as a rootstock for sweeter citrus species. Bergamot orange (*C. bergamia*), such as 'Bouquet', is cultivated for its oil, which flavors Earl Grey tea. Sweet orange (*C. sinensis*) is divided into a number of subtypes. Round or sweet oranges are

Choose dwarf shrub cultivars to grow citrus fruits in small gardens.

# GRAPEFRUIT, LEMON, LIME, ORANGE
*continued*

often grown for juicing. 'Hamlin' and 'Valencia' are popular cultivars. Navel oranges get their name from a small secondary fruit at the stylar end of the main fruit. Early to ripen and easy to peel, navel oranges are large and seedless. 'Washington' cultivars are the most popular. Blood oranges, such as 'Moro', have a high concentration of red pigments in the peel and pulp. Coloration varies with climate. Low-acid oranges, such as 'Succari' and 'Lima', are available; the juice is sweet but not as flavorful as that of acidic cultivars. Trifoliate oranges *(C. trifoliata* syn. *Poncirus trifoliata)* are small, shrubby deciduous plants that have naturalized in the southeastern United States. The small, bumpy fruits are too sour to eat, but the plant is often used as a dwarfing rootstock for other citrus plants because of its cold hardiness. A citrange is a *trifoliata × sinensis* hybrid developed for

resistance to root rot, nematodes, and tristeza virus. It is hardy to Zone 8.
**PUMMELO:** Also called shaddock, *C. maxima* is a tropical ancestor of

**Mulch to conserve soil moisture and control weeds.**

grapefruit. It typically grows 16–50' tall but can be pruned for use as a dwarf type. The tree bears thorns as well as fragrant flowers, and the large, round to pear-shaped fruits have pale yellow to pink or red pulp that is not as sweet as that of grapefruit—sometimes even bitter in cool climates. 'Chandler' is a good cultivar for warm zones. 'Hirado' is more cold hardy. Aging the fruits up to 3 months increases juice and flavor. Young trees are sun sensitive, and root rot can be a problem at any stage of maturity. Control common and brown aphids to prevent the spread of tristeza virus. Eliminate scale, which can cause sooty mold.

# RECOMMENDED CITRUS VARIETIES FOR HOME GARDENS

**CA = CALIFORNIA; DS = DESERTS; FL = FLORIDA; GC = GULF COAST; HI = HAWAII; TX = TEXAS**

## NAVEL ORANGE

'Cara Cara' and 'Washington' (CA, DS, FL, GC, HI, TX); 'Everhard' (TX)

## SWEET ORANGE

'Diller' (FL, GC); 'Hamlin' (DS, FL, GC, HI, TX); 'Marrs' (DS, FL, GC, HI, TX); 'Parson Brown' (DS, FL, GC, HI, TX); 'Pineapple' (DS, FL, GC, HI, TX); 'Shamouti' (DS, CA); 'Trovita' (DS, CA); 'Valencia' (CA, DS, FL, GC, HI, TX)

## BLOOD ORANGE

'Moro' (CA, DS, FL, GC, HI, TX); 'Sanguinelli' (CA, DS, FL, GC); 'Tarocco' (CA, DS)

## SOUR ORANGE

'Chinotto' and 'Seville' (CA, DS, FL, GC, HI, TX)

## MANDARIN ORANGE (& TANGERINE)

'Ambersweet' (CA, FL, GC); Calamondin (CA, DS, FL, GC, HI, TX); 'Changsha' (GC, TX); Clementine (CA, DS, FL, GC, HI, TX); 'Dancy' (DS, FL, GC, HI, TX); 'Encore' (DS, FL, GC); 'Fairchild' (DS, CA, GC); 'Honey' (DS, FL, GC, HI); 'Kara' (CA); 'Kinnow' (CA, DS); 'Page' (DS, FL, GC, HI); 'Pixie' (CA); Satsuma (CA, FL, GC); 'Wilking' (HI)

## LEMON

'Eureka' (CA, DS); 'Improved Meyer' (CA, DS, FL, GC, HI, TX); 'Lisbon' (CA, DS); 'Ponderosa' (DS, FL, GC)

## LIME

'Bearss', 'Mexican', and 'Rangpur' (CA, DS, FL, GC, HI, TX); 'Nitta' (HI)

## GRAPEFRUIT

'Duncan' (FL, GC); 'Flame' (FL, GC); 'Marsh' (CA, DS, FL, GC, TX); 'Melogold' (CA, DS); 'Oroblanco' (CA, DS); 'Redblush' (CA, DS, FL, GC, HI, TX)

## PUMMELO

'Chandler' (CA, DS, FL, GC, HI, TX)

## TANGELO

'Minneola' and 'Orlando' (CA, DS, FL, GC, HI, TX)

## TANGOR

'Temple' (FL, HI, TX); 'Murcott' (CA, FL)

# CORIANDER, CILANTRO

*Coriandrum sativum* *kor-ee-AN-drum sa-TY-vum*

**Cilantro thrives in hot weather but may also survive winter in a cold frame.**

**ZONES:** NA
**SIZE:** 5–24"h ×
4–10"w
**TYPE:** Herbaceous
hardy annual
**GROWTH:** Fast

**LIGHT:** Full sun to
part shade
**MOISTURE:** Average
**FEATURES:** Edible
leaves (cilantro),
seeds (coriander),
and roots

**SITING:** Direct-sow seeds after the last frost date in average, well-drained, slightly acid soil in a location where plants can remain; they have a deep taproot and are not tolerant of transplanting. Cilantro can be interplanted with peas, beans, peppers, and tomatoes.

**CARE:** Keep seeds and seedlings evenly moist. Gradually thin seedlings to about 1' apart. Water during dry weather. Plants tend to bolt in hot, dry conditions, so make successive plantings 2–4 weeks apart to maintain a steady crop all summer long. Plant again in autumn for spring harvest in warm climates. Plants can often be overwintered in a cold frame in northern gardens and will grow well indoors sown directly into deep pots.
**PROPAGATION:** Grow from seed.

**Cut stems as needed or harvest whole plants to thin crowded plants.**

**HARVEST:** Thin out whole plants as needed, or begin picking leaves from the lower part of the plant when several stems have developed. The lower leaves, called cilantro or Chinese parsley, look similar to Italian flat parsley and have more of the desired spicy flavor than the upper foliage, which resembles dill. The flowers are tiny white or lavender umbels and are edible; however, their presence indicates that the plant is past its flavor peak. Add leaves to cooked foods just before serving; heat dissipates the flavor. The leaves can be dried for later use, but the flavor is much milder. Leaves are best used fresh and can be stored for up to 2 weeks in the refrigerator. Cut the heads when the seedpods begin to turn brown. Hang the heads upside down in paper bags to catch the seeds. Use some whole or ground as coriander, a common ingredient in many Asian and Middle Eastern cuisines. Save some seeds for the next planting.
**PESTS AND DISEASES:** No significant pest problems affect cilantro.
**RECOMMENDED CULTIVARS:** 'Santo' is among the most popular cultivars for fresh leaves because it is slow to bolt.

# HAZELNUT

*Corylus spp.* *KOR-ih-lus*

**Hazelnuts, or filberts, have tough shells that must be cracked open.**

**ZONES:** 2–9
**SIZE:** 8–15'h ×
10–20'w
**TYPE:** Deciduous
perennial shrub or
small tree

**GROWTH:** Slow
**LIGHT:** Full sun to
part shade
**MOISTURE:** Average
**FEATURES:** Edible
seeds (nuts)

**SITING:** Filberts do best in deep, fertile, slightly acid, sandy loam. Plant them 10–20' apart to allow for air circulation. They tolerate some shade but produce more nuts in full sun.
**CARE:** Most types require cross-pollination by another cultivar for successful fruiting. Prune minimally to remove dead or

damaged wood and to maintain shape for best harvest. Prune severely every fourth or fifth year to restore plant vigor. Yield will be reduced that year but much improved in following years. Water in periods of drought or in particularly dry climates.
**PROPAGATION:** Hazelnuts grow best from layering; also from seed, or sprouts from root suckers.
**HARVEST:** Most filberts start to bear at 4 years and are productive for many decades. The nuts are ready for harvest from August to October; pick them as soon

**In order to thwart squirrels, pick the nuts as soon as you can twist open their papery coverings.**

as you can easily twist open the papery covering. Let the nuts dry in the sun for several days. The husk is thin but tough and must be cracked to get to the nutmeat inside. The white nutmeats are covered with a thin, papery reddish-brown covering similar to that on peanuts. Store the dried nuts in airtight packaging in cool but not freezing temperatures for up to a year.
**PESTS AND DISEASES:** European filberts are susceptible to eastern filbert blight, which is caused by a fungus. American types are less susceptible but can serve as the host. All types are susceptible to filbert bacterial blight, which is spread by water splash and contaminated tools. Prune and remove infected wood immediately and water and feed affected trees to maintain vigor. Use malathion or insecticidal soap to control aphids, whiteflies, weevils, and galls. Use netting if necessary to protect nuts and catkins from birds and squirrels.
**RECOMMENDED CULTIVARS:** Plant 'Bixby' and 'Potomac' hybrids together for cross-pollination. 'Winkler', an American hazelnut hybrid (*C. americana*), is self-fruitful. Hazelberts (*C. americana* ×*avellana*) work well as shrubs.

# MUSKMELON
*Cucumis melo melo* *kew-KEW-mis MEE-lo*

**Pick crenshaw and other winter melons when the smooth skin turns pale.**

ZONES: NA
SIZE: 1'h × 10–20'w
TYPE: Annual vine
GROWTH: Average
LIGHT: Full sun
MOISTURE: High
FEATURES: Edible fruits

SITING: Plant seeds or seedlings in full sun in light, fertile, well-drained, slightly acid soil and rich in organic matter. Soil temperature should be at least 60°F for transplants and 70°F for seeds to germinate. Choose a location protected from strong winds and large enough to accommodate the long vines, which grow to 10' or more. Direct sow seeds in hills 4–6' apart, six seeds per hill, 1–2 weeks after the last frost date, or start indoors in peat pots 1 month before the last frost date and transplant 1' apart in rows 3' apart

2 weeks after the last frost date. Melons cross-pollinate easily. Crossed seed will be fertile, so keep varieties separated in the garden if you want saved seeds to be true. CARE: Thin hilled seedlings to two or three plants per hill. Water thoroughly and consistently, especially while the plants are

in flower and developing fruits. Water in dry climates or during periods of drought, to provide at least 1" of water per week. Be sure leaves that wilt in the hot midday sun have enough moisture to recover at night. Black plastic mulch helps to increase the soil temperature and

**Muskmelons, often called cantaloupes, give off a strong aroma when ripe.**

conserve moisture. You can use organic mulch around plants to conserve moisture, but apply it after the soil temperature reaches 70°F. Weed by hand until the foliage is large enough to shade out new weeds. Feed at planting time, again when fruits start to set, and about 2 weeks after fruit-set with a low-nitrogen fruit plant food high in phosphorus, potassium, magnesium, and boron. Support trellised melons in slings made from strong netting or mesh fabric. Protect ripening melons from damp ground, especially overnight, by placing them on inverted pots, boards, or pieces of cardboard. If fruits are still ripening when nighttime temperatures begin to decrease in autumn, place melons on cardboard covered with aluminum foil or other reflective material to concentrate daytime heat and encourage quick maturation. Melons grow best when air temperatures average 70°F. Cool or cloudy weather and too much moisture during fruit development lessen flavor.
PROPAGATION: Grow from seed.
HARVEST: Depending on the variety, melons ripen from mid- to late-summer or early autumn, about 35–55 days after pollination. Muskmelons (often called

**Honeydews picked a bit too early can be ripened at room temperature.**

## MUSKMELON
*continued*

cantaloupes) and true cantaloupes give off a distinct odor when ripe. The skin color of ripe muskmelons becomes lighter under the netting, changing from green to tan or yellow. If a melon of mature size can be easily separated from the vine, it is ripe. Harvest carefully to prevent damaging the vines. The winter melons—honeydews, casabas, and crenshaws, which grow best in warm, dry zones—are ready to cut from the vine when their smooth green skin turns pale and the blossom ends are slightly soft. If they are picked a few days early, simply store them at room temperature until they are fully ripe. Store muskmelons and cantaloupes for up to a week in the warmest part of the refrigerator. Winter melons will keep for up to a month in the coldest (but not freezing) part of the refrigerator. All melons are best eaten fresh in slices or in cubes or balls in salads. They can also be made into juice, preserves, and pickles. Slices with the rind removed can be kept in the freezer for up to 1 year.

**PESTS AND DISEASES:** Striped and spotted cucumber beetles are the most significant pests; they spread bacterial wilt. See additional information about them on this page. Aphids carry cucumber mosaic virus; knock them off with water from the hose, or dust the plants with rotenone if the infestation is severe. Most varieties are resistant to squash bugs, but pick off and destroy any you see. Choose varieties resistant to fusarium wilt, anthracnose, black rot, gummy stem blight, and powdery mildew. Apply labeled fungicides if necessary to control these problems, and remove and destroy any plants that become infected. Crop rotation also helps to control disease.

**RECOMMENDED CULTIVARS:** Determine the number of suitable growing days in your area and choose cultivars developed for that particular climate. 'Ambrosia' is a medium-size muskmelon with a small seed cavity and sweet, juicy flesh. It's mildew resistant and a good choice in average and warm climates. 'Passport' is an early-maturing green-fleshed variety. In short-season zones, try 'Sweet 'n Early', with bright salmon flesh. 'Burpee's Early Hybrid' crenshaw is a large yellow-green melon with pink flesh. Southern-zone gardeners will appreciate the enormous 'Morning Dew' melon, which grows up to 12 pounds. In northern zones try 'Honey Pearl', a medium-size pale gold honeydew with almost white flesh. 'Casaba Golden Beauty' has spicy-sweet almost white flesh. For true European cantaloupes, which have rough or warty skin without netting, grow 'Charentais', an early, small melon, or 'Savor', a small grayish-green melon with sweet orange flesh. Both are resistant to fusarium wilt and powdery mildew.

**Provide early season warmth with plastic tunnels.**

**Handpick and destroy cucumber beetles.**

**Reflective material under the fruit hastens ripening.**

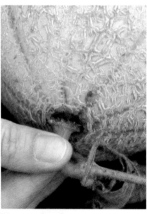

**Ripe muskmelons separate easily from the vine.**

# CUCUMBER BEETLES

**C**ucumber beetles are ¼"-long winged insects with black stripes or spots on their backs. Adults feed on many vegetables but primarily on cucumber and melon flowers, leaves, and fruit, and larvae eat the roots. As adults feed, they may transmit an incurable bacterial wilt from one plant to another, affecting nonresistant melons and cucumbers. The bacteria survive in the digestive tract of beetles that have overwintered in the ground. Bacterial wilt causes vines to wither and die within a week or two. Protect young plants with sealed row covers or cones. Examine flowering and fruiting plants regularly; pick off and destroy any beetles you see. Treat heavily infested plants weekly with rotenone dust. Flying insects, including honeybees, pollinate cucumbers and melons, and cucumber beetles have natural predators, such as wasps, so use an insecticide only if an infestation is severe. Insecticides may kill all insects, including the beneficial ones. Cucurbits, plants of the gourd family, are prone to pesticide injury, so be sure to use a product specifically labeled for cucumbers or melons, and follow the instructions carefully to avoid injury.

# CUCUMBER

*Cucumis sativus* kew-KEW-mis sa-TY-vus

**Pick cucumbers frequently to encourage more fruits.**

**ZONES:** NA
**SIZE:** 12–72"h × 12–18"w
**TYPE:** Annual bush or vine

**FORM:** Fast
**LIGHT:** Full sun
**MOISTURE:** High
**FEATURES:** Edible fruits

**SITING:** Choose a warm, sunny location with humus-enriched soil that drains well. Direct-sow seed when soil and air temperatures reach at least 60°F, planting 1½" deep and 2' apart in rows 2–3' apart (those to be trellised can be as close as 10" apart), or in hills of five to seven seeds. In short-season areas, start seeds indoors 4 weeks before the last frost date and transplant after the last frost date. Use black plastic to warm the soil in short-season climates to prevent transplant shock. In warm climates two or three successive plantings may be possible. Cucumbers can be interplanted with cole crops, corn, peas, beans, radishes, carrots, tomatoes, and herbs.

**CARE:** Thin hilled plants to three per hill. Hand-weed carefully around the shallow-rooted plants to reduce competition for moisture and nutrients. Use row covers to protect young plants from pests and cold. Remove covers when vines begin to bloom. Check plants daily for signs of infestation. Train vining types onto trellises or other supports. The soil should be continuously moist. Plants should receive ½" of water per week or more during periods of high heat. Fruits from plants allowed to dry out will taste bitter. Spread organic mulch when seedlings are several weeks old.

**PROPAGATION:** Grow from seed.

**HARVEST:** Cucumbers grow quickly and are ready to pick 50–70 days after planting. Harvest when they are about 8–12" long for slicing varieties and as small as 2" for pickling types. Larger fruits will have more and harder seeds. Picking frequently also encourages more production. Snip the stems with garden scissors. Small-fruited types will produce almost all at once. Be sure to pick every day to prevent fruits from becoming too large. Eat all varieties

fresh in salads and soups or use them for pickling. Fresh cucumbers can be stored in the refrigerator for up to 2 weeks. Cucumber soup can be frozen for up to a year.

**PESTS AND DISEASES:** Cucumbers are susceptible to a wide variety of problems, but new hybrids have been developed for disease resistance. Choose cultivars that have been bred specifically for your climate. Avoid pesticides to prevent killing beneficial pollinators. Striped and spotted cucumber beetles are the most significant pests; they spread bacterial wilt. Aphids carry cucumber mosaic virus; knock them off with water from the hose or dust the plants with rotenone if the infestation is severe. Most varieties are resistant to squash bugs, but pick off and destroy any you see. Choose varieties resistant to fusarium wilt, anthracnose, black rot, gummy stem blight, and powdery mildew. Apply labeled fungicides if necessary to

control these problems, and remove and destroy any plants that become infected. Crop rotation also helps to control disease. Bitterness often develops in fruits that are stressed. Water to avoid moisture stress and select bitter-free varieties.

**RECOMMENDED CULTIVARS:** 'Little Leaf' pickling cucumber sets fruit without pollination and will climb up supports without tying. It yields well even during dry spells. In short-season areas try 'Northern Pickling', which produces fruit in 45–50 days. 'Marketmore' and 'General Lee' cultivars are among the most popular slicing types, producing 8–9" fruits in 55–60 days. 'Diva' is an awarding-winning seedless type that cucumber beetles don't seem to like. In cool climates try seedless 'Socrates'. Extralong burpless 'Suyo Long' and 'Tasty Jade' must be trellised to support the 12–15" fruits. Try 'Spacemaster' or 'Salad Bush' compact bush types in small gardens or patio containers.

**1** Plant bush varieties in hilled-up soil, 5–7 seeds per hill.

**2** Thin the seedlings to 3 per hill and remove any weeds.

**1** Train vining cucumbers onto a fence or trellis for support.

**2** Long-fruited cultivars have room to develop when grown on a trellis.

# PUMPKIN, SUMMER & WINTER SQUASH

*Cucurbita* spp.  *kew-KUR-bih-tuh*

**Large winter squashes (*C. maxima*) often win giant pumpkin contests.**

**ZONES:** NA
**SIZE:** 2'h × 10'w
**TYPE:** Annual bush or vine
**GROWTH:** Fast to average

**LIGHT:** Full sun
**MOISTURE:** High
**FEATURES:** Edible fruits

**SITING:** Choose the sunniest and largest site so plants can spread unimpeded. The soil should be slightly acid, drain easily, and be amended with lots of well-composted manure. Direct-sow seed when soil and air temperatures reach at least 70°F. Plant bush types 1½" deep and 4' apart in rows 4' apart, or in hills of five to seven seeds. Plant vining squashes 2' apart in rows 4' apart, and large pumpkins 4' apart in rows 8' apart. In short-season areas start seeds indoors 4 weeks before the last frost date and transplant after the last frost date. Use black plastic to warm the soil in short-season climates to prevent transplant shock. Interplant rows with corn or herbs.

**CARE:** Squash and pumpkins have high moisture and nutrient requirements. Feed twice a month with water-soluble plant food for vegetables. Maintain consistently moist but not waterlogged soil. Moisture-stressed plants are more susceptible to pests and diseases and have lower yields. Hand-weed carefully to avoid disturbing the tender vines. If fruit set it poor, hand-pollinate flowers with a small brush or swab to ensure fruiting. Handle plants and fruits only when they are dry to avoid injuring them or spreading pathogens. Because winter squash and pumpkins rest on the ground a long time while they mature, slip a piece of

**Jack-o'-lanterns are typically carved from hard-shelled orange winter squashes.**

cardboard or another barrier underneath each fruit to prevent rot. In short-season areas or late in the growing season anywhere, remove blooms that appear after there are fruits maturing elsewhere on the vines. Pinching out those flowers and even the tips of the vines encourages the plant to direct its energy into the existing fruits. Trellis winter squash to save space; suspend fruits in strong netting or mesh bags securely tied to the supports. Or let vines run out of the garden and onto a patio or lawn if there is space. If frost is predicted, pick any ripe fruits and cover the others with mulch or blankets overnight.

**PROPAGATION:** Grow from seed.

**HARVEST:** Summer squash taste best when picked small—zucchinis, crooknecks, and straightnecks at about 6" long and scallops

**Pinch out small fruits to promote the growth of larger ones.**

**Slip a barrier between fruit and ground to prevent rot.**

# PUMPKIN, SUMMER & WINTER SQUASH
*continued*

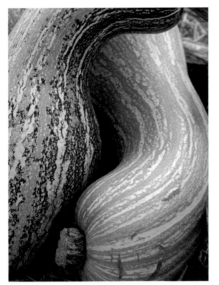

'Striped Crookneck Cushaw' is grown for its flesh and seeds.

Some cucurbit cultivars have been bred for resistance to squash bugs, a major pest.

at about 3" across. Pick some every day when plants are at the height of production. Use a clean, sharp knife to cut the stems about 1" above the fruits. Eat them uncooked—sliced, chopped, or grated into salads or as crudités. Use medium-sized fruits in stir-fries or steamed as a side dish. Store them for up to 2 weeks in the refrigerator. Slices can be blanched, towel-dried, and frozen for up to 6 months for later cooking uses. The bigger summer squashes are allowed to grow, the tougher their flesh and seeds will be. Any fruits

that escape detection and grow to enormous size can still be used. Remove the seeds and grate the flesh for use in baked goods, soups, and stews; or cut the fruits in half lengthwise, hollow out the halves, and fill them with stuffing as a main dish. Summer squash blossoms are also edible; try them lightly sautéed as an appetizer. Try to pick mostly male blossoms (with slender flower stalks)

for cooking and leave the female blooms to produce fruit. Leave winter squash and pumpkins on the plants until they are mature; they will not ripen further once picked and do not taste good immature. Use a clean, sharp knife to cut the stems a few inches above the fruits. Carry the fruits carefully from underneath to prevent any nicks or bruises, which interfere with long-term storage. All winter types but acorn squash need to be cured before storing. Leave any harvested ones that you do not intend to eat immediately in a warm, humid location for several weeks. Wipe off any dirt or moisture before storing.

**PESTS AND DISEASES:** Squash bugs are the most significant pests. Winter squashes are especially susceptible. Choose cultivars that have been bred for resistance. Adult squash bugs are difficult to eradicate, so apply neem extract or carbaryl pesticide when you first see the nymphs. Avoid pesticides if possible to prevent killing beneficial pollinators. Squash bugs like to hide, so place a piece of cardboard beneath plants. Destroy bugs that congregate on the underside of it and remove and destroy any infested vegetation. Buttercup and cushaw squashes can be decimated by squash vine borers. Crop rotation can help control them. Remove and destroy any dead vines to interrupt the borers' life cycle.

Buttercup types are winter squashes related to hubbards.

The dry flesh of butternut squash, *C. moschata*, stores well.

Hubbard squashes, *C. maxima*, come in many colors, including blue.

# PUMPKIN, SUMMER & WINTER SQUASH

*continued*

**Acorn-type squashes have hard shells and yellow-orange flesh.**

Cucumber beetles are also troublesome pests; they spread bacterial wilt. Aphids carry mosaic virus; knock them off with a stream of water from the hose, or dust the plants with rotenone if the infestation is severe. Choose varieties resistant to fusarium wilt, anthracnose, rots, leaf spots, gummy stem blight, and powdery mildew. Apply labeled fungicides if necessary to control these problems and remove and destroy any plants that become infected. Crop rotation also helps to control the spread of soilborne disease.

**RECOMMENDED CULTIVARS:** Squashes, pumpkins, and gourds belong to the cucurbit family but are not always called by their accurate names. The so-called summer squashes *(C. pepo),* including bush-type summer crooknecks, straightnecks, pattypans, pumpkins, and vining gourds can cross with one another. If you grow pumpkins and summer squash in your garden, don't save the seeds. 'Black Beauty' is an early, prolific, tender zucchini. 'Yellow Crookneck' is an easy-to-grow heirloom favorite. 'Golden Scallopini Bush' is a productive pattypan squash that can be eaten fresh or stored like a winter squash for later use. 'Sunburst Scallop' is a good pattypan for small gardens. 'Cornell's Bush Delicata' is an early-maturing, disease-resistant green-and-cream-striped squash with flesh similar to that of sweet potato. Only the flesh is eaten, like a winter squash, and the plant is open pollinated, so you can save the seed. Spaghetti squash is another *C. pepo* type eaten like a winter squash. Spaghetti squashes are so-called because the cooked flesh can be raked out in slender ribbons with the tines of a fork and served as a pasta substitute. To save space in the

***C. moschata* acorn cultivars grow on vines or bushes.**

garden, try 'Tivoli', a bush-type cultivar. In warm climates try chayote squash, or mirliton *(Sechium edule),* which grows on a perennial vine. The smal, pear-shape fruits are white to light green, smooth or wrinkled, and prickly but contain only one seed, like an avocado. Cook them as you would summer squash.

Bottle gourd *(Lagenaria siceraria)* is a cucurbit with night-blooming white flowers. The tan or brown skin hardens into a tough shell as the fruits mature. They can be eaten like summer squash if picked when they are less than 6" long. They can tolerate a light frost but take

**Pumpkins, gourds, and squashes all belong to the same family.**

**Use black plastic mulch to warm the soil before planting.**

# PUMPKIN, SUMMER & WINTER SQUASH
*continued*

**Summer squashes (*C. pepo*), like this yellow zucchini, are the immature fruits of true pumpkins.**

much longer to cure than other gourds. Yellow-flowered cucurbita gourds have colorful hard shells and are popular in autumn centerpieces. Grow them as you would winter squash, but soak the hard seeds overnight before planting to hasten germination. Because they are lighter weight than other squashes, they are ideal for growing on a fence or trellis. Leave them on the vines to ripen, but pick them before any possibility of frost. Then wipe them clean and let them dry in a warm room with good air circulation, which can take from a week to several months depending on the size of the gourd.

Gardeners can grow *Luffa acutangula,* a cucurbit vine with fruits somewhat similar to okra. The small, immature fruits can be cooked as a vegetable but are more often left on the vine to full maturity, when they turn brown and dry. The large fruits are then soaked in water until the peel can be removed and the seeds emptied

through a cut in one end. What remains is a scratchy sponge substitute perfect for use in the shower or bathtub.

True squashes are called winter squashes and include the very large orange-skinned cultivars grown for pumpkin contests. 'Big Max' (*C. maxima*) and 'Atlantic Giant' are known for their size, but their stems are soft and they do not make good jack-o'-lanterns. 'Rouge Vif d'Estampes' is a flattened, heavily creased, deep red-orange type sometimes sold as 'Cinderella' pumpkin. For small spaces, try 'Small Sugar', which grows to only 8 pounds. Other *C. maxima* types include hubbards, which come in a variety of colors, such as 'Red Kuri' and 'True Green Improved'. For a distinctive two-tiered,

**Male zucchini flowers are a culinary delicacy served sautéed or deep-fried.**

**Harvest crooknecks when they are no more than 7" long for best flavor.**

colorful squash, try 'Turk's Turban'. For acorn squashes, try *C. pepo* 'Table Queen' (vine) and 'Table King' (bush). *C. moschata* 'Puritan' and 'Zenith' are good butternuts. 'Sweet Mama' is a tasty buttercup. 'Blue Banana' and 'Jumbo Pink Banana' have dry, sweet flesh.

Southern gardeners grow 'Green Striped Crookneck Cushaw' (*C. mixta*) for its tasty pumpkin seeds, but the pale creamy yellow-orange flesh is perfect in soups and baked goods. 'Tricolor Cushaw' is attractively streaked with white, green, and orange. 'Japanese Pie' or 'Chinese Alphabet' is a black fruit with white flesh.

**Pick pattypans at about 3".**

**Hand-pollinate blossoms for high yields.**

**Keep fruits picked to promote new ones.**

# LEMONGRASS

*Cymbopogon citratus* sim-bob-POH-gon sy-TRAY-tus

Grow lemongrass as an annual in northern climates where it is not hardy.

**ZONES:** 9–11
**SIZE:** 3–6'h × 5–8'w
**TYPE:** Herbaceous perennial
**GROWTH:** Average

**LIGHT:** Full sun
**MOISTURE:** Average
**FEATURES:** Edible leaves, essential oil

**SITING:** Plant 4' apart each direction in full sun, in sandy or other well-draining, fertile, slightly acid soil. Cut back the tops of transplants to about 4" to encourage root growth.

**CARE:** Maintain plants at the desired size by frequent pruning and harvesting. Divide plants at 4–8 years to restore their vigor. Water in dry climates and periods of drought. Protect plants from frost. Those in Zone 9 may go dormant during the winter; water them occasionally if there has been no rain. Grow lemongrass as an annual in Zones 5–8. Dig a clump to bring indoors for winter use and for a supply of new outdoor plants next spring. Cut a potted plant back to 8" to encourage growth of the bulbous ends and maintain the plant at a manageable size indoors.

**PROPAGATION:** Grow from root or plant divisions or from side shoots.

Snip leaves near the base or dig whole stalks to use the bulbous ends.

**HARVEST:** Cut leaves at the base anytime, or dig up a whole section to use the entire stalk. Steep the leaves for an herbal tea or add to soups and stocks as you would bay leaves. The tender white bulbous ends are chopped and used in Asian cuisine and baked goods. The chopped pieces can be frozen for up to a year. Hang leaves upside down in a dark room to dry them for later use. Citral, commercially extracted from the plant's essential oil, is used in perfumes and cosmetics and to flavor soft drinks.

**PESTS AND DISEASES:** The plant's volatile oils are a natural pesticide that repels insects; they also have natural antimicrobial and antifungal properties.

**RECOMMENDED CULTIVARS:** East Indian lemongrass (*C. flexuosus*) matures faster and has a higher content of citral, the essential oil that gives lemongrass its distinctive lemony aroma. West Indian lemongrass is the type most commonly grown for culinary use. The stalks are more numerous and the bulbous ends are larger. Citronella (*C. nardus*) is a close relative of lemongrass and the source of citronella oil, used as an insect repellent. It is not edible.

# ARTICHOKE

*Cynara scolymus* SIN-uh-ruh SKOLL-ih-mus

Artichokes, also known as globe artichokes, can be grown as annuals or perennials.

**ZONES:** 8–10
**SIZE:** 3–5' h × 4–6'w
**TYPE:** Herbaceous tender perennial
**GROWTH:** Average

**LIGHT:** Full sun
**MOISTURE:** High
**FEATURES:** Edible leaf base and flower buds

**SITING:** After the last frost date, direct-sow with seed that has been soaked for 48 hours and held at 35–40°F for 4 weeks in loose (not shredded) sphagnum moss. Better results are likely with transplants held at 40°F for 2–4 weeks. Artichokes grow best in humid areas where they can receive the required amount of time at temperatures below 50°F. They prefer a deep, fertile, well-drained location. Where grown as perennials, space the plants 3–4' feet apart in rows 6–10' apart. For use as annuals, space 2–3' apart in rows 3–4' apart.

**CARE:** Keep seedlings and transplants consistently moist until they are established. Use water-soluble plant food just before planting and again 6–8 weeks later. Feed perennials in subsequent years when they bud in spring. Hot, dry weather may cause the buds to open prematurely. Mulch heavily with compost in summer to maintain soil moisture and with straw to overwinter plants in Zones 8 and 9. Plants become less productive after the fifth or sixth year; replace with new plants grown from suckers.

**PROPAGATION:** To obtain suckers for transplanting, cut off shoots from around the base of the parent plant when they are 8–10" long, making sure each has a piece of root attached. Plant the suckers 4" deep at the spacing recommended above.

**HARVEST:** Cut the edible flower buds when they are still immature and about 3–4" in diameter. After harvesting, prune the entire plant back by one-third to encourage a new crop of buds for fall harvest.

**PESTS AND DISEASES:** Obtain clean planting stock to avoid transmission of crown and bud decay diseases. Curly dwarf virus causes stunted growth. Botrytis, a fungal disease, can be a problem if humidity and moisture are too high. Choose cultivars developed for resistance to these diseases.

**RECOMMENDED CULTIVARS:** 'Green Globe Improved' grows best from crown divisions and is the best choice for perennial plants. 'Imperial Star' can be grown from seed and is both heat and cold tolerant.

Harvest immature flower buds when they are 3–4" in diameter.

# CARROT

*Daucus carota sativus* *DAW-kus ka-RO-tuh sa-TY-vus*

Miniature carrots grow well in containers and in gardens with heavy soil.

Cultivars come in a wide variety of shapes, sizes, and colors.

Thinning young carrots gives others a chance to grow larger.

**ZONES:** NA
**SIZE:** 6–12"h × 6–12"w
**TYPE:** Biennial grown as annual
**GROWTH:** Fast to average

**LIGHT:** Full sun to part shade
**MOISTURE:** High
**FEATURES:** Edible taproots and leaves

**SITING:** Choose a sunny location with loose, fertile, sandy loam that has been worked deeply and raked free of any rocks. Direct-sow carrot seeds in rows 12" apart 2–4 weeks before the last frost date, or in late summer and autumn for winter and spring crops in warm climates. Wet the soil before planting to help keep the tiny seeds from blowing away. Scatter unpelletized seed along a row and cover with ¼" of fine soil. Sow pellets ½" apart and ½" deep. Water again gently with a mist to keep from disturbing the seeds. Rows can be interplanted with lettuces, beans, peas, tomatoes, and peppers. Carrots grow well in raised beds; small cultivars can be grown in containers.

**CARE:** Keep seeds evenly moist to ensure germination, which can take up to 3 weeks, especially if seeds are pelletized for uniform sowing. If the soil dries between waterings, cover the rows with a layer of burlap to help retain moisture until the seeds germinate; water right through the burlap. Thin seedlings to about 3" apart; plant more seeds if necessary to fill in gaps in rows. Weed carefully by hand between rows to remove competition for moisture and nutrients. After the roots are well established, hoe lightly. Use straw or other organic mulch between rows to retain moisture and minimize weeds, but keep it off the leafy tops.

**PROPAGATION:** Grow from seed.

**HARVEST:** Begin pulling carrots as soon as they are at full color. This is also a good way to thin rows to give the remaining carrots a chance to grow larger. In northern zones, wait until after the ground has begun to freeze before digging the rest of the carrots; the cold will

increase their sweet flavor. Carrots can also be overwintered in the ground. Cut off the green tops to about 1" and mulch the plants heavily. In extremely cold-winter areas, use a coldframe as well as mulch. Carrots are low in calories and a good source of vitamin A. Although they are delicious as crudités and chopped, sliced, or grated raw into salads and slaws, they are actually more nutritious cooked, which makes their calcium available. They can be steamed, grilled, baked, stir-fried, and microwaved or cooked in soups, stews, and stocks. Try them boiled and mashed like potatoes. Many herbs and spices, including dill, chervil, fennel, mint, cumin, and ginger, enhance their flavor. Chop the leafy green tops into soups, casseroles, and stews. When keeping carrots in the refrigerator, cut off the green tops to prevent moisture loss and store in a plastic bag.

**PESTS AND DISEASES:** None are significant in home gardens.

**RECOMMENDED CULTIVARS:** For small gardens, containers, or where soil cannot be worked deeply, try 'Kinko', a 4" carrot

ready to harvest in 50–55 days, or 'Round Romeo', a petite, smooth-skinned, ball-shaped cultivar about 1–1½" in diameter. It's a good choice for children learning how to garden, and is ready to harvest in 55–60 days. Easy-to-grow, short, early carrots ready in 65–70 days include 'Danvers Half Long', 'Scarlet Nantes', and 'Chantenay' cultivars. 'Oxheart' is a good choice for growing in heavy soil; carrots are 4–5" long and wide and can weigh up to one pound apiece. Sweet 'Napoli' is recommended for fall sowing; 'Ithaca' can be sown summer or fall and is good for juicing or storage. Both grow to about 7" long. For traditional long carrots that are good fresh or stored, grow 'Tendersweet', 'Sugarsnax', or 'Bolero', all ready to harvest in 70–80 days. If your garden soil is deep and loose, try 'Japanese Imperial Long', which holds the world's record for the longest carrot. It will grow to at least 1' long in 90–100 days. 'Yellowstone' is another extra long variety and is bright canary yellow. 'BetaSweet' has maroon skin and an orange interior, which makes attractive carrot sticks and slices.

**1** To overwinter carrots in the ground, first cut off the green tops.

**2** Mulch the carrots with a thick layer of straw for protection.

# PERSIMMON
### *Diospyros* spp. *dye-AH-spih-rohs*

**Asian cultivars have larger fruits than American types but are less hardy.**

**ZONES:** 5–9
**SIZE:** 15–60'h × 10–20'w
**TYPE:** Deciduous tree
**GROWTH:** Average
**LIGHT:** Full sun to part shade
**MOISTURE:** Average
**FEATURES:** Edible fruits, valuable hardwood

**SITING:** Persimmons adapt to any fertile soil as long as it drains well. Space trees 20' apart. Choose cultivars according to your climate. Asian or Japanese persimmons (*Diospyros kaki*) are hardy to about 10°F but produces larger fruit than American cultivars, which are hardy to –25°F.

**CARE:** Young trees need consistent moisture to develop properly. Water mature trees in dry climates. Thinning fruit is unnecessary and impractical for large trees but can help to reduce cleanup around smaller trees. Remove any weak or willowy branches in late winter. Prop up fruit-laden branches to prevent breaking. Some types may bear fruit only in alternate years.

**PROPAGATION:** Graft Asian cultivars onto American persimmon (*D. virginiana*) rootstock for enhanced cold tolerance.

**Thinning isn't necessary but branches heavy with fruit may need supporting.**

Propagate American cultivars from bud grafts or root cuttings. Both male and female trees are required for pollination.

**HARVEST:** Trees begin to bear fruit at 3–6 years in autumn and may be fruitful for many decades. The flesh is bitter and astringent until fully ripe. Frost does not improve or harm the flavor. Eat ripe Japanese persimmons out of hand or cut in half and eat with a spoon, with or without lemon juice or sugar. The fruit tastes best chilled. Add the flesh to salads, ice cream, yogurt, or make it into jams. The puréed pulp is used in baked goods and can be frozen for up to 2 years. Freeze whole ripe fruits or dry for long-term storage.

**PESTS AND DISEASES:** Persimmons in the home garden are relatively insect free, although birds and raccoons eat the fruit. Keep debris from trees raked and composted to avoid pest infestations.

**RECOMMENDED CULTIVARS:** 'Early Golden', 'John Rick', and 'Meader' are reliable American cultivars. Japanese types include astringent 'Maru' types and 'Eureka', which become nonastringent when ripe, and nonastringent types 'Fuyu' and 'Great Wall'. 'Gailey' is often planted as a cross-pollinator.

# LOQUAT
### *Eriobotrya japonica* *eh-ree-oh-boh-TRY-uh juh-POH-nih-kuh*

**Cover ripe fruits with a bag to prevent sunburn and moth infestation. Loquat is also known as Japanese medlar.**

**ZONES:** 8–10
**SIZE:** 15–30'h × 15–30'w
**TYPE:** Evergreen shrub or tree
**GROWTH:** Slow
**LIGHT:** Full sun to part shade
**MOISTURE:** High
**FEATURES:** Fragrant flowers, edible fruits

**SITING:** Loquats are adaptable to all moderately fertile soils that drain well. Plant them in spring 20–30' apart.

**CARE:** Apply soluble plant food three times during active growth or use slow-release fruit tree spikes. Mulch with composted manure. Water when flower buds swell and again several times during harvest season. Thin flowers and fruits to increase the size of remaining fruit. Enclose fruit clusters in paper bags to prevent sunburn (purple staining) in hot climates. Prune after harvest to prevent alternate-year bearing. Weed around young trees by hand and around mature trees with light hoeing.

**PROPAGATION:** Bud-grafted trees produce fruit most quickly, in 3–5 years.

**HARVEST:** Loquats typically bloom in fall and fruit in spring. The fruits mature about 90 days after flowering. The best indication of ripeness is full color. Use a clean, sharp

**Loquat can be trained as an espalier to save space in the garden and take advantage of extra warmth from the wall.**

knife or clippers to cut the fruits; leave their stalks attached to avoid tearing the skin. Store at room temperature for up to 10 days or refrigerate for up to 2 weeks.

**PESTS AND DISEASES:** Caribbean fruit fly is a problem in Florida; keep the area underneath and around the tree cleared of fallen fruit. Fire blight (Southeast) and pear blight (West) bacteria may infect trees. Remove and destroy any affected branches at least 6" below the visible infection using loppers sterilized between cuts with bleach or rubbing alcohol. Pick off and destroy any caterpillars. Codling moth may be a problem in California; scrape the cocoons off the bark in late winter and spray with dormant oil. Tie the developing fruits in paper bags to prevent moths from laying eggs on them. Spray dormant oil in winter to combat aphids and scales. Cover trees with netting to protect fruit from birds.

**RECOMMENDED CULTIVARS:** In the Southeast, try 'Tanaka', which is partially self-fertile and more cold hardy than average. 'Advance' is a late-fruiting, blight-resistant natural dwarf about 5' tall, often used as a pollinator for other cultivars. In California, 'Golden Red' is popular.

# ARUGULA

*Eruca sativa* *eh-ROO-kuh sa-TY-vuh*

Arugula, or roquette, is a spicy green often found in mesclun mixes.

**ZONES:** NA
**SIZE:** 3–6"h × 3–6"w
**TYPE:** Annual
**GROWTH:** Fast
**LIGHT:** Full sun to part shade
**MOISTURE:** Average
**FEATURES:** Edible leaves

**SITING:** Choose a sunny or partly sunny location with rich, well-drained soil. Direct-sow seed ¼" deep and 1" apart in rows 8–12" apart, or broadcast seed and cover with ¼" of fine soil 4 weeks before the last frost date or in late summer for a fall crop. Sow small amounts once a month for continuous harvest and to replace plants that have bolted during hot weather.

**CARE:** Thin seedlings to 8" apart when they are 3–4" tall. Protect plants with shade cloth in intense summer sun. Water during dry periods. Sidedress rows with compost or well-rotted manure. Arugula tolerates a light frost but does best if protected under plastic tents or cold frames.

**HARVEST:** Plants that reach maturity while temperatures are cool have the best flavor. Begin harvesting from the center of the plants 3–6 weeks after sowing, or pull whole plants to thin rows. The youngest leaves have the best sweet-spicy flavor. Use them in salads, on sandwiches, in pesto and salsa, and added to soups and stews just before serving. Store unwashed leaves in plastic bags for up to 2 weeks.

**PROPAGATION:** Grow from seed.

**PESTS AND DISEASES:** Use row covers to protect seedlings from beetles that chew on the leaves.

**RECOMMENDED CULTIVARS:** 'Astro' and 'Runway' are two early, vigorous forms.

**1** Grow arugula in a cold frame for harvest throughout the winter.

**2** Pick the center leaves or pull whole plants as needed.

# PINEAPPLE GUAVA

*Feijoa sellowiana* *fay-YO-uh sell-oh-ee-AY-nuh*

Pineapple guavas have attractive blossoms that develop into fruits that drop to the ground when ripe.

**ZONES:** 8–11
**SIZE:** 8–15'h × 8–15'w
**TYPE:** Evergreen shrub or small tree
**GROWTH:** Slow
**LIGHT:** Part shade
**MOISTURE:** Average
**FEATURES:** Edible flowers and fruits

**SITING:** Choose a partially shaded site to protect the tender fruits from hot midday sun. Pineapple guava does best in rich organic acid loam that is well drained. Plant large cultivars 15–20' apart.

**CARE:** Pineapple guava grows well in subtropical climates with low humidity. The flavor of the fruit is improved by cool weather. Some cultivars are more heat tolerant, but all types need watering during extremely hot or dry weather to develop fruit and prevent internal decay. The root system is shallow, so weed by hand or hoe carefully. Use a low-nitrogen fruit plant food at flowering. Prune lightly after harvest to encourage new growth; fruit sets on young wood. Thinning helps air circulate and makes harvesting easier. Remove low-hanging limbs to keep fruit at least 12" off the ground. In mild-winter areas protect from spring frosts.

Plant feijoa where the tree will be shaded from midday sun.

**HARVEST:** Shrubs propagated by air layering or grafting will fruit the second year; plants grown from seed in the third to fifth year. Fruits drop to the ground when ripe. Almost-mature fruits can be picked and allowed to finish ripening at room temperature but will decay after only a few days. Keep unbruised fruits for up to a week in cool storage.

**PROPAGATION:** Grow pineapple guava by air-layering or grafting, or from seed.

**PESTS AND DISEASES:** Scale may cause sooty mold. Use dormant oil in winter if infestations are heavy. Fruit flies are attracted to the strong aroma of ripening fruit. Keep the ground beneath and around the tree cleared of dropped flowers, fruits, and other debris. High humidity may cause fungal infections. Treat with a fungicide labeled for the specific problem.

**RECOMMENDED CULTIVARS:** If you have room for just one pineapple guava, plant 'Edenvale Improved Coolidge', a self-fertile cultivar. In warmer climates try 'Pineapple Gem', which matures earlier. It is self-fruitful but bears more heavily if cross-pollinated. In large gardens grow an 'Apollo' and a 'Gemini' together for fruit from mid- to late season.

# FIG

*Ficus carica* FY-kus KARE-ee-kuh

**Wear gloves to handle unripe figs, which exude gummy latex.**

**ZONES:** 7–9
**SIZE:** 10–30'h × 10–30'w
**TYPE:** Deciduous tree

**GROWTH:** Medium
**LIGHT:** Full sun
**MOISTURE:** Average
**FEATURES:** Edible fruits

**SITING:** Choose a sunny location with well-drained soil. Figs grown for drying do best in sandy soil. Space trees 10–25' apart depending on the cultivar and the soil type. In climates where temperatures fall below 20°F, grow figs in 10- to 15-gallon half barrels or other large containers so you can move them indoors in winter.

**CARE:** One-year-old cuttings will fruit within a year of transplanting. Shade young trees from hot midday sun. Apply low-nitrogen plant food twice a year to in-ground trees or use slow-release fruit spikes for trees in containers. Water during hot or dry weather to prevent premature fruit drop, but do not allow trees to stand in water. Stop watering after harvest. Prune heavily in fall or winter when trees are dormant to remove buds of the early-season (breba) crop and increase the main crop. Trees are fruitful for up to 15 years.

**Insect pollinators enter the open end of the developing flower to pollinate it.**

**PROPAGATION:** Figs are best propagated by cuttings of mature wood. Use rooting hormone and plant cuttings within 24 hours. They may also be started by air layering or seed.

**HARVEST:** Unripe fruits are gummy with latex which can irritate your skin, so wear gloves when working with your trees. Most cultivars bear two crops each year; the breba crop produces acid fruits inferior to those of the main crop that follows. Ripe fruits become soft and turn downward.

**PESTS AND DISEASES:** Protect fig trees from root-knot nematodes with a thick layer of mulch, or use a labeled nematicide for serious infestations. Prolonged high humidity or drought may invite scale insects. Scrape them off the bark. Pick off and destroy leaves infected with rust and follow clean cultivation practices.

**RECOMMENDED CULTIVARS:** 'Celeste' produces one heavy crop of short duration, and rarely produces a breba crop. It is more tolerant of cold than heat. 'Brown Turkey' has a small, early breba crop and a large main crop in midsummer. 'Black Mission' and 'Kadota' cultivars are preferred for dried or candied figs.

# FLORENCE FENNEL

*Foeniculum vulgare azoricum* feh-NIK-yoo-lum vul-GARE-ee az-OR-ik-um

**Grow Florence fennel as you would celery, with plenty of plant food.**

**ZONES:** NA
**SIZE:** 2'h × 1'w
**TYPE:** Annual
**GROWTH:** Average
**LIGHT:** Full sun

**MOISTURE:** Medium
**FEATURES:** Edible leaves and bulbs (swollen leaf bases)

**SITING:** Florence fennel is adaptable to any soil but does best in neutral soil prepared as you would for celery—deep, loose, and heavily amended with organic matter. Direct-sow seed in warm climates ½" deep and 4" apart in rows 18" apart, or start seed indoors 3 weeks before the last frost date and transplant after that date. Like its relative the carrot, fennel grows well in raised beds.

**CARE:** Florence fennel grows like celery but forms a broad bulblike structure where the leaf bases swell at ground level. To provide ample room for the bulbs to grow, thin seedlings to 8" apart. Fennel is frost sensitive and has a tendency to bolt in hot midsummer weather. Water during dry periods to help prevent bolting. Like celery, fennel is a heavy feeder. Use a balanced soluble plant food or sidedress with manure tea every 2 weeks. Mulch

**Dig the whole plant when the bulb of the swollen stem is 3" in diameter.**

between rows to conserve moisture, keep the soil cool, and combat weeds. When the bulbs reach about 2" in diameter, blanch them by mounding soil or mulch around the entire plant, leaving just the feathery top uncovered.

**PROPAGATION:** Grow from seed.

**HARVEST:** The leaves are ready to harvest when they are about 18" tall. Bulbs are fully formed (about 3" in diameter) in 80–100 days. Dig the whole plants at that size and store in the refrigerator until needed; fennel becomes tough and stringy if left in the ground. Cut off the roots and the tops of the tallest leaves. Pull apart the bulb sections.

**PESTS AND DISEASES:** No significant problems affect Florence fennel.

**RECOMMENDED CULTIVARS:** 'Zefa Fino' has a large bulb and is slow to bolt. In northern zones, try 'Orion', which matures in 75–80 days. The perennial herb common fennel (*F. vulgare dulce*) does not form a swollen base and is grown instead for its feathery, anise-flavored foliage and seeds, which are used to flavor cheese, sausage, eggs, cabbage, sauerkraut, liqueurs, and breads.

# KUMQUAT

*Fortunella margarita* *for-tyew-NEL-la mar-gub-REE-tub*

**Many kumquat cultivars are sweet enough to eat straight from the tree.**

**ZONES:** 8–10
**SIZE:** 6–15'h × 6–15'w
**TYPE:** Evergreen shrub or small tree

**GROWTH:** Slow
**LIGHT:** Full sun
**MOISTURE:** Average
**FEATURES:** Fragrant flowers, edible fruits

**SITING:** Grow in deep, well-drained, acid silty soil in a sunny area protected from strong winds and located where you can water in dry weather. In hot climates, choose a site protected from midday sun. Plant kumquats 8–12' apart, or 5' apart for use as hedges. Some kumquats are thorny, so locate them well back from paths.

**CARE:** Like citrus, *Fortunella* species need consistently moist soil but should not be held in standing water. On mature trees, prune dead and damaged wood and any branch that interferes with the growth of scaffold limbs. Hedge pruning may be necessary on tightly spaced trees to maintain a manageable shape for harvesting. Pull weeds manually or till lightly. Feed several times a year from late autumn to midspring, increasing the amount of plant food as trees mature. Use foliar sprays to add needed micronutrients.

**Plant kumquat in containers for the deck or patio.**

**HARVEST:** Kumquats are ripe when they are fully colored. Eat unpeeled. Eat 'Nagami' and 'Meiwa' fresh out of hand; 'Marumi' is less sweet and better used for preserving. To store fruits, let them cure for a few days to lose some moisture, then dry them or can them in syrup.

**PESTS AND DISEASES:** Container plants are susceptible to mealybugs. Wash them off with a sharp stream from the hose or spray with insecticidal soap. Kumquats are attacked by common citrus pests, and in unfavorable conditions may be infected by rots, spots, gummosis, and anthracnose.

**RECOMMENDED CULTIVARS:** 'Nagami' bears oval yellow-skinned fruit and grows to 15'. It is the most common kumquat, bearing the sweetest fruit in hot summers but also tolerant of light frost. *F. japonica* 'Marumi' bears round orange-skinned fruit and is a better choice for northern zones. *F. japonica* 'Meiwa' is a dwarf but has large, sweet fruits, the best choice for eating fresh. It grows well in containers. Try limequat 'Eustis' or 'Tavares', and orangequat 'Nippon'. All three are well suited to containers.

# STRAWBERRY

*Fragaria* spp. *fra-GARE-ee-uh*

**Choose strawberry cultivars bred for successful growing in your region.**

**ZONES:** 3–10
**SIZE:** 6"h × 18"w
**TYPE:** Herbaceous perennial

**GROWTH:** Average
**LIGHT:** Full sun
**MOISTURE:** High
**FEATURES:** Edible berries

**SITING:** Choose a warm, sunny, elevated location for adequate surface drainage, preferably in well-drained loam or sandy loam. In areas with heavy soil, plant strawberries in raised beds at least 6" deep. Amend all soils with well-rotted compost or manure. Space plants 18–24" apart in rows 2–4' apart depending on the size of the strawberry bed and how much access you need for maintenance and harvest.

Day-neutral types (those that bear fruit regardless of daylength) can be planted closer together. Position plant crowns at the soil surface, then spread out the roots and firm soil over them. Another method is to scoop out a shallow pocket of soil for each plant, make a small mound of soil in the center with the top of the mound level with the bed level, and place the plant on top of the mound so the roots drape out and over the mound and into the pocket. Cover the roots with soil and water thoroughly after planting. Strawberries can also be planted in containers, such as

strawberry pots, which makes maintenance and pest control much easier.

**CARE:** Keep nursery-bought plants moist and cool until you are able to plant them. If possible, grow a green manure crop such as oats in the location you want strawberries the year before building a bed, especially if your bed is located where sod has grown previously. Till the cover crop under in autumn and begin a program of weed control. Keep the beds free of weeds for maximum yield. Herbicides usually aren't necessary for most home gardens, which can be

**Strawberries adapt well to container culture. Opt for a traditional strawberry pot with pockets or another roomy container.**

**Strawberries offer rich rewards for a small investment of time and attention. Fresh fruit from the garden excels in flavor.**

# STRAWBERRY
*continued*

Use strawberries as a double-duty ground cover: They provide attractive erosion control and a delicious harvest.

Alpine strawberry varieties make up in flavor what they lack in size. As a garden edging, they're a gem.

weeded by hand or with a hoe or tiller.

Begin pinching flowers off spring-planted strawberries as soon as they develop to encourage plant growth and early formation of runners for new plants. If the bed becomes a solid mat of plants, cut or till 8" open areas between the rows. For everbearing and day-neutral types, pinch off flowers until July 1, then allow the plants to bloom and fruit. In beds with limited space, follow the spaced-row system. Position the runners to develop rows 18–24" wide. When rows are as densely planted as you want them, cut off new runners as they develop. If not kept in check, runners quickly overtake the bed, forming dense mats that drain energy from everbearing plants, which reduces fruiting. If your growing area is large enough, you can train runners for rows of new plants each year and turn under the oldest rows, a practice that helps to maintain high yields. Day-neutral strawberries put out few runners, so they can be planted anytime and closer together, up to 12" apart in each direction. Remove any runners that do form. In a few years the plants will have multiple crowns and begin to have lower yields. Then you can let runners develop to replace the older plants.

Apply a balanced water-soluble plant food as buds develop; dry plant food particles caught on plants can burn them. Carefully follow label instructions for the product you choose in order to apply the correct rate for the size of your bed. You can also use well-rotted manure around first-year, spring-planted strawberries. Renovate your strawberry bed as soon after harvest as possible to control pests and diseases. Mow or cut the leaves close to the ground but without cutting into the crowns. Till or cut back the edges of the rows to about 12" wide. Continue weeding and apply a broadleaf herbicide, if necessary, after harvest and again when the plants are dormant. Apply a balanced water-soluble plant food to help bud formation for next season. Keep weeding until the plants are dormant and the ground has begun to freeze, then mulch for winter with clean straw. Remove the mulch in early spring so the ground can warm up and drain well. Install row covers to discourage pests. Protect plants from late-spring frosts with mulch and row covers.

**PROPAGATION:** Grow from runners.
**HARVEST:** Begin harvesting most types of strawberries the year after planting—about 14 months from planting in northern zones and 9 months in the South. Highest yields will come from the youngest plants. Berries

Rake off mulch in early spring so the ground warms quickly and drains well.

Berries are ripe when they attain full color, regardless of size.

# STRAWBERRY
*continued*

**1** Renovate beds after harvest by mowing the leaves close to the ground.

**2** Then till between rows to trim plants and control weeds.

**3** Apply a broadleaf herbicide and balanced plant food, then mulch well.

will be ready to pick about a month after the plants bloom. Day-neutral plants will be ready to harvest about 90 days after planting. Berries are ripe when they attain full color for their cultivar, regardless of size. Ripe berries left on the plants will quickly become overripe and start to decay, which attracts pests, so take all the ripe berries each time you pick. Pick berries as often as every other day. Pinch the stems between your thumbnail and forefinger, leaving the leaf cap and short stem attached. Store unwashed berries in the refrigerator for up to a week. Enjoy fresh berries out of hand; sliced, sugared, and served with milk or cream; in salads and on breakfast cereal; and as the essential ingredient in strawberry shortcake. Use them in pies and other baked goods; for juice, jam, jelly, and marmalade; and added to ice cream, yogurt, and smoothies. Freeze strawberries for up to a year for use in cooked recipes.

**PESTS AND DISEASES:** Purchase new plants guaranteed to be disease free rather than taking runners from a friend's yard that might be contaminated with insects or viruses. Strawberries are particularly susceptible to botrytis fruit rot (gray mold), leaf spot, and leaf scorch. All can be controlled with fungicides, clean cultivation practices, and attention to soil drainage. To control gray mold, apply fungicide every 10 days for as long as the weather is wet after the plants bloom. Strawberries are also susceptible to red stele root rot and verticillium wilt. Plants infected with red stele have roots with a rotted-looking red core. Avoid root rot by purchasing resistant cultivars and plants guaranteed to be disease free. If plants become infested,

till them under after harvest and do not plant strawberries again in that location or anywhere that Solanaceae crops (tomatoes, peppers, potatoes, and eggplant) or other berries, melons, or roses have been planted. To avoid wilt, purchase resistant plants and use row covers to keep temperatures around the plants too high for fungi to survive. Root weevils may be a problem in some areas. Remove and destroy damaged plants after harvest and rotate the next crop of strawberries to another area. Clean cultural practices discourage sap beetles, which are attracted to damaged and decaying fruit. Regularly remove overripe or rotting fruit and any vegetative debris from the bed and compost it. Use row covers to discourage tarnished plant bugs. Aphids and spider mites can be washed off by hard rains or watering. If you must use a pesticide, do not apply when plants are blooming or fruiting. Use bait or traps for snails and slugs. Cover plants with tunnels made from chicken wire to keep rabbits, birds, chipmunks, and raccoons from eating the fruit.

**RECOMMENDED CULTIVARS:** Strawberries are cultivated to succeed in specific climates and conditions. Select cultivars bred for your locale. *F. ×ananassa* includes June-bearing, everbearing, and day-neutral strawberries. Everbearing strawberries do not actually fruit all season, especially in hot climates. They produce heavily in spring, sporadically or not at all during the summer, then again in late summer or early autumn, although generally not as prolifically as in spring. Pinch flowers of spring-planted everbearers until July 1. Early spring-bearing cultivars

include 'Earliglow', which has good flavor but modest yields; 'Northeaster', a heavier producer with a slightly grape aftertaste; and 'Avalon', a vigorous producer of large dark red berries. In northern zones, try the Canadian strain of 'Mohawk', which is resistant to red stele. In Southern California, 'Sequoia' may bear as early as December, and 'Douglas' produces large berries in early spring. For midseason berries, grow 'L'Amour' or 'Mesabi', best for eating fresh. 'Northwest' is a late midseason berry in the Pacific Northwest, good fresh or preserved. 'Shasta' is a fairly vigorous cultivar for California growing. For late-season berries, 'Clancy', 'Winona', 'Sparkle', 'Delite', and 'Marlate' are all good choices. Try 'Ozark Beauty' in northern zones. With plastic mulch and row covers, 'Quinault' can be grown as an annual in Alaska. Day-neutral strawberries flower and fruit anytime temperatures are between 40–80°F. You can allow them to fruit in the planting year. 'Tribute' and 'Tristar' are the most commonly grown cultivars. Their fruits are smaller and less prolific than other cultivars, but they are disease resistant and provide crops when other strawberries are not producing. 'Seascape' is a popular cultivar in California and can be grown elsewhere as an annual. *F. vesca* is a day-neutral alpine strawberry—a small-fruited type much like wild strawberry. Most alpine varieties are propagated from seed and often grown as ornamental plants. 'Improved Rugen' is hardy and produces no runners. It fruits heavily even in late summer, tolerates some shade, and grows well in containers.

# SOYBEAN
*Glycine max* GLY-seen max

**Like other legumes, soybeans are cultivated for use fresh and dried.**

**ZONES:** NA
**SIZE:** 12–24"h × 12–24"w
**TYPE:** Annual
**GROWTH:** Average
**LIGHT:** Full sun
**MOISTURE:** Average
**FEATURES:** Edible seeds (beans)

**SITING:** Soybeans are adaptable to many soil types but do not tolerate standing water. They do best in neutral to slightly acid, well-drained, warm soil. Use black plastic to warm the soil for a few weeks in advance of planting in short-season areas. Direct-sow seeds that have been soaked overnight and inoculated with bacteria to fix nitrogen in the roots. Plant them 1½" deep in moist soils and 2" deep in dry soils in hot climates, 2" apart in rows 24–30" apart. In raised beds they can be planted 12" apart in both directions.

**CARE:** Thin 3" seedlings to 4" apart and mulch to conserve soil moisture. Keep the soil consistently moist until pods have set. Weed by hand or lightly with a hoe, but avoid working among plants when they are wet to prevent injury and the spread of disease. Too much nitrogen interferes with production of pods and seeds. Protect from frost damage.

**Soak seeds overnight and inoculate them with rhizobial bacteria.**

**PROPAGATION:** Grow from seed.
**HARVEST:** For use as fresh beans, pick the pods as you would pick shelling peas—when they are filled out and still green. Steam them for a few minutes to make hulling easier. To store soybeans dried, wait to harvest them until the pods are dry but not split open. Dried soybeans are cooked like navy beans or processed into soymilk, flour, miso paste, or the meat substitutes tofu and tempeh. Dried soybeans can be stored in airtight containers for many years.
**PESTS AND DISEASES:** Bacterial blight is common in prolonged cool, rainy weather and can be made worse if too much nitrogen is present in the soil. Remove and destroy any infected plants. Japanese beetles will visit soybeans. Handpick the beetles if they are numerous. Cutworms, white grubs, grasshoppers, and other legume-loving pests may cause some plant damage, but infestations in the home garden are usually not severe.
**RECOMMENDED CULTIVARS:** 'Vinton', 'Butterbaby', and 'Envy' grow well in all areas. Field soybeans are not suitable as a vegetable.

# JERUSALEM ARTICHOKE
*Helianthus tuberosus* hee-lee-AN-thus too-bur-OH-sus

**Jerusalem artichokes, also known as sunchokes, are sunflower relatives, not artichokes and not from Jerusalem.**

**ZONES:** 4–10
**SIZE:** 2–8'h × 1–4'w
**TYPE:** Herbaceous perennial
**GROWTH:** Average but invasive
**LIGHT:** Sun to part shade
**MOISTURE:** Average
**FEATURES:** Edible tubers, attractive flowers

**SITING:** Plant Jerusalem artichoke outside the vegetable garden in a permanent area where you can control its spread or allow it to grow freely. Although it is not fussy about location, loose, well-drained, acid soil gives it the best start. Plant entire tubers or pieces that each contain an "eye." Plant them 4" deep and 18" apart in a single row at the back of a bed or along a fence 2–4 weeks before the last frost date, or as soon as the soil can be worked. In southern zones plant tubers in fall for a spring crop. Mature plants benefit from a windbreak.

**CARE:** Keep the soil consistently moist until plants are established and remove weeds by hand. Tubers sprout 1–3 weeks after planting. Each tuber sends up multiple stalks, which will eventually crowd out most weeds. Cut off the flower heads the first year to help keep energy in the tubers.

**Harvest the edible tubers in autumn after the soil is cold.**

Mulch plants in summer to conserve soil moisture or for protection during severe winters.
**PROPAGATION:** Grow by division.
**HARVEST:** Jerusalem artichoke is not from Jerusalem and is not an artichoke but a type of sunflower grown for its edible tubers, which can be sliced raw into salads, steamed or sautéed as a vegetable, or cooked like potatoes. You can harvest tubers anytime after the soil has cooled in late autumn. In northern zones wait until the foliage has turned brown and the ground has begun to freeze before digging the tubers. The cold improves their sweet, nutty taste. Dig the whole plant with a garden fork; tubers that remain in the soil will become next year's plants. Dig only what you will use within a few days; tubers stored in the refrigerator are not as tasty as those freshly dug. Brush off the dirt and clean the tubers thoroughly under cold water with a scrubbing brush. Peeling is unnecessary.
**PESTS AND DISEASES:** None are significant.
**RECOMMENDED CULTIVARS:** 'Stampede' and 'Mammoth French White' are vigorous producers in all climates.

# SWEET POTATO
*Ipomoea batatas* *ip-oh-MEE-uh bah-TAH-tas*

Sweet potatoes, often confused with yams, can be grown as annuals.

**ZONES:** NA
**SIZE:** 12–30"h ×
12–24"w
**TYPE:** Perennial
herbaceous bush or
vine usually grown as
an annual

**GROWTH:** Average
**LIGHT:** Full sun to
part shade
**MOISTURE:** Average
**FEATURES:** Edible
tuberous roots

**SITING:** Moderately deep, friable, slightly acid, sandy loam is best. Plant sweet potato slips 3–4 weeks after the last frost date 12–18" apart in rows 48" apart for vining plants and 30" apart for bush types. Water with 4-12-4 starter solution to prevent transplant shock.

**CARE:** Cutting the vines while they are growing will cause the roots to sprout. Keep the soil consistently moist for proper growth and to avoid root cracks. If soil is poor, sidedress plants once with a low-nitrogen plant food. Sweet potatoes are drought tolerant for short periods. Avoid planting them in the same place more than once every 3 or 4 years to prevent soilborne diseases.
**PROPAGATION:** Grow from rooted slips.
**HARVEST:** Dig carefully, loosening the soil with a garden fork to avoid injuring the roots. Cure sweet potatoes for 2–3 weeks in a warm, humid area. Store cured roots

wrapped in newspaper in a dry location at 55–60°F. Do not store in the ground or the refrigerator; they are injured by chilling.
**PESTS AND DISEASES:** Diseases are more common in soil that is not acid enough. Purchase certified disease-free slips for planting. Use row covers to protect young plants from flea beetles and cutworms. Overwatering may attract root weevils.
**RECOMMENDED CULTIVARS:** 'Centennial' is a popular cultivar that is susceptible to rots. 'Allgold' has moist salmon-colored flesh and is resistant to stem rot. Choose bush types, such as 'Vardaman' and 'Porto Rico', for small gardens and containers.

Harvest when the vines are frosted.

Cut away the damaged foliage tops first.

Then dig the tubers with a garden fork.

# WALNUT
*Juglans spp.* *JUG-lanz*

Plant walnut trees away from other crops whose growth they inhibit.

**ZONES:** 4–9
**SIZE:** 60–100'h ×
60–100'w
**TYPE:** Deciduous
tree
**GROWTH:** Average

**LIGHT:** Full sun
**MOISTURE:** Average
**FEATURES:** Edible
nuts (seeds), oil from
fruit flesh, hardwood

**SITING:** Choose a sunny site with deep, fertile, well-drained, slightly alkaline soil. *Juglans* species secrete juglone in their tissues, which inhibits the growth of many other plants. Black walnut (*J. nigra*) and butternut (*J. cineria*) are particularly toxic to roses, potatoes, tomatoes, eggplant, and peppers, as well as pine and apple trees.

**CARE:** Keep the soil consistently moist until the trees are established, and for mature trees during dry spells. Prune the limbs to a central leader with lateral branches at least 18" apart. Examine trees regularly for signs of pests and diseases and treat problems immediately. Use foliar sprays to add needed minerals such as copper, zinc, manganese, and boron.
**PROPAGATION:** Named cultivars are bud-grafted to a rootstock.
**HARVEST:** Black walnuts drop while still in the husk, which is difficult to remove. Cut the husks off with a sharp knife or crush them underfoot—but wear gloves and

keep them off pavement, because the husks stain everything they touch. After hulling, rinse nuts with a garden hose and spread on shallow trays 2–3 nuts deep. Place the trays in a cool, dry, well-ventilated area out of direct sun for 2 weeks to cure the nuts. Store fresh nutmeats in a glass jar or plastic bag for up to 6 months in the refrigerator or up to 1 year in the freezer.
**PESTS AND DISEASES:** Walnut is prone to many blights and fungi, especially when stressed by improper culture and high heat. Choose cultivars that are disease resistant and bred for your climate. Walnut anthracnose defoliates trees in summer and blackens the nut kernels. Darker than usual husks may be a sign of insect damage. Aphids, scales, worms, caterpillars, flies, fall webworms, curculios, maggots, and twig girdlers can all be problems.
**RECOMMENDED CULTIVARS:** Some English or Persian walnuts (*J. regia*) are not self-fertile and need cross pollination. Self-fruitful 'Buccaneer' and 'Broadview' form large nuts. 'Rita' is a smaller self-fertile cultivar good for ornamental use. 'Carpathian' is extremely cold tolerant.

Drive over the tough husks to crush them open.

Wear gloves to avoid the dark pigment in husks.

# LETTUCE
*Lactuca sativa* lak-TOO-kuh sub-TY-vuh

Grow heat-tolerant bibb lettuce for spring and autumn harvests.

Serve early-season butterhead lettuce whole as an individual salad.

Iceberg and other crisphead lettuces require a long, cool growing season.

**ZONES:** NA
**SIZE:** 2–10"h × 2–8"w
**TYPE:** Annual
**GROWTH:** Fast
**LIGHT:** Sun to part shade
**MOISTURE:** High
**FEATURES:** Edible leaves

**SITING:** Start head lettuce indoors 6 weeks before the last frost date and transplant outdoors 3 weeks before it. Direct-sow other lettuces in early spring or fall. Choose a site with loose, fertile, slightly acid, sandy loam amended with well-rotted manure or compost and raked free of any dirt clods and rocks. Sow in wide rows or broadcast and cover with ¼" of fine soil.
**CARE:** Thin seedlings to 4–8" apart, or 12" apart for head lettuces, in rows 18" apart. Pull weeds by hand or hoe lightly to avoid disturbing the shallow roots. Keep the soil consistently moist but not waterlogged. Mulch the rows with organic matter to keep the soil cool and moist. Make successive plantings for prolonged harvest. Seedlings will tolerate a light frost.
**PROPAGATION:** Grow from seed.
**HARVEST:** Leaf lettuce is the fastest-growing type and can be picked when the leaves are as small as 2". Take leaves from the outside of the plants so new leaves will continue to form. When leaves are 4-6", pull the entire plant before it becomes tough and bitter. Pick outside leaves of butterhead and romaine or cut the entire head about 1" above the soil surface. A new head may grow. Pick head lettuce when the center is firm.
**PESTS AND DISEASES:** Purchase seeds, or plants from seeds, pretreated with fungicide to prevent damping off and downy mildew. Thin plants to the appropriate spacing to help prevent botrytis. Plants grown in raised beds are less susceptible to root rots and leaf drop. Handpick beetles and caterpillars; use row covers to protect seedlings from infestations. Wash away aphids with a strong stream from the hose.
**RECOMMENDED CULTIVARS:** Head lettuces need a long growing period in cool

Sow romaine in a cold frame for fresh lettuce until winter.

weather. They are the most difficult type to grow at home. 'Ithaca' is a heat-tolerant cultivar slow to bolt. 'Sierra' is an iceberg type that grows best in cool coastal areas. 'Rouge de Grenoblouse' is a loose, crisphead type that matures quickly and is bolt resistant. For early-season butterhead lettuce, try 'Boston' or 'Four Seasons'. 'Buttercrunch' and 'Summer Bibb' are heat-tolerant types for late spring and autumn. 'Bronze Mignonette' has frilly red-edged leaves and does well in hot climates. 'Tom Thumb' is a fast-maturing miniature bibb lettuce 3–5" tall. It interplants well and each plant can be served whole as an individual salad. Plant 'Winter Marvel'

Interplant leaf lettuces among taller crops that provide shade.

or 'North Pole' in autumn; they will overwinter with protection in mild climates. The looseleaf lettuces 'Salad Bowl', 'Oakleaf', and 'Red Deer Tongue' are heat tolerant but do best planted in the shade of taller crops, such as tomatoes. 'Black Seeded Simpson' is a good choice for early-season lettuce. 'Red Sails' has crinkly leaves with burgundy edges and is slow to bolt. Romaine types grow best in cool weather. 'Little Gem' is a 5–7" cultivar good for small gardens. Plant hardy 'Paris Island Cos' and red-tinged 'Rouge d'Hiver' in fall and protect them in a cold frame for lettuce until winter.

Snip individual leaves as needed for salads and sandwiches.

Pull entire plants by hand to avoid disturbing nearby plants' shallow roots.

# GARDEN CRESS
*Lepidium sativum* *lep-ih-DEE-um sub-TY-vum*

**Peppery garden cress is related to mustard greens. It is also known as peppergrass, curly cress, or broadleaf cress.**

**ZONES:** NA
**SIZE:** 3–12"h × 6"w
**TYPE:** Annual
**GROWTH:** Fast

**LIGHT:** Full sun to part shade
**MOISTURE:** High
**FEATURES:** Edible leaves and stems

**SITING:** Direct-sow anytime indoors in pots and keep in a bright location. Or broadcast in the garden, in a windowbox, or in a container in spring and autumn, and cover with a ¼" layer of fine soil. A small area—no more than 1–2' square—provides a lot of leaves. Garden cress does best in fertile, well-drained soil or potting mix to which well-rotted compost has been added. Interplant it with carrots, radishes, and lettuces.

**CARE:** Thin seedlings to 6" apart when they are 3" tall; use the thinnings in salads. Hand-weed to avoid disturbing shallow roots. Keep the soil continuously moist. Garden cress will bolt under moisture and heat stress. Leaves become bitter above 85°F. In hot climates protect from midday sun.
**PROPAGATION:** Grow from seed.
**HARVEST:** Seedlings are ready to thin in as little as 2 weeks. Cut or pull entire clumps when they are no more than 6" tall (about 2–4 weeks after seeding) for the best flavor and texture. Snip them into salads and use as garnishes. Garden cress is related to mustard; the leaves have a peppery aroma

**Protect cress from hot midday sun for best foliage and flavor.**

and taste. Cut plants will regrow, but make successive plantings of new seed for a continuous supply until frost.
**PESTS AND DISEASES:** Garden cress has no significant problems. Use row covers if insects bother young plants.
**RECOMMENDED CULTIVARS:** Like parsley, garden cress comes in flat and curly types. 'Cressida' and 'Persian' have flat leaves and are sometimes marketed as peppercress, although they are not of that species (*L. virginicum*). 'Wrinkled Crinkled' is a bolt-resistant curly type that looks like parsley. 'Presto' is a small, ruffled cultivar bred to taste like watercress. Although watercress (*Nasturium officinale*) is grown and used in much the same way as garden cress, it is not related. Plant it at the edge of a pond or stream where it can get some shade and the constant moisture it requires to thrive, or grow it in containers that you can set inside pans of water. Snip leaves or pull whole plants for use in salads, sandwiches, and soups. Another fast-growing plant with peppery leaves good in salads is nasturtium (*Tropaeolum majus*), sometimes called Indian cress. It is usually grown for its colorful flowers, which are also edible. Unlike garden cress and watercress, nasturtium grows best in poor soil and full sun.

# LOVAGE
*Levisticum officinale* *leb-VIS-tib-kum off-fib-sib-NAH-lay*

**Use lovage's tender leaves and stems in place of celery.**

**ZONES:** 3–7
**SIZE:** 2–4'h × 2–4'w
**TYPE:** Herbaceous perennial
**GROWTH:** Average

**LIGHT:** Full sun to part shade
**MOISTURE:** High
**FEATURES:** Edible seeds, leaves, and stalks; essential oil

**SITING:** Direct-sow seed after the last frost date in deep, fertile, consistently moist soil, or start indoors or in cold frames 4 weeks before the last frost date. Transplant seedlings when they are 3–6" tall to 4' apart

or use just a few plants as ornamentals at the back of perennial flower beds.
**CARE:** Keep the soil consistently moist and water during high heat or periods of drought. Remove flowers as they appear to stimulate growth of leaf stalks, or let some flowers develop so you can collect the dried seed. Lovage will self-sow if flowers

**Use the leaves as an herb or harvest whole stalks for use as a vegetable.**

go to seed. To collect seed, cut the seedheads with an inch of stalk attached and hang them upside down in bunches in paper bags to catch the seeds. Mulch lovage for overwintering in cold climates.
**PROPAGATION:** Grow from seed or by division in spring.
**HARVEST:** Lovage is ready to use about 90 days after sowing. Pick the tender leaves and stalks anytime during the growing season and use fresh in salads. Blanch the leaf stalks as a vegetable side dish, or chop the stems and use in cooking as you would celery. The leaves can be dried or frozen for use within 1 year. The dried seeds are used in pickles.
**PESTS AND DISEASES:** Lovage contains a highly aromatic essential oil that naturally repels insects. Maintain adequate space between plants to help avoid blights. If any stems rot or leaves turn yellow or reddish, pull and destroy the whole plant and sow seed in a new location.
**RECOMMENDED CULTIVARS:** Lovage is marketed under its common name.

# LYCHEE
### *Litchi chinensis* LEE-chee chi-NEN-sis

**Lychees are ripe when they reach their full cultivar color of red, pink, or amber. Litchi is a variant spelling of this plant.**

**ZONES:** 9–11
**SIZE:** 30–100'h × 30–100'w
**TYPE:** Evergreen tree
**GROWTH:** Slow

**LIGHT:** Full sun
**MOISTURE:** High to average
**FEATURES:** Edible fruits

**SITING:** Lychee grows best where summers are hot and wet and winters are cool and dry without frost. It is adaptable to a wide range of soils, including clay and alkaline ones, and can tolerate brief flooding but not salinity. It does best in deep alluvial loam with high acidity. Space trees at least 40' apart and 40' away from other trees and structures that might shade them.

**CARE:** Protect young trees from wind and high heat. Prune them to a central leader and remove any low and acute-angle branches. Add plant food to the planting hole and feed once a year until the tree is large enough to bear fruit, then feed only immediately after harvest. Bearing trees need less phosphorus than developing trees. Lychees require insects for good pollination, primarily honeybees, so avoid using pesticides. Water during hot months. Heavy rain or fog and hot, dry winds during flowering can cause blossom drop and splitting of fruit. Shaded portions of a tree will not bear fruit. Too much nitrogen causes fruits to crack.

**PROPAGATION:** Grow it by air-layering.

**HARVEST:** Air-layered trees fruit 2–5 years after planting and will bear for many decades. Fruits mature 4–5 months after flowering. Harvest every few days over a period of a few weeks. Yields vary with environmental conditions, cultivar, tree age, cultural practices, and availability of pollinators. Fruits are ripe when they reach the full cultivar color. The aromatic oval fruits are red, pink, or amber and look like strawberries hanging in clusters. The swelling of maturing fruit causes the warty bumps on the skin to flatten out somewhat. Clip clusters with some stem and leaves attached; pulling fruit will break the skin. Use a pruning pole to clip clusters overhead.

Fresh flesh is white, grayish white, or pinkish white and juicy. The seed comes out easily and is not edible. Lychee dries naturally; the skin turns brown and brittle and the flesh turns dark brown and wrinkly. The dried flesh is dark and rich, similar to a large raisin. Eat lychees fresh out of hand or peeled and pitted and added to salads, baked goods, and sherbet. Store fresh fruits in a cool, dry location with good air circulation to prevent rotting. They hold their color and quality for just a few days. Refrigerate them for up to 2 weeks, or freeze them whole after peeling and seeding. Thaw frozen lychees in tepid water and eat immediately before they discolor. To dry lychees, hang them up or layer them in mesh trays and store in a cool, dry area. To hasten the process, use a drying oven or a regular oven at low temperature. Dried lychees can be stored in tightly sealed containers at room temperature for up to a year.

**PESTS AND DISEASES:** Lychees are susceptible to algal leaf spot, leaf blight, dieback, and mushroom root rot. Avoid planting them where oak trees once grew. Birds, bats, and bees can damage ripe fruits. Raccoons and rodents are attracted to the aroma of ripe fruit. Use netting if necessary to protect the fruit from invaders. Grasshoppers, katydids, and crickets may eat the foliage. Other damaging insects include stinkbugs, borers, aphids, scale, and twig-pruners.

**RECOMMENDED CULTIVARS:** Some lychees leak juice when the skin is broken. Those that don't are most desirable and are referred to as "dry and clean." 'Brewster', 'Peerless', and 'Bengal' withstand light frosts and are good choices in Florida. They fruit midseason. In Hawaii 'Kaimana', 'Kwai Mi', and 'Groff' are popular cultivars that fruit in August and September. 'Groff' and 'Kwai Mi' (or 'Mauritius') are also popular in California, along with 'Amboina', which ripens in spring.

# TOMATO
### *Lycopersicon esculentum* ly-ko-PER-si-con es-kew-LEN-tum

**Plant early season cultivars for harvest while other types are still growing.**

**ZONES:** NA
**SIZE:** 8–72"h × 8–36"w
**TYPE:** Annual
**GROWTH:** Average

**LIGHT:** Full sun
**MOISTURE:** High
**FEATURES:** Edible fruit

**SITING:** Tomatoes are adaptable to many soil types but grow best in deep, highly fertile, well-drained, slightly acid, loamy soil. Work the soil thoroughly before planting, amending it with well-rotted compost or manure. Although tomato seeds can be sown directly into the garden, most home gardeners purchase transplants. For a head start on the growing season, seed can be started indoors in greenhouse conditions 6–10 weeks before the planting date. Plant seedlings in a sunny location after the last frost date. Plant 1½–2' apart for small bush tomatoes and 3–4' apart for larger types if not staked. Add a handful of well-rotted compost to each hole as you plant. Water thoroughly and use 4-12-4 starter plant food to prevent transplant shock. In cool zones warm the soil with black plastic before setting out transplants.

**CARE:** In hot climates new transplants may need to be shaded until they are established. Protect them from strong or cold winds. Add stakes or cages at planting time to avoid injuring roots later. Training indeterminate plants up stakes or growing them inside stiff wire cages elevates the foliage for better air circulation and holds the fruits off the ground. Also, caged tomatoes tend to be more productive. Make sure that openings in cages are large enough to reach through for harvest and that stakes are at least 8' tall, 1" in diameter, and of sturdy wood or metal. Sink each stake at least 1' deep and about 4" away from the plant. Begin tying the

# TOMATO
*continued*

Midseason tomatoes are great for slicing fresh or cooking.

**1** Add a handful of compost to each hole as you plant.

**2** Plant leggy transplants deeply in a trench. New roots will form on the stem.

**3** Stakes and cages promote air circulation and keep fruits off the ground.

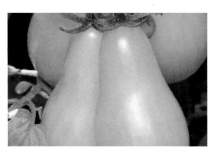

Yellow tomatoes are higher in sugar than red ones but don't keep as well.

stem to the stake when the terminal end is tall enough to droop over toward the ground. Use strips of soft cloth or garden twine to tie the stems in figure-eight loops so that they are not in contact with the stakes. Check staked indeterminate plants regularly for suckers—side branches that form in the joints where leaves join the stems—and pinch them out just beyond the first two leaves that develop. Do not prune determinate tomatoes. Tomatoes need plenty of water to develop juicy fruits and maintain resistance to disease. Use organic mulch around plants to control weeds and conserve soil moisture, especially during midsummer. Feed with a water-soluble tomato plant food such

as Miracle-Gro Water Soluble Tomato Plant Food, according to package directions. Feed plants grown in containers with tomato plant food according to package directions or use a potting mix with plant food already in the mix.

**PROPAGATION:** Grow from seed.

**HARVEST:** Begin picking tomatoes when they have reached full cultivar size and color. Tomatoes will continue ripening off the plant and even in the dark. The pigments that give fruits their distinctive color do not develop well in high temperatures, so tomatoes harvested during midsummer may have more yellow coloration than in cooler weather. Pick any fruits remaining on the vine when the first autumn frost is predicted. Green tomatoes can be fried or pickled. Those that have even a hint of yellow may continue to ripen if held in a dark, warm location (about 65°F) in single layers between sheets of newspaper. Check them once a week or so for ripe fruits, and remove any tomatoes that are decayed or show no signs of ripening. Another method is to

pull up whole plants and hang them upside down in a cool area, where fruits can continue to ripen on the vine. Once picked, ripe fruits can be stored for up to another 2 weeks at 55°F. They also can be stored in the refrigerator but will not taste as good as those stored at cool room temperature. Tomatoes are high in vitamins A, C, and K. They also contain lycopene, a powerful antioxidant. Enjoy fresh tomatoes right off the vine, in salads, on sandwiches, and cooked in soups, stews, and casseroles. Use them fresh or cooked in salsas and slow-cooked into tomato sauce and catsup. Many cooks immerse tomatoes in almost-boiling water for 30–60 seconds, depending on fruit skin thickness, to remove the peel. Use only firm, fully ripe tomatoes for canning. Low-acid tomatoes, which are actually higher in sugar than they are lower in acid, are safe to can as long as they are ripe.

**PESTS AND DISEASES:** Tomatoes are susceptible to a wide variety of diseases and physiological disorders caused by environmental stress. Choose cultivars bred

**1** Blossom end rot, a common problem, is a symptom of calcium deficiency.

**2** Keeping the soil consistently moist helps prevent blossom end rot.

**3** Spread mulch over the soaker hose to conserve soil moisture.

Keep ripe tomatoes picked to encourage more fruits to develop.

# TOMATO
*continued*

for resistance to disease and tolerance of problems common to your geographical area. Among the most common diseases are anthracnose, early blight, Septoria leaf spot, tobacco mosaic virus, fusarium wilt, and verticillium wilt. Typical physiological problems include blossom-end rot, caused by moisture extremes; blossom drop, caused by temperature extremes; skin cracking, caused by hot, rainy periods following dry spells; sunscald, caused by overexposure to the sun on one side of the fruit; and catfacing, a puckering and scarring at the blossom end of fruit caused by cool weather or herbicides. Excessive nitrogen, extreme temperatures, dry soil, or too much shade causes poor fruit set. Too much soil moisture can cause blotchy ripening. Puffiness—a condition where the inside of the fruit cavity does not fully develop—can be the result of temperature extremes at pollination, too much nitrogen, not enough sun, or too much moisture.

Use cardboard collars around tomato transplants to discourage cutworms. Handpick and destroy Japanese beetles and hornworms. Control fruitworms and stinkbugs with a labeled insecticide.

**RECOMMENDED CULTIVARS:** Determinate tomatoes grow to a genetically predetermined, compact height, then produce clusters of flowers at the growing tip. The plants set fruit along the stem within 2–3 weeks and the fruits ripen almost simultaneously. Tomatoes labeled "semideterminate," "strong determinate," or "vigorous determinate" produce a heavy crop, as do regular determinates, but then can be pruned back for a light second crop in late summer to early autumn. Many paste and early-season tomatoes are determinate. Although many paste tomatoes are good eaten fresh, they are most often used for cooking because of their lower moisture content.

Indeterminate tomatoes continue to grow throughout the season because the terminal end of the stem produces leaves instead of flowers. New flowers appear continuously along the side shoots and bloom as long as growing conditions are favorable. For a steady supply of tomatoes all season, plant some indeterminate types. To have ripe tomatoes in the shortest amount of time, choose early-season varieties. Late-season cultivars include the types that grow to immense size, but many of those are susceptible to skin cracking. For ornamental value, choose small-fruited types, which can be grown in hanging baskets or patio pots, or grow some of the many varieties bred for unusual colors.

**Big beefsteak tomatoes ripen late in the season and are worth the wait.**

**Choose disease-resistant cultivars developed for use in your region.**

## DETERMINATE TOMATOES

**SMALL FRUITED:** 'Tumbler' is a hybrid developed for hanging baskets (50 days). 'Gold Nugget' is an early yellow cherry tomato (55 days). 'Tiny Tim' is a compact plant suitable for flowerpots (60 days). 'Patio' is a popular dwarf hybrid for small gardens or containers (70 days). 'Micro-Tom' produces miniature fruit on plants 5–8" tall (75 days).

**EARLY SEASON:** New hybrids of 'Bush Early Girl' are small and disease resistant and bear big, flavorful fruit in 55 days. 'Orange Blossom' bears large, mild-flavored orange-yellow tomatoes (60 days). In areas where summer nights are cool, try 'Oregon Spring Bush' (60 days). 'Silvery Fir Tree', a Russian heirloom tomato, does well in overcast coastal areas (60 days). 'Matina' produces small to medium-size fruits in 60 days, but they taste as rich as late-season beefsteak tomatoes. 'Taxi' is a compact grower with sweet bright yellow fruit. It is cold tolerant and adaptable to all soil types (65 days).

**MIDSEASON:** 'Celebrity' is a disease-resistant midseason cultivar with 7–8-ounce fruits. It does best in areas with consistent moisture (72 days). In the South grow 'Heatwave', which yields best when daytime temperatures are above 90°F (70 days), or 'BHN-444', a high-yielding hybrid with resistance to spotted wilt virus (75 days). 'Sun Chaser' and 'Sunmaster' are flavorful, disease-resistant varieties that also perform well in high heat (75 days). 'Homesweet' and 'Rutgers' are widely adaptable, disease-resistant cultivars

(75 days). 'Shady Lady' is popular in hot climates because its ample foliage protects the fruit from sunscald (75 days). 'Burbank' is an heirloom slicing tomato on a compact plant that needs no support (75 days).

**LATE SEASON:** 'Bradley' is a favorite canning tomato in southern zones (80 days). 'Ace 55' produces high yields of medium-size tomatoes (80 days). 'Super Bush' bears large, meaty fruit all season but is only 3' tall and wide and requires no stakes or cages (85 days). 'Long-Keeper' lives up to its name, producing long clusters of medium-size light orange-red tomatoes that keep for several months if stored properly after picking (85 days).

**PASTE:** 'Roma' (75 days) and 'LaRoma' (60 days) have rich, meaty, almost seedless fruits on compact, disease-resistant vines. Use them for cooking. In northern climates try 'Bellstar' (3–4 ounces), developed in Canada, or 'Oregon' (6–8 ounces), both cold-tolerant cultivars that bear full-flavored fruits that are good fresh or in sauce (60–65 days). 'Ropreco' is ideal for canning and sauces (70–75 days). 'Windowbox' is a good choice for container growing. Its small fruits are good fresh or cooked (70 days). 'Health Kick' is a 4' plant that bears medium-size plum-type tomatoes containing 50 percent more of the antioxidant lycopene than other tomatoes (75 days). 'Jersey Devil' has long, tapered bright red fruits shaped like peppers (80 days).

# TOMATO
*continued*

## INDETERMINATE TOMATOES

**SMALL FRUITED:** 'Grape' is a sweet, early, disease-resistant and heat-tolerant cultivar (55 days). 'Sunsugar' has sugary-sweet bright orange fruit (60 days). 'Sugar Snack' is a cherry-size hybrid that produces high yields all season (65 days). 'Sweet Million' is an improved version of 'Sweet 100', with the same flavor but better resistance to disease (65 days). 'Jolly' is a prolific bearer of extra sweet fruits whose tips are pointed like peaches (70 days). 'Isis Candy' has sweet, cherry-type yellow-gold fruits streaked with red (70 days). 'Red Pear' is less commonly grown than 'Yellow Pear' but is equally good in salads or right off the vine (80 days). 'Ceylon' is a 2" tomato that looks like a miniature beefsteak variety and has a rich, almost spicy flavor (80 days).

**EARLY SEASON:** 'Early Girl' is a popular early slicing tomato that adapts well to almost any climate and is disease-resistant (55 days). 'Early Cascade' bears clusters of fruits not much larger than cherry types. It provides a steady supply all season (55 days). 'Lime Green Salad' is a small plant with 3–5-ounce tangy chartreuse fruit that adds interest to salads. It grows well in containers (60 days). 'Tigerella', sometimes called 'Mr. Stripey', bears big yields of small red tomatoes with clearly defined yellow-orange stripes that look good in salads (60 days). 'Fireworks' and 'Siletz' are the largest red slicing tomatoes available early in the season (60 days). 'Moskvich' produces medium-size fruits that taste as rich as late-season tomatoes (60 days). In warm climates try 'Jetsetter' and 'Miracle Sweet' hybrids, which are vigorous producers and highly resistant to disease (65 days).

**MIDSEASON:** 'Champion' was bred specifically as a slicing tomato. It is disease resistant and bears high yields of fruits larger than 'Early Girl' and earlier than 'Better Boy' (70 days). 'Sioux' is an heirloom variety of average size but exceptional flavor; it yields reliably even in hot weather (70 days). 'Giant Valentine' has heart-shaped fruits that look like a cross between a paste tomato and an oxheart type. They stay sweet and juicy even in mediocre growing conditions (75 days). 'Pink Ping Pong' is a prolific bearer of fruits that match its name, but they are juicy and flavorful (75 days). 'Big Boy' and 'Big Girl' hybrids are longtime favorites because of their large,

meaty fruits produced all season (75 days). 'Big Beef' hybrid is disease resistant and keeps producing large tomatoes even at the end of the season (75 days). 'Cabernet' is a tall, vigorous greenhouse tomato that produces flavorful fruit outdoors too (75 days). 'Ugly' is the popular commercial beefsteak tomato recently made available to home gardeners (75 days). 'Paul Robeson' is a richly flavored deep maroon heirloom black tomato (75 days). 'Green Zebra' has unusual and attractive mottled fruit that is ripe when the skin gets a yellow blush. The light green flesh is tangy (75 days).

**LATE SEASON:** 'Moneymaker' is a medium-size greenhouse variety that does best in extremely humid areas (75–80 days). 'Brandywine' and 'German Johnson' hybrids are heirloom beefsteak varieties with very large dark pink fruit often weighing a pound or more apiece. Both come in curly- and potato-leaf (flat-leaf) types. They do best in temperate zones; potato-leaf plants may slow production during extremely hot weather (75–90 days). 'Beefmaster' is popular for its flavorful fruits that weigh up to 2 pounds apiece (80 days). 'Costoluto Genovese' is a deeply ribbed Italian heirloom tomato that does well in hot weather (80 days). 'Supersonic' does well in temperate areas and requires stakes or other supports for

its substantial vines and 8–12-ounce fruits (80 days). 'Pink Ponderosa' (80 days) is a longtime favorite beefsteak type with fruits up to 2 pounds apiece. To prevent sunscald grow plants in wire cages rather than staking them to poles and pruning out side shoots. 'Mortgage Lifter' is not quite as big but is pink and meaty and has few seeds (85 days). 'Purple Calabash' is a medium-size black tomato with a flattened, deeply ribbed shape, nearly true purple color, and a winey taste (80–90 days). 'Hawaiian Pineapple' is a yellow-orange beefsteak tomato with a distinctly pineapple flavor when ripe (90–95 days). 'Martian Giant' produces sweet scarlet-red fruits that weigh up to a pound apiece (90–100 days). 'Big Rainbow' has huge golden-orange fruits streaked with red (90–100 days).

**PASTE:** 'Super Marzano' is an improved hybrid of 'San Marzano.' Plants are tall with 5"-long fruits (70 days). 'Sausage' produces long, curved, meaty tomatoes good for cooking (75–80 days). 'Italian Red Pear' has 6-ounce pear-shape tomatoes with thin skin and sweet flavor, good for eating fresh or cooked (80 days). 'San Marzano' is an heirloom plant with heavy yields of small, flavorful tomatoes (80–90 days). 'Amish Paste' produces sweet, oblong, oxheart-type heirloom tomatoes (85 days).

## TOMATO DISEASE-RESISTANCE ABBREVIATIONS

Seed packets and seedling tags are often marked with one or more of the following abbreviations, indicating that the cultivar has been bred for specific resistance to one or more viruses, bacteria, fungi, or physiological problems. Combinations of V, F, and N are the most important to look for, but choose cultivars bred for resistance to problems common to your geographic area.

| | |
|---|---|
| ASC = alternaria stem canker | LB = late blight |
| BC = bacterial canker | N = root-knot nematode |
| BSK = bacterial speck | PM = powdery mildew |
| BST = bacterial spot | PVY = potato virus Y |
| BW = bacterial wilt | Si = silvering |
| C1, C2, etc. = leaf mold | St = gray leaf spot |
| CMV = cucumber mosaic virus | TEV = tobacco etch virus |
| CR = corky root | ToMV = tobacco mosaic virus |
| EB = early blight | ToMoV = tobacco mottle virus |
| F1, F2, etc. = fusarium wilt races | TW, TSWV = spotted wilt virus |
| FCRR = fusarium crown and root rot | TYLC = tomato yellow leaf curl |
| | V = verticillium wilt |

# MACADAMIA
*Macadamia integrifolia* mak-uh-DAY-mee-uh in-teg-rih-FOH-lee-uh

**Choose macadamia trees hybridized for best flavor and yields.**

**ZONES:** 9–11
**SIZE:** 15–40'h × 20–30'w
**TYPE:** Woody evergreen tree
**GROWTH:** Slow
**LIGHT:** Full sun to part shade
**MOISTURE:** High
**FEATURES:** Edible seeds (nuts)

**SITING:** Macadamias are suitable for tropical and subtropical climates only. Choose a sunny area where the brittle trees will be protected from wind. Space them at least 30' apart. Macadamias are adaptable to a wide range of soils, but the location must be well-drained and not saline.
**CARE:** Consistent moisture is crucial, particularly from time of nut set to harvest. Young trees need more water than mature ones, and all need watering in heat and drought. Long periods of high heat reduce yields. Saturate the soil annually in areas with low rainfall. Macadamias are not hardy; trees are killed below 25°F, flowers below 30°F, and young trees even by light frost. Where bees are not active,

macadamias may need cross-pollination by hand. Different types grow naturally into different mature shapes but can be pruned to maintain a rounded form. Train all types to a central leader, because macadamias tend to produce multiple trunks that split.
**PROPAGATION:** Macadamia is best grown from grafts, or from air layering or cuttings.
**HARVEST:** Grafted trees bear within 2–8 years and continue producing for 8–10 years before yields levels off. Mature nuts fall to the ground. Collect them on a tarp spread under the tree. Use a long pole to knock down mature nuts that are out of reach. Shaking the tree can bring down immature nuts and cause brittle limbs to break. Remove the husks and cure the nuts by spreading them in single layers on trays kept in a dry location out of direct sun for 2–3 weeks. Finish drying them in the oven at 100–110°F for about 12 hours. Check them frequently to make sure they aren't

**Collect fallen nuts from the ground. Dry them in a shady location for several weeks.**

cooking, and stir them to distribute the heat evenly. Crack dried nuts with a nutcracker. Roast whole or halved nuts for 45–50 minutes in a shallow pan, stirring frequently, just until they start to turn light golden brown. Salt the nuts if desired and allow them to cool completely, then store them in airtight containers at cool room temperatures, or double-wrap and store in the freezer.
**PESTS AND DISEASES:** Macadamias are naturally resistant to avocado root rot and are sometimes planted to replace avocados damaged by fungus. They are susceptible to anthracnose in humid climates. Thrips, mites, and scales may be a problem, but avoid using pesticides that can kill bees, which are needed for pollination.
**RECOMMENDED CULTIVARS:** *M. integrifolia* is a tropical species with creamy-white flowers in early summer, high yields, and good heat tolerance. 'Keauhou' is popular in Hawaii because it is resistant to anthracnose. 'Keaau' is wind resistant and yields even more highly. *M. tetraphylla* is a subtropical species with large racemes of pink flowers and rough-shelled nuts. It flowers August through October, often simultaneously with fruiting, and produces one main crop. The nut quality is more variable and the yields are not as high, but the taste is sweeter. 'Cate' is a popular cultivar in California, ripening in October and November. Hybrids of the two species such as 'Vista' and 'Beaumont' combine the best qualities and are the most reliable choices for home gardens.

# APPLE, CRABAPPLE
*Malus* spp. MAY-lus

**'Gala' is a sweet, midseason apple popular in many zones.**

**ZONES:** 3–10
**SIZE:** 6–40'h × 2–40'w
**TYPE:** Deciduous tree
**GROWTH:** Average
**LIGHT:** High
**MOISTURE:** Average
**FEATURES:** Fragrant flowers, edible fruits

**SITING:** Choose a sunny, protected site with deep, fertile, slightly acid soil that drains well and is not in a low-lying area where frost may collect. A gentle slope (no more than 20 degrees) provides the best drainage. Apple trees are intolerant of salinity. Plant in early spring in northern climates and anytime the trees are dormant in warm zones. Use two or more cultivars that bloom at the same time to ensure cross-pollination and a variety of fruits, or choose a self-pollinating cultivar if you have room for just one tree. Planting holes should be wide and deep enough that the roots are not crowded or bent. Plant so the graft is at least 2" above the soil to prevent the wood above the graft from rooting. Space trees as far apart as they will be tall when mature, or as close as 6' for

hedgerows. Spur-type cultivars can be planted closer together. Make a trench in a ring around the edge of each hole as a reservoir for water.
**CARE:** Use no plant food at planting. Cut back young trees by about one-third to just above a bud. Cut back any branches by up to one-third to a bud that faces out. Remove any buds growing between branches or in crotches. Hand-weed an area 4–6' around the trunk. Use mulch to control weeds and conserve moisture in a circle as wide as the drip line, but keep it away from the trunks of trees. Use nutritional foliar sprays to correct mineral deficiencies. In dry conditions water newly planted trees until they are well established. Water mature trees according to your soil type—as often as once a week

# APPLE, CRABAPPLE
*continued*

**Trees with multiple grafts make it possible to harvest a variety of apples from one tree.**

in areas with sandy soil—and make sure the entire area beneath the canopy is wet to a depth of 18". Most apple cultivars are hardy, but flowers and fruitlets are damaged below 30°F, so protect trees from late frosts. Train young trees to a modified central leader and thin the branches to 1–2' apart. Train early-bearing trees while they are young. Thin fruit on full-size apple cultivars by hand to one per spur. Prune moderately each year during the dormant season. Prune for wide crotch angles, which are stronger and less prone to breaking. Feed mature trees with low-nitrogen fruit tree spikes. Remove water sprouts in summer to maintain an open canopy that sun can penetrate. Dwarf trees have a shallow root system, so they must

be staked, often permanently, or espaliered against a wall or other support.

**PROPAGATION:** Grow by grafting. Dwarf and semidwarf types are most often grafted to East Malling or Malling-Merton rootstocks; standard-size varieties are grafted to young apple seedlings.

**HARVEST:** Expect to wait 3–5 years for your first full harvest. Fruits ripen 70–180 days from bloom, depending on the cultivar. Pick apples by hand to avoid bruising them. A ripe apple separates easily from the fruiting spur and has firm flesh. A soft apple is overripe but can still be used in cooking. Late-season varieties are the best for long-term storage at cool room temperatures. Some types, such as Cox, McIntosh, and Jonathan, decay if stored in the refrigerator.

**PESTS AND DISEASES:** Early-ripening cultivars are the most susceptible to apple maggot. Plant late-season trees, especially in warm climates, and regularly pick up dropped fruit from the ground around the tree. Use insecticidal soap or dormant oil spray in late winter before bud swell to

**Failure to thin fruitlets to one per spur on full-size cultivars results in crowded apples.**

control codling moths, plum curculios, scale, leaf rollers, mites, and aphids. Use a delayed dormant spray when bud tips are ¼" long. Removing water sprouts reduces aphids. Use pesticide sprays only when the petals fall but not while the trees are in bloom to avoid killing pollinating honeybees. Rake up and destroy leaves and other debris, especially during summer fruit drop, to control apple scab and pests. Avoid apple scab by choosing resistant cultivars and planting where air circulation

**Rake up dropped fruit, leaves, and other debris to prevent apple scab and discourage pests.**

**Branches heavily laden with fruits may need to be propped up to avoid breaking.**

# APPLE, CRABAPPLE
### *continued*

is good. Use sulfur spray as directed on infected trees. Bitter rot and botryosphaeria canker are fungal diseases that cause stem and twig cankers, which should be pruned out and destroyed. Tart cultivars such as 'Granny Smith' tend to resist rots better than soft, sweet-fleshed types such as 'Red Delicious'. Corking is caused by insufficient calcium. Overpruning results in succulent growth that is susceptible to fire blight, a bacterial disease that occurs most often in warm, humid climates. Fly speck and sooty blotch may appear on fruits in summer during hot, humid periods but can usually be removed with scrubbing. Eastern red cedar (*Juniperus virginiana*) is a host of cedar-apple rust, a fungal disease that can cause defoliation and poor fruit quality. If there are red cedar trees on or adjacent to your property, be sure to choose apple cultivars labeled for resistance to cedar-apple rust. In cool, humid climates choose cultivars resistant to powdery mildew, a fungus that causes a bumpy brown netting on developing fruits. Use hardware cloth or plastic guards around the lower part of tree trunks to prevent rabbits and mice from eating the bark.

**RECOMMENDED CULTIVARS:** Apple *(Malus sylvestris ×domestica)* is the most widely adapted of all temperate-zone fruit trees. Choose from among more than 1,000 apple varieties in cultivation today, including new introductions as well as heirloom varieties and a wide range of possibilities in between. However, many cultivars have chilling requirements that must be met for fruits to develop properly.

**Low-chill** varieties, suitable for Florida, California, and Arizona, need only 100–400 hours below 45°F. Try 'Anna', similar to 'Red Delicious', for a crop in June, and plant another early bloomer to ensure pollination. 'Dorsett Golden' is an early-season cultivar and self-fruitful. 'Tropic Sweet' is lighter red than 'Anna' and sweeter. Fruits can be stored in the refrigerator for up to 2 months.

**Moderate-chill** varieties need about 400–700 hours below 45°F. 'Macoun' is a deep red McIntosh-type apple resistant to fire blight and hardy to Zone 4. 'Granny Smith' bears tart green apples in late October to early

**'Granny Smith' is more resistant to rots than many red apples and thrives in hot weather.**

November that store well. The tree thrives in hot climates with long summers and is a good pollenizer.

**High-chill** varieties need at least 700–1,600 hours below 45°F. Such trees are hardy and do not thrive in hot climates. 'Liberty' is highly disease resistant and bears medium to large reddish gold fruits in early October that are good fresh or cooked and store well. It is interfruitful with 'Royal Empire', a popular cider apple.

Almost all apple cultivars require other apple cultivars for pollination. Some cultivars—such as 'Jonagold', 'Mutsu' ('Crispin'), 'Spigold', 'Winesap', 'Gravenstein', and sports of 'Stayman'—are poor pollinizers. They can be pollinated by other cultivars but cannot be used to pollinate others. If you have room for only one apple tree, choose a cultivar that is self-fruitful. 'Priscilla' is a disease-resistant bright red over yellow apple with an unusual spicy flavor, and it stores well. 'Prima' is yellow with a bright red blush and a rich flavor. Ready for harvest in early September, it keeps a month or more at cool temperatures. 'Dorsett Golden', an early-season cultivar similar to 'Golden Delicious' in appearance and flavor, needs only 100 hours of chilling. 'Gordon' is another low-chill cultivar popular in warm climates, where it bears from August through October. It has red stripes over green skin and tastes good fresh or cooked.

Many of the most well-known apple cultivars have been made better through hybridization. Look for improved strains of these old favorites and be sure to check pollination

requirements. 'Calville Blanc d'Hiver' apples (800–1,000 hours of chilling; mid-October) have pale yellow to white skin when ripe but are often harvested green and allowed to mature in storage. They are excellent for cooking and cider. 'Cortland' (800–1,000 hours; mid-September) develops many small branches, so it requires more pruning than other types but is hardy to Zone 3. 'Esopus Spitzenberg' (800 hours; late September to early October) is prized for its crisp flesh and rich flavor. 'Delicious' and 'Golden Delicious' (700 hours; October) have a tendency to develop weak crotches. Thin excess fruitlets or fruits will not develop characteristic colors. 'Jonathan' (700–800 hours; early October) is self-fruitful but susceptible to fire blight. 'Lodi' (800–1,000 hours; early August) is similar to 'Yellow

**Columnar apples are single-trunked upright hybrids that bear full-size apples.**

# APPLE, CRABAPPLE
*continued*

**Pick your own apples, using a reliable, old-fashioned tool with an extended arm.**

**Wear your apple-picking bag over a shoulder and tote up to a bushel of apples.**

Transparent' but keeps better. McIntosh (900 hours; early September) bears early and produces best in cool climates. It is partially self-fruitful. New strains have improved color, flavor, and disease resistance. 'Melrose' (800–1,000 hours; mid- to late October) is a cross of 'Jonathan' and 'Delicious' and partially self-fruitful. Its extra large fruits make fruit thinning a requirement, and regular pruning is necessary to keep them from being shaded so much that their red color doesn't develop. Similarly, 'Rome Beauty' (1,000 hours; November) must be thinned and pruned for best harvest. A good choice for cool climates because it blooms late, it is excellent for cooking.

Many more recent cultivars and strains are also available. 'Zestar' (August) is an excellent all-purpose white-fleshed red apple that is hardy to Zone 3. 'Crispin', also called 'Mutsu' (600 hours; mid- to late September), is an extremely sweet yellow-green apple that is good fresh or in pies. It does best in Zones 5–9. 'Fuji' (600 hours; mid-September) is a good pollenizer with large, sometimes russeted fruits that store for up to 6 months. It's a popular cultivar in California. 'Sun Fuji' bears fruits with an orange-pink blush over yellow skin that ripen in October (Zones 5–8). 'Gala' (600 hours; September) is a sweet midseason apple popular in many zones. Thinning is difficult because the tree blooms over a long period. The fruits are small and

sometimes pale red. 'Galaxy Gala' and 'Scarlet Gala' have been bred for better color. 'Gala' Mitchell and Buckeye strains (early September) are hardy to Zone 3. All are best consumed within a month or two.

'Gravenstein' strains (700 hours) are good fresh or cooked and bear early in the season, but they require pollinizers. 'Braeburn' (700 hours; October to November) is a self-fruitful tree that bears late. Its fruits are green blushed with red and have a better flavor than 'Granny Smith'. 'Empire' (800 hours; September) is a self-fruitful cultivar good for hot summer climates; it is a reliable pollinizer. 'Jonagold' (700-800 hours) is a compact tree with juicy, sweet, all-purpose red fruits that ripen in early October. 'Honeycrisp' (800–1,000 hours; September) has sweet, juicy red over gold fruits best eaten fresh. 'Stayman Winesap' (800 hours; October) is a favorite red baking and cider apple in Zones 5–8 that keeps well. 'Idared' (800–1,000 hours) is hardy to Zone 4, blooms early,

and ripens in late October. The bright red fruit has aromatic white flesh that is excellent in desserts. 'Goldrush' is a disease-resistant tart yellow apple that ripens in late October. It keeps well, and the flavor sweetens in storage. **Columnar apples** such as 'Scarlet Sentinel', 'Golden Sentinel', and 'Northpole' are hybrids that grow as single-trunked, branchless trees that produce full-size apples along the length of the trunk. They are easy to maintain at 8' or less in containers, suitable for deck or patio gardening. They require about 800 chilling hours and bear in September. Plant one of each to ensure pollination if other apple trees are not present in the landscape. **Red-fleshed** apples are prized for their ornamental value; their blooms are abundant and colorful like those of pink- and red-flowering crabapples. Their full-size fruits can be almost oblong and colored rose over greenish yellow to entirely dark red. The flesh is pink to dark red and has an intense sweet-tart flavor. 'Hidden Rose' bears medium to large greenish-yellow apples flushed with a hint of red in early October. The flesh is dark pink. 'Scarlet Surprise' bears dark red fruit with deep purple-red flesh in mid- to late August. Even the leaves and bark of the tree have a red cast. It requires about 800 chilling hours and needs a pollenizer.

**Homegrown apples may not always have a picture-perfect appearance, but they boast flavor, color, and freshness that can't be beat.**

# APPLE, CRABAPPLE

*continued*

Crabapples are *Malus* species with highly ornamental flowers and small, sour fruits less than 2" in diameter. Like larger-fruited species, they grow slowly and do best in consistently moist, slightly acid soil. Because they flower profusely, crabapples are often interplanted with standard apples to ensure pollination. Most have moderate chill requirements. White-flowering varieties are the most disease resistant and the best pollenizers. Crabapples grown for their fruit include Siberian crabapple (*M. baccata*) which grows best in Zones 2–7. 'Jackii' is the most popular. *M. sargentii* cultivars, such as 'Sargent' and 'Tina', are dwarf types and the most disease resistant of all crabapples. *M. ×zumi* var. *calocarpa* 'Golden Hornet' is a self-fertile white-flowered tree with golden-yellow fruit, but it is not entirely disease-resistant. Unlike standard apples that need regular pruning and thinning, prune crabapples only to control their

size and shape and to encourage growth. Prune just after the petals fall for best results.

To grow crabapples as ornamentals and pollenizers for standard apples, choose cultivars guaranteed to bloom annually and hold their fruit through winter. Also select cultivars resistant to apple scab and fire blight. Those with larger fruit, such as 'Transcendent' or 'Whitney', which is sweet enough to be eaten fresh, are easier to pick for culinary use but may drop some fruit in summer and autumn. Harvest or rake up fallen fruit to discourage pests and prevent disease.

'Holiday Gold' is a good pollenizer that holds its yellow fruit until spring and is resistant to scab. 'Adirondack' is a tall, upright type with persistent red fruits. 'Jewelberry' is an excellent choice for small spaces. 'Professor Sprenger' is among the taller crabapple cultivars and has orange-red fruits. 'Ormiston Roy' is also tall and has yellow fruits with an orange blush.

**Large-fruited crabapples are easier to pick than small types but may drop more fruit.**

'Sargent' and 'Tina' are short, wide-spreading shrub-type cultivars with persistent red fruits. 'Evereste' and 'Winter Gem' ('Glen Mills') are highly disease-resistant trees that produce abundant crops of showy red fruits.

# MANGO
## *Mangifera indica*  man-JIF-er-a IN-di-ka

**Protect mangoes from sunburn in hot climates and water trees weekly.**

**ZONES:** 9–11
**SIZE:** 30–100'h × 50–100'w
**TYPE:** Nearly evergreen tree
**GROWTH:** Fast
**LIGHT:** Full sun to part shade
**MOISTURE:** High
**FEATURES:** Edible fruits

**SITING:** Plant at the top of a slope for the best drainage and good air circulation, and provide a windbreak or stake young trees. In desert locations plant mangoes in the shade to prevent sunburn of fruits. In cooler zones plant them on the south side of the house for maximum sun and warmth. Mangoes grow well in almost any moderately acid soil but not in heavy clay or other wet soils.

**CARE:** Mangoes thrive only in frost-free zones. Night temperatures above 55°F are required for pollination. Water trees weekly in warm weather to keep the soil consistently moist until fruit is harvested. In the desert, trees may need daily watering until harvest. Hard water can cause fruit flesh to be stringy. Mangoes are sensitive to chemical plant foods but need regular applications of nitrogen and iron. Work fish emulsion or composted manure into the soil around the trees every 2 weeks until July. Wear gloves while working with mango trees; the leaves and fruit skins contain a toxic sap that can cause a painful dermatitis. Prune trees in late winter or early spring to control size and shape. To avoid alternate-year bearing, remove some flower clusters in years when blooms are too abundant. Thinning the fruit also helps to encourage annual bearing.
**PROPAGATION:** Grow by grafting or from nursery-grown trees.
**HARVEST:** Fruits mature 100–180 days after the flowers bloom. They are oval or kidney shape. Ripe fruit skin is pale green or yellow blushed with red and is soft to the touch. Tree-ripened fruits have the best flavor. Pick fruit from late-bearing trees if temperatures fall; ripen indoors with

the stem ends down in trays covered with a damp cloth to prevent shrinkage. Keep at cool room temperatures not below 50°F. Ripe fruits can be refrigerated for up to 3 weeks.
**PESTS AND DISEASES:** Anthracnose is often a problem in wet, humid weather. Choose cultivars with resistance or use copper spray or fungicide. Too much nitrogen causes shriveling at the fruit apex, called "soft nose." Control fruit flies and sand weevils by keeping dropped fruit and vegetative debris around the trees picked up and destroyed. Use dormant oil or insecticidal soap to control scale, mites, and mealybugs.
**RECOMMENDED CULTIVARS:** In Hawaii 'Pairi' is popular for greenhouse and home-garden growing but is not as reliable an annual producer as 'Gouveia'. In Florida try 'Kiett', which is mildew resistant, or fiberless 'Kent'. 'Edward' grows well in all interior locations. 'Earlygold' is an anthracnose-resistant, very early bearer for coastal areas. All mangoes are self-fertile, so you can plant just one tree if space is limited. 'Brooks' is a late-bearing, anthracnose-resistant, somewhat dwarf cultivar suitable for outdoor container growing.

# MINT
*Mentha* spp. *MEN-thuh*

Common spearmint is best known for its aromatic oil used in mints and gum.

**ZONES:** 4–10
**SIZE:** 1–4'h × 1–4'w
**TYPE:** Herbaceous perennial
**GROWTH:** Fast
**LIGHT:** Full sun to part shade
**MOISTURE:** Moderate
**FEATURES:** Edible leaves

**SITING:** Choose a sunny location with rich, well-drained, slightly acid soil or muck. Plant rooted stem cuttings or runners 3" deep and 2' apart in fall or spring. Space different cultivars far apart to avoid cross-pollination. Northern climates get the right amount of sun for the best mint oil production.

**CARE:** Remove flowers as they appear and pinch back the stems to encourage bushier growth. Keep the area around mint free of weeds and grass, which reduce yields and may affect flavor. Mint can be mowed and will quickly come back. Set boards 12" deep in the soil around the plants to slow the spread of runners. If space is limited, grow mint in a container to control its growth. To overwinter indoors cut the plant back to

Pineapple mint is as popular for its variegated foliage as it is for its distinctive fruity fragrance.

6" and leave it outside through autumn for proper chilling.

**PROPAGATION:** Grow from stem cuttings or divisions.

**HARVEST:** Mint oil is stored in glands on the undersides of leaves and is at its peak in mid-June to late September. Pinch out the topmost leaves as needed all season. Cut the leaves and the flower tops when plants start to flower; hang them upside down to dry in small bundles, or spread them loosely in a shallow tray. When the stems are brittle, remove the leaves and flowers and store in airtight containers.

Add fresh leaves to brewed tea while it is still hot, or snip leaves into fruit salad, ice cream and sherbet, and any dish containing peas. Mix with yogurt and diced cucumber for a refreshing salad dressing. Chop or process just before serving; leaves turn dark quickly. Mint is also made into sauce and jelly as an accompaniment to lamb and game meats. It is often a key ingredient in many Asian, Mediterranean, and Middle Eastern dishes. Fresh leaves can be frozen to retain their bright color. Use dried leaves in tea.

**PESTS AND DISEASES:** Most are not significant in home gardens. Knock off mites and aphids with a spray from the garden hose, being careful to spray the undersides of leaves. Choose cultivars with improved resistance to verticillium wilt and mint rust. Avoid using pesticides when plants are in bloom; the flowers attract beneficial bees and flies that pollinate many plants and trees.

**RECOMMENDED CULTIVARS:** Common spearmint (*M. spicata*) and peppermint (*M. piperita*) are best known for their aromatic oils, used to flavor beverages, candies, and medicines. Others rich in menthol include field mint (*M. arvensis*), Japanese mint (*M. arvensis* var. *piperascens*), horsemint (*M. longifolia*), orange mint (*M. ×piperita* 'Citrata'), and water mint (*M. aquatica*).

Austrian and Vietnamese mints (*M. ×gracilis*), curly mint (*M. spicata* 'Crispa'), Moroccan mint (*M. spicata* 'Moroccan'), 'Bowles' (*M. ×villosa alopecuroides*), red raripila mint (*M. ×smithiana*), and 'Kentucky Colonel' (*M. ×cordifolia*) are all used in cuisine. 'Kentucky Colonel' is often used in mint juleps.

Flavored mints are prized for their distinctive fragrance and often variegated foliage. Among the most popular are apple mint (*M. suaveolens*), pineapple mint (*M. s.* 'Variegata'), ginger mint (*M. ×gracilis* 'Variegata'), and chocolate mint (*M. ×piperita* 'Chocolate').

Some mints form low-growing mats that make excellent ground covers. Corsican mint (*M. requienii*) has tiny leaves on plants only 1" or so tall but releases a strong menthol fragrance when touched and is not invasive. It should be treated as an annual in northern zones. Pennyroyal (*M. pulegium*) grows to 18" tall and spreads rapidly, like most mints. Its oil has long been used as an insect repellent, but pennyroyal is not edible.

**1** Root stem cuttings in peat pots and transplant them in spring or fall in full sun to part shade.

**2** Pinch out the topmost leaves to encourage bushier plants, and enjoy the trimmings in tea or food.

# BANANA

*Musa acuminata* and *M.* ×*paradisiaca*  MEW-sa a-kew-mi-NA-ta, M. pair-uh-dee-zee-AH-kuh

**Bananas and plantains are heavy feeders that require lots of plant food.**

**ZONES:** 9–11
**SIZE:** 5–25'h × 5–25'w
**TYPE:** Herbaceous perennial
**GROWTH:** Average
**LIGHT:** Full sun
**MOISTURE:** High
**FEATURES:** Edible fruits

**SITING:** Choose a warm, sunny, protected location with deep, moist, rich, slightly acid soil that drains well. Bananas do not tolerate standing water or salinity and will not thrive in sand or heavy soil. Plant suckers or large chunks of corm in holes 3' wide and 2' deep amended with well-rotted compost. Space plants as far apart as they will be tall at maturity.

**CARE:** Bananas and plantains are heavy feeders, so maintain soil nutrients with fruit tree plant food spikes and monthly applications of compost or manure mulch in a wide circle under the plant but not touching it. Soil that is infertile or too acid will decrease yields. Mulch is also necessary to conserve soil moisture and control weeds. Keep the soil moist but not waterlogged. In dry climates water deeply a few times a year to leach the soil of excess mineral salts. *Musa* has shallow roots but huge leaves up to 9' long and 2' wide that make the plants top-heavy, so protect them from wind. Strong breezes may also shred leaves, which interferes with plant metabolism. Nearly all types stop growing in temperatures below 55°F. Plants die back to the ground in freezing temperatures, but the underground rhizomes survive to 25°F. Wrap young trees in blankets if frost is predicted. Grow dwarf plants indoors in full sun where air circulates well and temperatures are consistently above 65°F.

Cut off all but one stalk (actually a pseudostem made up of clustered leaf stalks) per plant and keep new suckers pruned off at ground level. When the main stalk is 6–8 months old, allow one new sucker to develop for the following season. Prop up the fruiting stalk when it begins to bend over from the weight of developing fruit. Use a sturdy forked pole or two

stakes fastened together to form an X to hold the bunch. If there are more than six clusters of fruits ("hands") on a bunch, remove the terminal male bud several inches below the last hand to encourage fuller fruits. After harvest cut the current season's fruiting branch back to the ground.

**PROPAGATION:** Grow from suckers, pieces of budded corm, or nursery transplants.

**HARVEST:** Plants are mature 1–3 years from planting, depending on the method of propagation, and bear fruits 10–24 months from planting. Cut clusters of plump fruits that are still green with a clean, sharp knife and hang them to ripen in a dry, shady area or indoors at warm room temperatures for 1–2 weeks. Individual fruits ("fingers") left on the plant will split open as they ripen and the fruit will decay rapidly. Banana fruits, which technically are berries, are highly perishable when ripe but can be peeled, cut into chunks, and frozen in plastic bags for later use in cooking. They also can be dried but should not be refrigerated. Bananas are preferred for eating out of hand and in desserts; the more nutritious plantains are used primarily in cooking because their flavor is milder. Ripe raw bananas are used in fruit salads, on sandwiches, and in beverages, desserts, and baked goods. Unripe bananas can be boiled, fried, or grilled in their skins. Green or ripe plantains are most often peeled, sliced, fried in oil, and

sweetened as an accompaniment to a main dish. They can also be cooked, mashed, and incorporated in a sweet or savory casserole.

**PESTS AND DISEASES:** Few pest problems develop in home gardens. Control nematodes and weevils if they are present.

**RECOMMENDED CULTIVARS:** Choose plants bred for your climate. 'Gros Michel' is a popular but somewhat disease-prone tall cultivar in Hawaii. 'Lady Finger', a tall plant with small sweet fruits, grows well in Florida and Hawaii. 'Bluggoe' and 'Ice Cream' are often grown for use as cooking bananas. 'Silk' is a medium-size plant with abundant apple-scented fruits that keep well. For deck or patio growing, try 'Dwarf Cavendish', a hardy, wind-resistant clone that bears full-size fruits on plants only 5–8' tall. It grows well in containers and indoors in greenhouse conditions. Several *Musa* species provide ornamental appeal as well as tasty fruit. 'Red' (also called 'Red Fig', 'Red Cuban', and other names) is a tender, large plant that takes 18 months to mature but bears purple-red fingers that become orange-yellow and aromatic as they ripen. 'Orinoco' is a medium-size plant popular in California that produces sparsely; the fruit flesh is salmon pink. It is best used like a plantain, in cooking. 'Macho' is a popular plantain in Florida. 'Common Dwarf' and 'Maricongo', a tall plant, are widely grown.

**1** Spread well-rotted compost or manure in a wide circle under the tree once a month for high yields.

**2** Mulch helps to hold moisture in the soil and controls weeds. Keep the soil wet but not waterlogged.

# BASIL

*Ocimum basilicum* OS-i-mum ba-SIL-i-kum

**Basil is easy to grow in any size garden and can be harvested all season.**

**ZONES:** NA
**SIZE:** 1–3'h × 1–3'w
**TYPE:** Annual
**GROWTH:** Fast
**LIGHT:** Full sun
**MOISTURE:** Average
**FEATURES:** Edible leaves and flowers

**SITING:** Choose a sunny location with rich, moist, friable, slightly acid soil that drains well. Plant seeds or seedlings in the garden 12–36" apart after the last frost date. Basil is highly adaptable and grows well almost anywhere, including raised beds and containers. It does well when interplanted with tomatoes.

**CARE:** Basil is very tender; growth slows in cool weather and leaves may wither and discolor if nighttime temperatures are consistently below 45°F. Keep plants inside cloches or cold frames in cool zones or anytime frost is predicted. Pinch out the tops of newly planted tall seedlings to about 6" to promote root growth. Cut or pinch off flowers as they appear to encourage bushier growth. Keep the soil around plants consistently moist and weed free. Sidedress plants with well-rotted compost and use mulch to conserve soil moisture.

**PROPAGATION:** Grow basil from seed.

**HARVEST:** Begin harvesting basil as soon as there are at least four sets of true leaves. Pinch out the topmost set of leaves and any flowers as needed for use in salads, tomato-based recipes, and pesto, a paste made of basil, garlic, nuts, and oil and used on pasta, pizza, and bread. Snip large leaves or add small whole ones into cooked dishes just before serving to preserve basil's spicy anise flavor. Substitute basil leaves for lettuce on sandwiches for a tangy treat. Store unwashed basil as you would lettuce, but only for a day or two; basil begins to decay as soon as it is picked. Preserve fresh leaves and flowers in vinegar and olive oil to prevent oxidation. Basil can be processed with oil and stored in the freezer for up to 2 years or in the refrigerator for up to 3 months. If you use only part of what you have stored, cover any unused portion with more oil. Basil can be dried but is not as flavorful and colorful as when it is preserved with oil. At the end of the growing season in temperate climates, pull up the plants by their roots and harvest any remaining leaves before the first frost date. In hot zones basil can be cut back to 6" above ground and regrown several times in one year before the final harvest.

**PESTS AND DISEASES:** Many insects are attracted to basil, but no common insecticide is labeled for use on edible herbs. Discourage pests by keeping mulch from touching the plants, and remove and destroy any leaves that look unhealthy. Spray off aphids and mites with a garden hose. Basil is susceptible to fusarium wilt in hot, humid weather; look for cultivars bred for resistance and plant them in soil that drains well. Remove and destroy infected plants, including the roots and surrounding soil.

**RECOMMENDED CULTIVARS:** There are dozens of basil types with variations in leaf size, coloration, fragrance, and growth habit. 'Aroma 2', with 2" leaves, and 'Nefar', with 4" leaves, are two traditional Genovese-type basils that make excellent pesto. 'Italian Large Leaf' has a slightly sweeter taste than 'Genovese', which smells a bit like cloves. Both have 4" leaves on plants 2–3' tall. 'Genovese Compact Improved' has small leaves on an 18" tall plant suitable for container growing. 'Napoletano' has large, frilly light green leaves that look good in salads and on sandwiches. 'Fino Verde' bears flavorful 1" leaves on compact plants only 18" tall. 'Spicy Bush' forms dense mounds of 1" leaves on plants up to 12" tall. 'Greek' is the smallest basil of all. Its ¼" to ½" leaves on plants 6–9" tall make it a perfect choice for container growing. 'Red Rubin' has eye-catching foliage. The bronze-purple Italian-type leaves grow to 4" long on compact 2' plants. The frilly leaves of 'Purple Ruffles' are almost brown by comparison but taste and smell strongly of cloves and licorice. The plant is compact and grows well in containers. 'Osmin Purple' has a sweet, almost fruity fragrance. The 2" leaves are glossy and slightly ruffled; the flowers are lavender. The plants are sometimes variegated green and purple. 'Magical Michael' has medium-long red-veined green leaves and burgundy flowers with a sweet, fruity taste. 'Sweet Thai' basil has reddish-purple stems and flowers and spicy 2" leaves. 'Thai Magic' has larger, milder-tasting leaves and bright magenta flowers that give it extra appeal as a landscape ornamental. 'Holy Basil' (*O. tenuiflorum*), typically grown only as an ornamental, has slender purple and green leaves and purple flowers. 'Mexican Spice' has distinctive reddish-brown stems and flowers in addition to its unmistakable aroma and flavor of cinnamon. The dark green leaves are small and glossy. 'Sweet Dani' is a tall plant with large olive-green leaves that taste and smell lemony. 'Mrs. Burns' Lemon' (*O. basilicum citriodora*) is an old Mexican variety with a sweet lemon flavor. 'Lime' basil (*O. americanum*) adds a strong lime flavor and aroma to Thai or Mexican cuisine and is also good minced and added to sherbet.

**Red- or purple-leaved cultivars have a strong anise or clove flavor and are as ornamental as they are tasty.**

**Harvest basil early and often, pinching out the topmost leaves and any flowers to encourage new growth.**

**Thai and cinnamon basils have reddish-brown stems and flowers and a spicy aroma and flavor.**

# OLIVE

*Olea europaea* *oh-LAY-uh yur-OH-pee-uh*

**Pick green olives for curing when they reach full cultivar size.**

**ZONES:** 8–11
**SIZE:** 15–35'h × 15–35'w
**TYPE:** Evergreen tree or shrub
**GROWTH:** Slow

**LIGHT:** Full sun
**MOISTURE:** Low
**FEATURES:** Fragrant flowers, edible fruits (olives)

**SITING:** Plant olive trees in full sun in well-drained, alkaline soil with as much space between them as possible and away from sidewalks or patios where fallen fruit will leave stains. Choose a site where breezes can help to pollinate the flowers. Olive trees will not thrive in waterlogged soil or high humidity but are tolerant of high pH and salinity.
**CARE:** Water olive trees deeply once a month in dry climates. Feed with tree spikes until fruit set. Thinning the crop as soon as possible after fruit set to 2 or 3 per foot will increase the size of remaining fruits. Pruning at least annually is necessary to control height and ensure annual bearing. Olives bear on the previous year's growth and never on the same wood twice, so current fruiting wood can be removed after harvest. Prune suckers and low branches to achieve a single trunk, or enourage the attractive gnarled appearance of multiple trunks by staking suckers at the desired angles. Because they can withstand severe pruning, olive trees can be maintained at small size in containers or pruned to espaliers for use in limited spaces. Protect trees from spring frosts that will kill the blossoms. Green fruit is damaged below 30°F, ripe fruit below 25°F.
**PROPAGATION:** Grow from cuttings or plant grafted trees.
**HARVEST:** Trees begin to bear about 4 years after planting and are long lived—up to hundreds of years. Fruits mature in 6–8 months. Pick olives to be cured while green when they have reached full cultivar size. Harvest olives for other uses anytime thereafter, keeping in mind that the riper the olives, the more easily they are bruised in handling. Cure the fruits in processing marinades to remove the tannins which cause bitterness, then pack them in oil for long-term storage.
**PESTS AND DISEASES:** Peacock spot, a fungal disease, may occur in wet years. Olive knot, a bacterial disease, spreads during prolonged rainy spells. Clean tools after every use and sterilize them between pruning cuts to avoid spreading disease. Use commercially available traps to kill olive fruit flies and keep the ground around the trees cleared of fallen fruits and vegetative matter, which will also help to prevent verticillium wilt. Avoid chemical sprays; their odors are retained in olive flesh.
**RECOMMENDED CULTIVARS:** Most olives require at least 200–300 chilling hours (about 2 weeks below 45°F) to set fruit properly. Choose a self-pollinating type if you have room for just one tree. 'Ascolano' is a hardy, disease-resistant tree with light-colored olives ready in late September or early October. 'Manzanillo' and 'Barouni' are shorter, spreading trees. 'Mission' grows quite tall but bears small black olives with high oil content in late October or early November. It is susceptible to peacock spot but resistant to olive knot and quite hardy. The large blue-black fruits pickled and sold commercially as "black olives" come from the tender 'Sevillano' tree.

# SWEET MARJORAM

*Origanum majorana* *or-IG-ah-num mah-jor-RAY-nuh*

**Marjoram can be used in place of oregano but is sweeter and milder.**

**ZONES:** 8–11
**SIZE:** 12–18"h × 12–18"w
**TYPE:** Perennial grown as annual
**GROWTH:** Average

**LIGHT:** Full sun to part shade
**MOISTURE:** Average
**FEATURES:** Edible leaves and flowers

**SITING:** Choose a sunny or mostly sunny, well-drained location. Marjoram is adaptable but does best in light, fertile, slightly alkaline soil. Plant divisions 12" apart after all danger of frost has passed.
**CARE:** Sweet marjoram is the most tender of the *Origanum* species but can be grown as an annual. It is well suited to container growing and looks especially attractive in hanging baskets. Cut the trailing stems frequently to encourage bushier growth. Protect from midday sun in hot climates. Marjoram dries out quickly, so keep the soil consistently moist but not waterlogged. Dig and divide plants every few years when they become woody. Overwinter in mild climates by covering plants with mulch, or dig and divide plants in autumn and pot some for use indoors.
**HARVEST:** The leaves have a sweeter, milder flavor and aroma than those of oregano. Marjoram can be used in place of oregano, but because of its sweetness can also be used in soups, herb butter, and egg dishes as well as to flavor spinach, beans, and other vegetables. Try it in addition to or in place of sage in poultry stuffing and pork sausage. Snip leaves fresh into salads or cooked dishes just before serving. Hang the stems upside down to dry in a cool, dark location with good air circulation. Pull the leaves from the stems when they are completely dry, crumble them, and store in airtight jars. Dried marjoram retains its flavor better than dried oregano.
**PROPAGATION:** Grow by division or from stem cuttings. It is slow to start from seed.
**PESTS AND DISEASES:** None are significant.
**RECOMMENDED CULTIVARS:** 'Sweet Max' is a tall, upright marjoram with yellow-green leaves. 'Erfo' has pale grayish-green leaves that have a balsamlike fragrance. Hardy marjoram, sometimes sold as Italian oregano (*O. ×majoricum*), is a cold-tolerant hybrid of wild oregano and sweet marjoram that is both pungent and sweet. Pot marjoram (*O. onites*), typically grown as an ornamental, is not as flavorful as sweet marjoram.

# GREEK OREGANO
*Origanum vulgare hirtum* *or-IG-ah-num vul-GARE-ay HEER-tum*

Oregano is a cold-hardy perennial with fragrant, spicy leaves.

**ZONES:** 5–11
**SIZE:** 12–24"h × 24–40"w
**TYPE:** Semiwoody perennial
**GROWTH:** Average
**LIGHT:** Full sun
**MOISTURE:** Average
**FEATURES:** Edible leaves and flowers

**SITING:** Choose a sunny location with well-drained soil. Oregano is adaptable but does best in light, fertile, slightly alkaline soil. The more sun it receives, the more pungent the flavor of the leaves. Space plants 24" apart.

**CARE:** Oregano's purple or pink flowers attract bees and butterflies, but the leaves are best picked just before the buds open.

Divide plants every few years when they become woody. To obtain two large harvests, cut the whole plant back to 3" just before it flowers, then again in late summer. Water only during periods of drought to avoid root rot.

**HARVEST:** Cut succulent stems as needed, and snip fresh leaves into salads or cooked dishes just before serving. Oregano has a particular affinity with members of the Solanaceae family—potatoes, tomatoes, eggplants, and peppers—and is a key ingredient in many Mediterranean poultry and lamb dishes. Hang stems upside down to dry in a cool, dark location with good air circulation. Pull the leaves from the stems when they are completely dry, crumble them, and store in airtight jars. Fresh leaves can also be frozen for later use.

**PROPAGATION:** Grow by division or from stem cuttings; growth is slow from seed.

Clip or pinch off oregano above the woody stems.

Tie the stems into small bunches and hang upside down to dry.

When they are dry, strip the leaves from the stems for storing.

**PESTS AND DISEASES:** None are significant.

**RECOMMENDED CULTIVARS:** 'Aureum', sometimes sold as creeping golden marjoram, has yellow-green leaves. 'Aureum Crispum' has curly golden leaves and pink flowers. Try 'Compactum' for a low-growing aromatic and edible ground cover that rarely blooms. 'Thumbles Variety' forms low, small mounds of gold and green variegated foliage. 'Kaliteri' has spicy silver-gray leaves. 'White Anniversary' is a tender cultivar with variegated green and white foliage. Italian oregano (*O.* ×*majoricum*) is a hybrid of wild oregano and sweet marjoram that is both pungent and sweet but also hardy.

# PASSIONFRUIT
*Passiflora edulis* *pass-i-FLOR-a ed-YEW-lis*

Carpenter bees help to carry passionfruit's heavy pollen. It is also known as purple granadilla.

**ZONES:** 10 and 11
**SIZE:** To 50'h
**TYPE:** Woody evergreen perennial vine
**GROWTH:** Fast
**LIGHT:** Full sun
**MOISTURE:** High
**FEATURES:** Showy, fragrant flowers; edible fruits

**SITING:** Choose a sunny location protected from strong winds. Passionfruit does best in neutral-pH sandy loam enriched with organic matter well in advance of planting. The plants are highly susceptible to root and crown rots, so good drainage is essential.

Plant them 4'–8' apart and next to a fence, trellis, or tree for support.

**CARE:** Prune lightly after the last harvest to control excess growth. The purple passionfruit tolerates more pruning than the yellow. Purple types flower twice a year, in spring and fall. Yellow types flower just once, in spring or fall, depending on location. Passionfruit pollen is large and heavy; only bees are sturdy enough to carry it from flower to flower. In the absence of bees, pollinate the flowers by hand using a small brush or swab. To cross yellow and purple vines, use the purple as the receptacle plant. For best results with cross-pollination in home gardens, plant two vines of different parentage. Keep the soil continuously moist for best fruiting. Use a soluble, high-potassium plant food at a rate of 3 pounds per plant four times a year. Too much nitrogen causes brown rot and fruit drop. Hand-weed to protect the shallow roots from damage. Protect plants when frost is predicted.

**HARVEST:** Passionfruit vines begin to bear 1–3 years from planting. Fruits turn from green to deep purple or yellow in 70–80 days, then fall to the ground. Pick them when they have achieved full cultivar color or gather from the ground each day; they are highly perishable. Ripen yellow passionfruits at room temperature in plastic bags to retain humidity. Store unwashed fruits in plastic bags in the warmest part of the refrigerator for up to 1 week.

**PROPAGATION:** Grow from cuttings, grafts, or seeds, or by air layering.

**PESTS AND DISEASES:** Choose hybrids of purple and yellow types to avoid woodiness, a viral disease transmitted by aphids, as well as fungal infections and nematode infestations. Keep fruit and vegetative matter picked up from the ground around the vines. Avoid insecticide sprays, which kill carpenter bees. Remove, destroy, and replace diseased plants.

**RECOMMENDED CULTIVARS:** Yellow passionfruit (*P. edulis flavicarpa*) is fungus and nematode resistant, so it is widely used as a rootstock. The fruit of the purple vines is juicier and less acidic. 'Brazilian Golden' bears large yellow fruits that are slightly tart. 'Kahuna' has very large purple fruits with sweet flesh. 'Red Rover' is a cross of 'Kahuna' and 'Brazilian Golden'.

# PARSNIP

*Pastinaca sativa* pab-stib-NAH-kub sub-TY-vub

**Parsnips can be overwintered in the garden and dug as needed.**

**ZONES:** NA
**SIZE:** 6–12"h × 6–12"w
**TYPE:** Biennial grown as annual
**GROWTH:** Average
**LIGHT:** Full sun to part shade
**MOISTURE:** Average
**FEATURES:** Edible taproots

**SITING:** Direct-sow parsnip seed in rows ½" deep and 12–18" apart in deep, loose, rich, slightly acid soil in spring or early summer. Make sure the soil is free of rocks and clumps of dirt.
**CARE:** Keep the seeds consistently moist. Germination is slow, especially in cold soil. If the soil dries too much between waterings, cover the rows with a layer of burlap to help retain moisture until the seeds germinate. Thin the seedlings to 12" apart. Water only in times of drought and use a soluble high-potassium plant food once a month. Plant more seeds if necessary to fill in gaps in rows. Weed carefully by hand between rows to remove competition for moisture and nutrients. After the roots are well established, you

**Organic mulch conserves moisture in summer and protects plants in winter.**

can hoe lightly. Use mulch between rows to retain moisture and deter weeds.
**HARVEST:** Dig spring-planted parsnips beginning in late September. Wipe free of dirt and store unwashed like carrots in the refrigerator for up to 2 months. Their flavor is improved by a few frosts, so you can store them in the ground under mulch and harvest as needed throughout the winter.
**PROPAGATION:** Grow from seed.
**PESTS AND DISEASES:** Crop rotation helps to control blights and molds. Use floating row covers to protect young plants from leafhoppers and keep the soil free of all weeds.
**RECOMMENDED CULTIVARS:** 'Hollow Crown', also called 'Long Guernsey Smooth', is the old-time standard and a reliable yielder. 'Harris Model' holds its white color after harvest. 'Gladiator' is a sweet hybrid with excellent disease resistance. 'White Gem' grows in all soil types. 'Javelin' has been bred for canker resistance. Try 'Premium', a short-rooted variety, if you garden in a short-season zone or have heavy soil. 'Cobham Improved' is a good choice for overwintering in the ground.

# AVOCADO

*Persea americana* PER-see-ub ub-mer-ib-KAY-nub

**Space avocado trees far enough apart that they do not touch at maturity. Avocado is also known as alligator pear.**

**ZONES:** 9–11
**SIZE:** 8–60'h × 6–40'w
**TYPE:** Briefly deciduous tree
**GROWTH:** Fast
**LIGHT:** Full sun
**MOISTURE:** Average
**FEATURES:** Edible fruits

**SITING:** Choose a protected, sunny location with deep, rich, friable soil. Avocado is adaptable to all slightly acid soils and will even grow in alkaline soil in Florida and Hawaii. The site must have excellent drainage. Space trees so that they will not touch at maturity. Plant at any time of the year except in the high heat of midsummer.
**CARE:** Use a transplant starter solution at the time of planting, then a balanced plant food every 2 months except when the tree blooms and fruits. Hand-weed and water frequently until the roots are established. Use foliar sprays to correct mineral deficiencies. Prune to control size. Water only in times of drought. Maintain a wide circle of organic mulch under the tree canopy but not touching the trunk. Protect trees from frost.
**HARVEST:** Grafted trees usually bear 1–3 years after planting. Avocados will not ripen on the tree but should be picked when they have reached full cultivar size. Fully mature fruits may drop but can be bruised or split open as a result. Because the trees bloom over a long period, fruits will not mature all at once. Skins will darken or lose their glossy sheen when mature. Pick the largest, fullest ones first, using clippers to cut the stems. Fruits will ripen at room temperature in 5–10 days. Hasten ripening by placing an avocado in a paper bag with an apple or a banana. To preserve half a fruit for later use, leave the seed in, moisten the exposed flesh with citrus juice, and wrap tightly in plastic wrap. Store whole ripe avocados in the refrigerator for up to 1 week.
**PROPAGATION:** Grow by grafting.
**PESTS AND DISEASES:** Choose cultivars bred for resistance to problems in your locale. Avoid using insecticides, which also kill the insects necessary for pollination. Use fungicides to prevent rots in humid areas.
**RECOMMENDED CULTIVARS:** Guatemalan and Mexican types grow best in California and tolerate some cold. 'Edranol' is a disease-resistant tree with sweet, nutty fruits borne over a long period. Mexican trees bloom in winter and are ready to harvest the following summer or fall. 'Hass' is the standard Mexican avocado popular in California but is being replaced by hybrids that are more pest resistant, such as 'Lamb Hass' and 'Sir Prize'. West Indian varieties thrive in the high humidity and salinity of Florida and Hawaii and are less hardy, but they bloom in spring and the fruits ripen in the same year. The fruits of 'Russell', a West Indian type recommended for home gardens, ripen in late summer.

# PARSLEY
*Petroselinum crispum* peh-troh-seh-LY-num KRIS-pum

'Moss Curled' is the most popular type of parsley in home gardens. It is also known as curly-leaved parsley.

**ZONES:** NA
**SIZE:** 8–24"h × 8–24"w
**TYPE:** Biennial grown as annual
**GROWTH:** Fast
**LIGHT:** Full sun to part shade
**MOISTURE:** Average
**FEATURES:** Edible leaves and stems

**SITING:** Sow seeds or plant transplants in early spring. The location should have rich, moist, friable, well-drained, acid to neutral soil. Space transplants and seedlings 10–18" apart in each direction. Parsley also grows well in a pot, outdoors or indoors, in a sunny spot.

**CARE:** For a steady supply, sow seeds in spring and fall. When seedlings develop their first true leaves, thin to 10" apart. Parsley seed is slow to germinate. Warm the seedbed with black plastic or use a cold frame to concentrate heat. Keep the soil evenly moist and weed free. Use a balanced soluble vegetable plant food on mature plants once a month. Use mulch around curly parsley to keep soil particles from gathering in the leaf crevices. To keep parsley productive, snip the full length of the stems regularly; remove flower stalks as soon as they begin to form. Late in the season, allow a plant to develop mature flowers and progress to form seeds. The plant may sow its own seeds and produce seedlings for next year's garden.

**HARVEST:** Harvest parsley and encourage new growth by cutting outer stems at least 1" above the soil as needed. The whole plant can be cut before winter or mulched for overwintering in the garden. Plants kept in an insulated cold frame continue to produce new stems until the following spring. Collect the seeds for a new crop or allow the old plants to self-sow. Leaves and stems can be refrigerated for up to 1 month or frozen for up to 1 year. To dry parsley, hang the stems upside down or spread them in a single layer on screens in a cool, shady, well-ventilated location. Use leaves, fresh or dried, in cooking. Its mild flavor blends well with many foods.

**PROPAGATION:** Grow from seed.

**PESTS AND DISEASES:** Avoid using insecticides, because parsley attracts swallowtail butterflies. Knock off aphids with a strong spray from the garden hose. Carrot weevils may overwinter on parsley or nearby carrot tops. Parsley is susceptible to bacterial spot and Septoria leaf spot. Both overwinter in crop debris and can be spread by wind, rain, or dirty tools. Parsley is also susceptible to aster yellows, a viral disease spread by leafhoppers. Protect young plants with floating row covers and keep the area around them weed free. Remove and destroy any infected plants.

**RECOMMENDED CULTIVARS:** 'Moss Curled' is the most popular curly-leaf parsley. 'Giant of Naples' is a flat-leaf Italian type. *Petroselinum crispum* var. *tuberosum*, turnip-rooted or Hamburg parsley, is grown for its fleshy, parsniplike root that has a parsley-celery flavor. Sow seeds in spring and harvest roots in fall.

Harvest parsley leaves and use them fresh, or flash freeze them on a cookie sheet, and then store in a freezer bag until use.

Some cooks prefer the sweeter flavor of flat-leaf parsley.

Cover plants with floating row covers to discourage pests.

Parsley is easy to grow in pots and hanging baskets.

# BEAN

*Phaseolus* spp. *fa-ZEE-o-lus*

**Scarlet runner beans have ornamental value as well as edible seeds.**

**ZONES:** NA
**SIZE:** 8–72"h × 6–24"w
**TYPE:** Annual
**GROWTH:** Fast

**LIGHT:** Full sun
**MOISTURE:** High
**FEATURES:** Edible seeds and immature pods

**SITING:** Choose a sunny location where legumes have not been grown in the last 3 years. Beans are highly adaptable but do best in rich, well-drained, friable, slightly acid to neutral soil. Plant seeds after all danger of frost has passed. In northern zones warm the soil with black plastic for rapid germination, or plant seedlings started indoors several weeks before the last frost date. Dust dampened seeds with rhizobial inoculant before planting to fix nitrogen in the soil for the crop that follows the beans. Plant all *Phaseolus* seeds except limas 1" deep in heavy soils or 1½" in light soils. Space seeds 2" apart in rows 24" apart. Plant limas later than other beans, when the soil reaches 65°F, and ½–1" deep. Plant pole beans 2" deep, 4–6 seeds per hill or 6" apart in rows 36" apart against a fence or trellis. Beans do well interplanted with corn, sweet potatoes, and tomatoes.

**CARE:** Beans do best where daytime temperatures are 70–80°F and may drop their blossoms above 85°F. They are also sensitive to frost. Temperatures below 35°F kill the flowers and pods. Create a tripod of three poles 6–8' tall for each hill of pole beans to climb. Cut off the terminal end of each vine when it gets to the top of the tripod to encourage branching. Tie string 5" above the ground between two short stakes on either side of each row of bush beans to hold the plants off the soil. Bean plants are tender and easily damaged by garden tools, so weed by hand if possible. Keep the soil consistently moist, but water only in the morning so the plants dry quickly, which reduces the potential for disease. Extremes in soil moisture result in malformed pods. To avoid injury to the plants and the spread of fungal spores, work around and harvest beans only when

they are not wet. Beans supply their own nitrogen but benefit from a monthly application of soluble plant food high in phosphorus and potassium.

**PROPAGATION:** Grow from seed.

**HARVEST:** Pinch or cut the pods off carefully to avoid uprooting the plant if it is still producing. Pick fresh beans at least every few days for optimum tenderness. Harvest dry beans when the pods are fully mature and have changed color. Dry pods may shatter and eject the beans, so put a sheet down between rows, or hold a pan underneath the plants as you pick. If you live in an area of high humidity, pull the plants when the pods have changed color and hang them upside down to dry in a well-ventilated area protected from rain. Immature pods of snap and pole beans are ready to harvest 6–9 weeks from planting. Eat them fresh—whole or cut, raw, steamed, boiled, or stir-fried—and blanch some for freezer storage or pressure canning. The pods of some shelling beans also can be eaten when immature. Horticultural beans are ready for shelling 8–10 weeks from planting. Use them uncooked or steamed in salads or added to soups and stews. Beans grown for their dried seeds are ready for harvest 12–15 weeks from planting. They are presoaked and slow cooked in soups, stews, and casseroles. Store fresh beans in a plastic bag for up to a week in the refrigerator. Dried beans can be stored in an airtight container in a cool, dry location.

**PESTS AND DISEASES:** Choose cultivars bred for resistance to bacteria and viruses and pretreated with fungicide for prevention of blights, rots, rusts, and anthracnose. Practice crop rotation to avoid diseases that persist in the soil. All beans are visited by a host of damaging insects, including aphids, thrips, beetles, weevils, mites, stinkbugs, and tarnished plant bugs. The Mexican bean beetle is the main pest in home gardens; it lays its eggs on the underside of bean leaves. Handpick and destroy eggs and larvae, or use neem oil for heavy infestations. Ask your local extension agent which other pests are most common in your locale and how to deter them. Avoid using insecticides; bean flowers attract beneficial ladybugs and predatory wasps and are pollinated by bumblebees.

**RECOMMENDED CULTIVARS:** Tepary bean *(P. acutifolius)* is a drought-tolerant species grown for its dried seeds. It grows well in desert climates. 'Blue Speckled' produces plump beans in 60–90 days. Scarlet runner bean *(P. coccineus)*, a climbing type, is

often grown only for its ornamental value, but the mature pods bear tasty shelling beans. 'Scarlet Emperor' has vivid red flowers that attract hummingbirds and bears long, stringless pods with large black- and purple-mottled white beans in 90–95 days. Lima bean *(P. lunatus)* typically thrives in areas with long, hot summers, but 'Fordhook' cultivars do well even in northern climates if the soil drains well. Green limas are ready to shell in 85 days or can be harvested at 95–100 days for dried butter beans.

Most of the beans that home gardeners grow are *P. vulgaris* determinate cultivars. For early fresh snap green beans, grow bush types that produce abundantly in 50–55 days. 'Tenderlake' is a good choice for home gardens. The pods are sweet and the plants are heat resistant. 'Xera' has attractive dark green pods with white seeds that are slow to develop. It was bred for exceptional heat tolerance but is adapted to most climates and is disease resistant. 'Indy Gold' is a wax-type bush bean that bears short, green-tipped vivid yellow pods with white seeds. 'Provider' can be eaten as a fresh green bean, or the seeds can be dried for soup beans. It is virus resistant.

**'Fordhook' cultivars grow well in northern climates where other lima bean varieties do not.**

'Normandie' is a French haricot-type, disease-resistant bean with pencil-thin pods that are excellent eaten fresh, steamed, stir-fried, or dilled. 'Dragon Tongue' has flat pale yellow pods with purple streaks that disappear when cooked. 'Royalty Purple' beans also turn green when cooked. Snap beans are still sometimes called string beans, but all contemporary cultivars are actually stringless. For a continuous fresh harvest of determinate beans, sow

# BEAN
*continued*

**Most home gardeners grow *P. vulgaris* snap beans like 'Provider' or 'Tenderlake', which are stringless.**

new seed every 2–3 weeks throughout the summer.

Most fresh snap pole beans are ready for harvest in 60–65 days but are indeterminate and continue to produce over several months. 'Black Seeded Blue Lake' is a vigorous producer of stringless pods that are good fresh, frozen, or canned. 'Cascade Giant' bears abundant stringless dark green pods mottled with purple. It is tolerant of drought and damp weather and is good for canning. 'Kentucky Wonder' is an old favorite variety with green pods and tan seeds. 'Romano' has wide, fat, stringless, tender pods with an excellent flavor cooked or canned. 'Triofono' purple pods turn green when cooked. 'Fortex' pods grow to 11" long but are tender at all lengths and a

good choice for home gardens. 'Northeaster' pods are large, flat, stringless, tender, and sweet.

Horticultural types bear large beans that are ready for fresh shelling in 75–80 days. 'Tongue of Fire' has red-streaked ivory pods and beans that can be eaten as snap beans when young or shelled fresh. 'Flagrano' has straight green pods with easy-to-shell light green seeds that can also be dried. 'Cannellini' is an old favorite half-runner type with long white pods and large, nutty-flavored white beans that are good in minestrone. It also can be shelled fresh when the pods are yellow-green.

Dried bush beans come in a wide variety of sizes and colorations, including pea or navy, field or pinto, great northern, black, butter (lima), and marrow types. They are ready to harvest in 90–105 days, which means they do best in long-season areas where the autumn is dry. 'Vermont Cranberry' has attractive red- and pink-mottled pods and beans that also can be shelled green at 75 days. 'Topaz Pinto' is a short, compact plant adapted to northern climates and easy to shell by hand. It is excellent for frijoles. 'Midnight Black Turtle Soup' is a tall upright plant

that bears small beans good for soups and canning. 'Yellow Eye' is a marrow type that becomes creamy when cooked. It makes tasty baked beans. 'Jacob's Cattle' is a good choice for short-season northern areas. Its kidney-shape white beans with dark red splotches are excellent in soups

**Unlike bush beans, pole beans are indeterminate and continue to produce throughout the season.**

and casseroles and can be shelled for fresh use at 85–90 days. 'Red Hawk' produces dark red kidney beans on erect, disease-resistant bushes. They are good for canning.

Not all beans belong to the genus *Phaseolus*. For information on soybeans, see page 87. For information on fava beans, see page 130. For information on adzuki beans, asparagus beans (or yard-long beans), cowpeas (or blackeyed peas), and mung beans, see page 131. Chickpeas *(Cicer arietinum)*, also called garbanzo beans, are neither beans nor peas but legumes called pulses. They require a long, dry, cool growing season of 100 days or more and do best in the coastal Southwest. The small pods bear just two seeds each so are not efficient producers for small home gardens. Seeds of 'Baron' are the traditional light golden brown color. 'Black Kabouli' is a vigorous producer of small, dark seeds.

**Provide support for bush bean pods by tying string to short stakes on either side of each row.**

**Pick snap beans every few days while they are still tender. Pinch or cut off the pods to avoid uprooting the plants.**

# DATE PALM
*Phoenix dactylifera* *FEE-nix dak-tee-LIH-fer-uh*

**Plant at least two date palm trees for the best yields.**

**ZONES:** 8-10
**SIZE:** 50–100'h × 20–30'w
**TYPE:** Evergreen tree
**GROWTH:** Slow

**LIGHT:** Full sun
**MOISTURE:** High
**FEATURES:** Edible drupes (dates), seeds, and terminal buds

**SITING:** In North America, date palm grows only in Arizona, California, Hawaii, and Mexico where days and nights are hot and the air is dry. It tolerates moderate salinity and does best in areas where the water table is high. Choose a site where fruit that drops will not create a maintenance problem. Plant the offshoots 25–30' apart.

**CARE:** Water newly planted offshoots frequently, and use mulch around the base to conserve moisture and reduce weeds. Protect young trees from cold weather with commercial wraps or old palm fronds wrapped around the trunks. Most date palms are dioecious—some trees are male and some are female—but just one male tree can produce enough pollen for up to fifty female trees. Hand-pollination guarantees the best results. The easiest method is to collect pollen from staminate (male) flowers on a sheet of white paper or in a white paper cup, then dip tiny wads of cotton in the pollen and insert them into the female flowers. Remove fronds in late summer as they turn brown, and cut off any sharp thorns at the leaf bases to make pollination and harvest less difficult.

**PROPAGATION:** Grow from offshoots of a mature female tree or nursery transplant.

**HARVEST:** Date palm begins to bear 3–5 years after planting, and may bear for 100 years. The fruits mature from green when unripe to reddish brown when fully ripe. Each tree produces 5–12 bunches, and each bunch may contain many hundreds of fruits, but they ripen at different times. Harvest the dates once a week as they become ready. Pick soft and semidry cultivars when they reach their preripe yellow, pink, or red color, then dry them in the sun to increase their sugar content and retard spoilage. Dry dates can be left on the tree to cure. Store them in plastic or glass in the refrigerator for up to a year, or freeze them for up to several years. Date seeds—one per fruit—can be roasted whole and eaten like nuts. Also, try the peeled and sliced terminal buds of branches, called hearts of palm, in vegetable salads and on pizza.

**PESTS AND DISEASES:** A wide variety of insects and animals are attracted to the fruits. Use labeled insecticides if necessary to control heavy infestations, and netting or paper bags to protect fruit clusters from animals.

**RECOMMENDED CULTIVARS:** 'Deglet Noor' is famous for its rich flavor and semidry texture. 'Medjool' is the best-known soft date in the United States. It is more tolerant of humidity than most cultivars. 'Thoory' is a dry date with large, firm, fruits that mature late in the season.

# TOMATILLO
*Physalis ixocarpa* *FY-sah-lis ix-oh-KAR-pa*

**Tomatillo fruits develop inside green or purple papery husks. It is also known as husk tomato.**

**ZONES:** NA
**SIZE:** 2–6'h × 2–6'w
**TYPE:** Herbaceous annual
**GROWTH:** Average

**LIGHT:** Full sun
**MOISTURE:** Moderate
**FEATURES:** Edible fruits (berries)

**SITING:** Choose a sunny location with rich, well-drained, slightly acid loam. Start seeds indoors and transplant outside when all danger of frost has passed in spring.

**CARE:** Tomatillos are grown just like tomatoes (see pages 91–94) and will sprawl across the ground if not staked or caged. Unlike tomatoes, however, tomatillo fruits develop inside green and purple calyces. Keep the soil around the plants moist but not waterlogged, and remove all weeds. Use a soluble tomato plant food twice a month.

**PROPAGATION:** Grow from seed.

**HARVEST:** Tomatillos begin to bear 60–80 days after transplanting and produce fruits for about 6 weeks. Ripe fruits are bright green, yellow, purple, or reddish, and the husks are light brown but not shriveled or dry. Unripe fruits have a slightly sticky surface. Tomatillos fall before they are ripe; collect them daily and allow the husks to finish drying for 1–3 weeks. Store individual unhusked fruits in a cool, dry location or pull the entire plant if frost is predicted and hang it upside down in a protected area until needed. Remove the husks and wash the fruits when they are fully ripe. You can store tomatillos in their husks in the refrigerator for up to 2 weeks.

**PESTS AND DISEASES:** Plant tomatillos where other Solanaceae crops have not been grown previously to avoid diseases that persist in the soil. Use cardboard collars around tomatillo transplants to discourage cutworms. Handpick and destroy Japanese beetles and hornworms.

**RECOMMENDED CULTIVARS:** 'Verde Puebla' plants grow 6–8' tall; stake or cage to hold the 1½" pale yellow-green fruits off the ground. They are ready to harvest in 75 days. 'Rendidora' cultivars have smaller but firmer lime-green fruits ready in 60–75 days. 'Cisneros' produces large green fruits in just 75 days. *P. philadelphica* 'Purple De Milpa' bears 2" fruits with a sharp, sweet flavor; they're good fresh or cooked. It bears later in the season, at about 90 days.

**Grow tomatillos just like tomatoes, starting the seed indoors 6–10 weeks before the last frost date in spring.**

# PEA

*Pisum sativum* PY-sum sub-TY-vum

Traditional shelling cultivars are called green peas, English peas, or garden peas.

**ZONES:** NA
**SIZE:** 1–6'h × 6–12"w
**TYPE:** Herbaceous annual
**GROWTH:** Fast
**LIGHT:** Full sun to part shade
**MOISTURE:** High
**FEATURES:** Edible pods and seeds

**SITING:** Plant peas in early spring in a location where they can be protected from midday sun if temperatures are higher than 80°F. Choose a sunny area of the garden where legumes have not been grown in the last 3 years. Peas are highly adaptable but do best in rich, well-drained, friable, slightly acid to neutral loam. They do well interplanted with corn, tomatoes, garlic, onions, and lettuce. Dust dampened seeds with rhizobial inoculant before planting to fix nitrogen in the soil for the crop that follows the peas. Plant the seeds 1" deep and 2" apart in rows 8–12" apart. In hot climates or areas with dry soil, try the trench-planting method for establishing peas. Dig a furrow about 2" wide and 4" deep across the front of whatever supports you will use. Lightly water the trench, then plant the seeds as above and cover them with 2" of soil. The trench serves as a catch for water as the seedlings grow. Gradually fill it in with more soil as they get taller.

**CARE:** Peas are cool-weather crops but plants can be damaged by a late frost. They tolerate brief periods of temperatures to 25°F, but prolonged exposure will interfere with later development. Flowers drop and vines wither in temperatures warmer than 80°F. All but the most dwarf pea plants require stakes, trellises, or other supports for the vines to climb. Keep the soil consistently moist and weed by hand to avoid disturbing tender vines and roots. Work around and harvest from vines only when they are not wet to avoid spreading disease. Keep mature peas picked regularly for best flavor and to promote the development of other pods.

**PROPAGATION:** Grow from seed.

**HARVEST:** English or shelling peas are ready to pick when the pods are fully rounded. The seeds are shelled from the pods and used raw in salads, steamed as a vegetable, or cooked in soups and stews. Store unshelled peas for up to 3 days and shelled peas for up to 7 days in the refrigerator. Shelled peas can be blanched and kept in the freezer for up to 1 year. Leave some pods to dry on the vine if you want to keep seed for next year's crop. Harvest snow peas when the pods are still flat and the seeds inside are small and undeveloped. Use them raw in salads or as crudités for dipping, or add to stir-fries for a crunchy texture. Pick snap varieties when the pods are plump and the seeds are fully developed. The pods of snap peas are edible and, like snow peas, are a fun addition to a platter of raw dipping vegetables. They are most often served steamed or sautéed with butter and herbs but also make a delicious pea soup. Store snow and snap peas in the refrigerator for up to 1 week or blanched and frozen for up to 1 year.

**PESTS AND DISEASES:** Peas may be susceptible to leaf spot or scab, blights and rots, fusarium wilt, powdery mildew, botrytis and other molds, damping-off, and mosaic virus. Choose cultivars bred for resistance to bacteria and fungi common in your area, and rotate legume crops each year to avoid diseases that persist in the soil. Beneficial insects control most aphids and thrips, but you can knock these pests off mature plants with a stream of water from the garden hose, or use insecticidal soap or neem oil spray if infestations are severe. Use floating row covers on young plants to discourage weevils. Tiny holes in pea pods may indicate an infestation by pea moths. Pick and destroy any yellowing pods and destroy all the plant debris after harvest.

**RECOMMENDED CULTIVARS:** Green peas, also called English peas, are cultivars grown for shelling. 'Dakota' is a very early variety ready to harvest in 50–55 days. The vines are short enough to be grown without supports. 'Caseload' is an extra sweet shelling pea ready in 55–60 days and slow to become starchy. 'Maestro' and 'Eclipse' are good choices for hot southern zones. They are disease resistant and ready in 60–65 days. 'Alderman', sometimes called 'Tall Telephone', grows to 5' or more tall and bears long pods, each with 8–10 extremely sweet peas in 75 days. 'Alaska' is a short-season variety ready in just 55 days and is best canned. 'Oregon Trail' (55–70 days) is a prolific producer of small pods with sweet peas, delicious raw or cooked. 'Little Marvel' (60–65 days) and 'Wando' (65–70 days) are popular home-garden cultivars because of their heat tolerance. Use them fresh, frozen, or canned.

*P. sativum* var. *macrocarpon* varieties are grown for their edible pods, called snow peas, which may require stringing. 'Oregon Giant' is a disease-resistant variety that produces sweet large pods in 60–70 days and throughout the summer. 'Sugar Pod 2' is a better choice for cool zones, bearing in 60–70 days. Other edible-pod varieties, called snap peas, are harvested after the seeds have filled out. 'Sugar Ann' is the earliest variety, ready to harvest in 50–55 days. 'Sugar Snap' produces plump, succulent pods in 60–70 days in both cool and hot weather. Remove the strings on the pods before eating or cooking them. 'Sugar Pop' and 'Sugar Daddy' are stringless varieties. 'Super Sugar Snap' is resistant to powdery mildew.

Direct-sow seed in early spring; peas do not transplant well.

All but the most dwarf plants require some type of support.

Harvest snow peas while the pods are still flat. Remove any strings.

Let the edible pods of snap peas fill out before harvesting them.

# STONE FRUIT

Trees in the genus Prunus bear the most commonly grown stone fruits in North America—plums, apricots, cherries, almonds, peaches, and nectarines. Stone fruits have in common a single hard seed called a pit or stone that is surrounded by juicy flesh. Most *Prunus* species are not native to North America and therefore require more effort to cultivate successfully in home gardens than apples or pears. Most types are susceptible to winter injury, although cherries and plums are generally the hardiest of the genus. All are attractive to pests and susceptible to diseases, and all must have systematic pruning to provide the highest yields. Although their abundant fragrant flowers alone are reason enough to include *Prunus* trees in the landscape, the extra effort to promote healthy fruits reaps delicious rewards.

## APRICOT

### *Prunus armeniaca* PROO-nus ar-men-ee-AY-kuh

**Apricot is susceptible to late spring frost damage because it blooms early.**

**ZONES:** 4–9
**SIZE:** 6–30'h × 6–30'w
**TYPE:** Deciduous tree
**GROWTH:** Slow
**LIGHT:** Full sun
**MOISTURE:** Moderate
**FEATURES:** Fragrant, showy flowers; edible fruits

**SITING:** Choose a protected, sunny site with deep, loose, well-drained, slightly acid soil. Plant the tree in a north-facing position if late spring frosts occur in your locale. Space standard varieties 25' apart, semidwarfs 15' apart, and dwarfs 6' apart. Use no plant food at planting.

**CARE:** Prune the new tree to a central leader with three or four scaffold branches at staggered intervals around the trunk (see pages 23–24). In the following year prune the scaffold branches back to form secondary branches. Rub or cut off any sprouts coming from the trunk. Cut the leader back even with the top scaffold branch when the tree has reached the desired height. Because apricot is an early bloomer, it is susceptible to late spring frost damage, which results in no fruiting. If possible cover trees if frost is predicted. Apricot does not tolerate drought. Keep the soil consistently moist but never waterlogged. Provide weekly deep watering during warm weather. Use tree plant food spikes if trees do not grow 1–2' each year. Prune lightly once a year after flowering to remove old fruiting spurs and control tree height. After normal fruit drop, thin to the healthiest fruit on each spur and leave 3" between fruits. Thin the branches of shrubby cultivars to allow sunlight to penetrate the interior of trees.

**PROPAGATION:** Grow from cuttings or by grafting.

**HARVEST:** European apricots begin producing at 4–5 years, Asian varieties as early as 3 years. Both may live 15–30 years or more, depending on care. Older varieties may drop ripe fruit, but newer hybrids need to be picked ripe from the tree. The velvety-skinned fruits look like miniature peaches and are ready to harvest when all green coloration is gone and the flesh is just starting to soften, usually in early July to mid-August. Pull off the fruit by twisting it up and away from the spur. Pick a few apricots from different parts of the tree and test them for full flavor before harvesting any others. Store ripe fruits in the refrigerator for up to 2 weeks.

**PESTS AND DISEASES:** Apricots are susceptible to the same problems as peaches. Prune out diseased and damaged wood immediately, and keep the ground around trees cleaned of dropped fruit and other vegetative matter that harbors pests and encourages disease. Most diseases can be avoided by choosing resistant cultivars and practicing clean cultural habits to keep pests away. If necessary, spray dormant oil

**Thinning fruits to 3" apart allows them to develop to full size.**

during winter to control serious infestations of peach tree borer; spray *Btk* at bloom time and during the summer to control the caterpillars. Cultivate the soil around the tree shallowly to destroy pupae. Avoid using insecticides while trees are in flower to protect pollinators. Use a fungicide spray at 10–14-day intervals until petal drop and again in autumn after leaf fall to prevent brown rot, twig blight, green fruit rot, and other infections. Use dormant oil in winter to control scale, mites, and borers. Use netting to protect trees from birds, and trunk wraps in winter to prevent rodent damage.

**RECOMMENDED CULTIVARS:** Choose apricots grafted to rootstocks that do well in your locale and cultivars bred for disease resistance. Their chilling hour requirements vary from 300 to 1,000. Popular European varieties include 'Stark Sweetheart', which has edible pits, 'Aprigold', 'Autumn Royal', 'Earligold', 'Wenatchee', and 'Puget Gold'. 'Blenheim' is a good choice for eating fresh or for drying and canning. Asian and hybrid types include 'Brookcot', 'Moongold', and 'Sunrise'. Manchurian apricot (*P. mandshurica*) is similar to Oriental bush cherry but grows to 25' tall and is not a reliable annual producer. Plant two for the best yield of 1" yellow-orange fruits. It is hardy to Zone 4. Japanese apricot (*P. mume*) is the small-fruited cultivar used to make plum sauce in Asian cuisines. It has showy red, white, or pink flowers, grows to 30' tall, and is hardy to Zone 6. Asian apricots are hardier than European varieties but may not fruit in climates where winter temperatures vary, such as in Zones 5 and 6. (Try 'Scout' in those zones.) Consistently cold or warm winters are required for fruiting. European apricots thrive where peaches grow, typically in Zones 8 and 9. Hybrids of apricots and plums called apriums, pluots, and plumcots combine the best features of each species.

# CHERRY

*Prunus spp.* PROO-nus

**'Lambert' is a hardy sweet cherry and a good pollenizer for other types.**

**ZONES:** 3–8
**SIZE:** 8–80'h × 6–50'w
**TYPE:** Deciduous tree
**GROWTH:** Slow

**LIGHT:** Full sun
**MOISTURE:** Average
**FEATURES:** Fragrant, showy flowers; edible fruits

**SITING:** Choose a sunny location at the top of a slope in deep, fertile, moist, well-drained, slightly acid soil. Plant the tree in a north-facing position if late spring frosts occur in your locale. Bush-type cherries can tolerate heavier and alkaline soils. Dig the hole to the same depth as the roots and somewhat wider than their mass when spread out. The bud union should be several inches above the soil. Firm the soil around the roots by hand to make sure there are no air pockets and water well. Space standard varieties 25–50' apart, semidwarfs 15–25' apart, and dwarfs 8–12' apart. Use no plant food at planting.

**CARE:** Train sour cherries to an open or vase shape (see pages 23–24). Train sweet cherries to a central leader. After planting, cut off all the side branches but leave the leader. In late winter or early spring of the second year, choose a branch about 3' from the ground for the top scaffold branch, then select a few more shoots at staggered intervals around the tree and not right above one another. Prune out all other branches, trim back the scaffolds to even their lengths, then cut back the leader to a point above the topmost scaffold where you want another one to form. In the following years, prune lightly but continue to develop new scaffold branches and remove any branches that compete. Branches become unfruitful after 3–5 years; prune them out. Feed mature trees with low-nitrogen fruit tree spikes, and water in dry weather, especially when the fruits are ripening. Remove water sprouts in summer to maintain an open canopy that sun can penetrate. Cut off suckers at ground level as soon as they appear.

Hand-weed an area 4–6' around the trunk. Use mulch to control weeds and conserve moisture in a circle as wide as the drip line, but keep it away from the trunks of trees. Use nutritional foliar sprays to correct mineral deficiencies. In dry conditions, water newly planted trees daily until they are well established.

Sour cherries are more tolerant of cold and heat and bloom later than sweet types, but protect both from frost damage. Either one may be killed below −20°F. Keep competing shrubs and trees pruned; too much shade makes even sweet cherries tart and less flavorful.

Sweet cherries are either crisp or soft fleshed. Crisp types are more desirable for cooking but tend to split as they ripen and become susceptible to brown rot. Sweet cherry trees can grow quite tall and are therefore more difficult to protect from birds. Put netting around the parts you can reach and let the birds have the cherries at the top, which is hard to harvest anyway. When training scaffolds, choose only wide-angled branches, which are less prone to breaking. Increase the angle of desirable young branches by weighting them down or using a wedge against the trunk.

**PROPAGATION:** Grow by bud grafting.

**HARVEST:** Sour cherries begin to bear 3–4 years from planting. Fruits ripen about 60 days after bloom, from late May to mid-June. Sweet cherries begin producing heavy yields in their fifth year and bear fruit in July. Store ripe cherries for up to a week in the refrigerator. Also called pie cherries, sour cherries are used for cooking only, because they are usually too tart to eat fresh from the tree. A few cultivars will become sweet if left on the tree until completely ripe.

**PESTS AND DISEASES:** Humidity and heat encourage fusarium wilt, rots, and molds. Clean cultural practices are essential to the health of cherry trees. Remove and destroy diseased fruit, leaves, twigs, and branches. Choose cultivars bred for your weather and soil conditions and with resistance to pests and diseases common in your locale. Varieties susceptible to brown rot are best grown in dry climates. Plum curculio, brown rot, fruit flies, leaf spot, and bacterial canker are common problems of cherry trees. See page 37 for information on spraying trees to prevent or control infection and infestation. Cover trees with netting to protect the fruit from birds. Use trunk wraps in winter to protect trees from gnawing rodents.

**RECOMMENDED CULTIVARS:** Sour cherries *(P. cerasus)* are self-fruitful and need about 1,000 chilling hours below 45°F. They are subdivided into two types: Morellos have

**Sweet cherries thrive in warm climates but most are not self-fruitful. Plant compatible pollenizers nearby to ensure a good crop.**

# CHERRY
*continued*

**Self-fruitful amarelle types are tart cherries good for cooking. They are also known as pie cherries.**

dark skin, red flesh, and acidic juice; amarelles have red skin, yellow flesh, and clear juice and are more disease tolerant. Choose varieties grown on dwarf rootstock to keep them to 10'. 'Montmorency' is a tart amarelle cherry that blooms late and ripens over a long season. For small gardens try 'Northstar', which has similar fruit on a genetic dwarf tree. 'Meteor' is a semidwarf amarelle tree that bears abundantly late in the season. 'Early Richmond' is an old-fashioned morello with small, acidic fruits. 'English Morello' is a large, hardy, late-bearing shrub with dark, acidic fruits that freeze well.

Acerola or Barbados cherry (*Malpighia glabra*) is a distantly related shrub or small tree 5–20' tall with pink or red flowers and juicy bright red fruits resembling cherries. Acerola blooms throughout the summer and bears several crops of fruit beginning the third or fourth year from planting. The fruits are too tart to be eaten raw but make excellent sweetened juice and preserves that can be frozen for later use. Duke cherries (*P. ×gondovinii*) are hybrids of sweet and sour cherries. 'Royal Duke' is a hardy and productive cultivar. The flavorful fruits are dark red with light, soft flesh. Because sweet cherries need 600–700 chilling hours, they grow well in mild climates—typically anywhere where peaches thrive. Most need a compatible pollenizer; ask your local extension agent

**Cover the parts of cherry trees that you can reach with netting to protect the fruits from birds and squirrels.**

or nursery grower which ones will work best together in your garden. 'Stark Gold' is a universal pollinator and hardy to Zone 4. 'Bing' is a well-known crisp-fleshed variety good for eating fresh but is susceptible to disease. 'Lambert' is hardier and more vigorous and can be used as a pollenizer. It has dark purple-red skin and pale flesh and is good for canning.

'Windsor' is another firm-fleshed dark red cultivar that is good fresh or processed and has disease resistance. 'Royal Ann' (also called 'Napoleon') is a large midseason yellow cherry blushed with red. Its sweet, firm flesh is good fresh or cooked. Choose 'Rainier' if you need an earlier tree with the same characteristics. Try self-fruitful 'Stella' or 'Starkrimson' which is both self-fruitful and a good pollinator, if your growing space is limited; or 'Black Tartarian', an early, soft-fleshed

cultivar, if you have room for two or more trees in a home garden.

Nanking cherries (*P. tomentosa*) are extremely cold-hardy shrubs with tart fruits good for canning or wine making. Oriental bush cherry (*P. japonica*) fruits in 2–3 years from seed, grows to 8', and is hardy to Zone 4. Other bush-type cherries that thrive in northern climates are pin cherry (*P. pensylvanica*) and chokecherry (*P. virginiana*). Orange-fruited chokecherry (*P. virginiana flava*) is a shade-tolerant native wild cherry adaptable to most soils. It grows 25–40' tall. All parts of the chokecherry except the ripe fruits are toxic. Western sand cherry (*P. besseyi*) cultivars 'Hanson', 'Amber', and 'Black Beauty' are hardy to Zone 3, and 'Brooks' grows in Alaska. They are cold and drought tolerant and rarely bothered by pests or disease.

# ALMOND
### *Prunus dulcis* PROO-nus DULL-sis

**Almond is the only *Prunus* tree grown solely for its edible seeds.**

**ZONES:** 8–10
**SIZE:** 10–30'h ×
8–25' w
**TYPE:** Deciduous
tree
**GROWTH:** Slow

**LIGHT:** Full sun
**MOISTURE:** Average
**FEATURES:** Lightly
fragrant, showy
flowers; edible
seeds (nuts)

**SITING:** Almond does best where summers are long, warm, and dry. Choose a sunny, elevated location with deep, fertile, well-drained, slightly acid soil. A shallow site is acceptable if irrigation is available. Keep the tree roots damp while you prepare the site. The hole should be deep enough for the roots to be spread out without being bent or crowded. The bud union of a grafted tree should be several inches above the soil line. Fill the soil in by hand, packing it around the roots for maximum contact. Water to eliminate air pockets, then add more soil. Use no plant food at planting.

**CARE:** Of all the *Prunus* trees, only almond is cultivated solely for its seeds. It is the first in its genus to bloom in spring. A dormant tree will survive a temperature dip into the teens, but protect a blooming tree from frost. Almond is deep rooted and thus drought tolerant, but prolonged temperatures over 80°F can cause bud failure the following season. Prune almond to an open shape or a modified leader shape and remove excess new branches (see pages 23–24). Unlike other *Prunus* trees cultivated for the flesh of their fruits, almond does not need to be thinned. Spread mulch around the tree to the drip line to keep the roots cool, but don't let it touch the trunk. Use a foliar zinc spray if soil analysis indicates the need.

**PROPAGATION:** Grow by grafting or from seed.

**HARVEST:** Trees begin fruiting in 3–4 years and can produce for 50 years or more. Fruits develop on shoot spurs, which are productive for up to 5 years and then should be pruned out. Pick when fruits split open, 180–240 days from flowering.

Spread a sheet or tarp beneath the tree and shake to loosen the fruits. Ripe fruits left on the tree attract pests. Hull the ripe fruits and spread the shells in single layers in trays in a dry, shady area with good air circulation. Almonds are ready to eat when the shells are brown and completely dry and the nuts are crunchy. Eat them raw or roasted, or use in baked goods and almond butter and as a topping for casseroles and desserts. Store dried nuts in plastic or glass at room temperature for up to 1 year and in the freezer for many years. Freezing nuts for 2 weeks kills any weevils or worms that may be present.

**PESTS AND DISEASES:** Avoid insecticides if possible to protect bees and other beneficial insects that pollinate fruit trees. Keep the area around the tree cleaned of dropped fruits and other vegetative matter that can harbor pests and diseases. Use a fungicide spray at 10–14-day intervals until petal drop and again in autumn after leaf fall to prevent brown rot, twig blight, green fruit rot, and other fungal infections.

For more information on spraying fruit trees, see page 37. Use dormant oil in winter to control scale, mites, and borers. Use netting to protect trees from birds, and trunk wraps in winter to prevent rodent damage.

**RECOMMENDED CULTIVARS:** Almonds are subdivided into bitter and sweet types and hard- and soft-shelled varieties. Most are self-sterile and require pollinators. They need only 250–500 chilling hours below 45°F. Sweet soft-shelled almonds are the type most often grown in home gardens in the United States. 'Cavaliera' is a very early cultivar suitable for areas with warm weather year-round. 'Nonpareil' is the most commonly grown midseason variety. It blooms in February and fruits in late August or early September. Use 'All-in-One', a self-fruitful semidwarf cultivar, as a pollenizer. 'Ferragnes' fruits in mid-September, 'Marcona' in late September, and 'Texas' in early October. 'Garden Prince' is a midseason self-fruitful genetic dwarf good for container growing.

**Almonds are ready to harvest when the fruits split open. Shake the nuts from the tree onto a sheet spread below.**

# PEACH
*Prunus persica* PROO-nus PER-sih-kuh

**Peach trees require long, hot summers and mild winters.**

**ZONES:** 4–8
**SIZE:** 6–20'h × 6–20'w
**TYPE:** Deciduous tree
**GROWTH:** Slow
**LIGHT:** Full sun
**MOISTURE:** Moderate
**FEATURES:** Edible fruits

**SITING:** Peaches and nectarines are the least hardy of the *Prunus* trees and the most demanding to grow, so plant them in a sunny, protected location. Plant in spring on the north side of your property if late spring frosts are a problem in your area; otherwise, a south-facing slope is the best site. In hot southern climates plant peaches and nectarines in autumn. They are shallow rooted, so they do best in rich, moist, well-drained, slightly acid soil. Choose 1-year-old trees about 4' tall and at least ½" in diameter grown on rootstock suitable for your climate. Container-grown trees can be planted at any time of year; plant bare-root trees in spring in areas with cold winters and in fall in areas with mild winters. Soak both in a weak solution of transplant starter for several hours before planting. Space them as far apart as they will be tall when mature. Prune out any dead or damaged wood, and cut away any roots that encircle the root ball. Remove any wires and ties, and make accommodation for stakes if they are needed. The holes should be large enough to accommodate the roots without crowding or bending them. The graft union should be several inches above the soil surface. The top layer of soil should be light and friable so the crown will dry quickly to prevent disease. Make a shallow trench around the tree 8–12" from the trunk to catch water.

**CARE:** Train trees to an open center as you would sour cherries (see pages 23–24). Keep the soil consistently moist but not waterlogged. High humidity increases the likelihood of brown rot. Spread several inches of well-rotted manure or mulch around the tree but away from the trunk to avoid pest and fungal damage and control weeds. Remove any sprouts and suckers. A healthy tree grows 12–24" a year; if yours does not, have the soil tested to determine its nutrient needs. Unnecessary feeding encourages new succulent growth, which is susceptible to frost damage and insect infestation. Trees bear on 1-year-old wood only, so prune out old wood each year while trees are dormant and dry. Thin fruits to 6" apart after normal fruit drop. Prop up sagging fruit-laden limbs to keep them from breaking.

**PROPAGATION:** Grow by grafting.

**HARVEST:** Peach and nectarine trees bear in 2–3 years. Fruits ripen in midsummer to midautumn, depending on cultivar and zone. Pick them when all green coloration is gone. Ripe fruits easily come off the tree with a slight upward twist, but handle them gently because they bruise easily. Store ripe fruit in the refrigerator for a few days. Pressure-can fruits for long-term storage. Sliced fruits bathed in lemon juice to retard discoloration can be stored in the freezer for up to 6 months.

**PESTS AND DISEASES:** Prune out sick and damaged wood immediately, and keep the ground around trees cleaned of dropped fruit and other matter that harbors pests and encourages disease. Most diseases can be avoided by choosing resistant cultivars and practicing clean cultural habits to keep pests away. If necessary, spray dormant oil during the winter to control serious infestations of peach tree borer, scale, and mites; spray *Btk* at bloom time and during the summer to control the caterpillars. Cultivate the soil around the tree shallowly to destroy pupae. Avoid using insecticides while trees are in flower to protect beneficial bees and other pollinators. Nectarines are more susceptible than peaches to plum curculio and brown rot, possibly because of their smooth skin. Use a fungicide spray at 10–14-day intervals until petal drop and again in autumn after leaf fall to prevent peach leaf curl, brown rot, twig blight, green fruit rot, and other infections. For more information on spraying fruit trees, see page 37. Use netting to protect fruit from birds and trunk wraps in winter to prevent rodent damage.

**RECOMMENDED CULTIVARS:** Peaches and nectarines differ by just one gene. Peach has the gene for fuzzy skin and nectarine does not. Most are self-pollinating and live only 10–15 years. Fruits are ready to harvest 2–3 years from planting. The flesh of most types is yellow but some are white. Peaches are further subdivided as freestone or clingstone. The pits are easy to remove in freestones but are still attached to the flesh in clingstone varieties. They bloom very early so are susceptible to frost. Choose cultivars with chilling hours appropriate for your area and bred for resistance to pests and diseases in your climate. Nectarine 'Garden Beauty' is a natural dwarf growing 4–6'. 'Durbin' is an early, disease-resistant variety good for southern gardens. 'Sunglo' bears large, juicy freestone fruits. 'RedGold' is a heavy-bearing, disease-resistant yellow freestone nectarine with bright red skin.

'Harbinger' is a very early, small yellow clingstone peach. Other early varieties include 'Early Redhaven', a peach that freezes well; 'Garnet Beauty', a yellow semifreestone type; and 'Florida King', a low-chill variety good for the South. Midseason varieties include 'Cresthaven', a yellow freestone resistant to browning; 'Polly', a semidwarf, self-fertile, white variety hardy to Zone 4; and 'Reliance', the most cold-hardy peach. 'Compact Redhaven' and 'Compact Elberta' are genetic dwarf peaches. Late varieties include 'Elberta', a large yellow freestone good fresh and canned; 'Belle of Georgia', an old-fashioned white-fleshed freestone cultivar; and 'Yakima Hale', a self-fruitful, large, flavorful yellow freestone. They ripen in late August.

**Nectarines are peaches without the gene for fuzzy skin.**

**Thin peaches and nectarines to 6" apart after fruit drop to give them room to develop fully.**

**Prevent peach leaf curl, rots, and blights with fungicide applications.**

# PLUM

*Prunus spp.* PROO-nus

**European plum cultivars bloom late and fruit late in the season.**

**ZONES:** 2–9
**SIZE:** 8–25'h ×
10–20'w
**TYPE:** Deciduous
tree
**GROWTH:** Slow

**LIGHT:** Full sun
**MOISTURE:** High
**FEATURES:** Showy,
fragrant flowers;
edible drupes

**SITING:** Choose a sunny, protected location with deep, rich, fertile loam. Plant plums on the north side of your property if late spring frosts are a problem in your area; otherwise, a south-facing slope is the best site. Plant 1-year-old dormant stock in spring in cold winter climates and in autumn in mild climates. Prune back to 3–4' tall and plant the tree at the same depth it grew in the nursery. Space standard-size trees 20' apart, semidwarf trees 15' apart, and dwarf trees and shrubs 8–10' apart. Spread a layer of well-rotted compost or manure around the tree and cover that with a couple inches of mulch to the drip line, but keep both away from the trunk.

**CARE:** Because European plums have deep roots, they can tolerate heavy soils. Japanese trees have shallower roots and can't tolerate waterlogged soil but are drought resistant. European plums should grow 12" a year, and Asian plums should grow up to 20". If not, have soil samples analyzed to determine the nutrient deficiencies before adding any amendments. Overfeeding encourages new succulent growth which is susceptible to pests and diseases. Train European plums to a central leader and Japanese plums and all shrub types to an open center (see pages 23–24). Prune after flowering to remove dead or diseased wood only. Fruits develop on long-lived spurs. European fruits develop toward the interior of the tree, so thinning branches promotes ripening. American plums are shrubby and need thinning to make harvest easier. Thin the fruits by hand after normal fruit drop, leaving only the best plum on each spur and 4–6" between fruits. Red cultivars need more thinning than blue ones, and

heavily fruiting branches may need to be propped up.

**PROPAGATION:** Grow by grafting.

**HARVEST:** Blue plums bear 4–5 years from planting and red ones 3–4 years. Most trees are productive for 10–15 years. Plums are ready to harvest when they come off in your hand with a gentle twist. Unripe fruit won't come off the spur without tugging. Sample a few from different parts of the tree before making a significant harvest. Japanese plums can be picked before they are completely ripe; they will continue to ripen off the tree. American plums are ready to harvest when they are soft. European plums must ripen on the tree but should be picked before they are mushy. Ripe plums left on the tree will rot. Store all types of ripe plums for up to 2 weeks in the refrigerator. European plums can be sundried whole for use as prunes. All sweet-fleshed varieties are excellent eaten out of hand or sliced in fresh fruit salads, and can be used for cooking and canning. Tart cultivars are good in jams, jellies, preserves, baked goods, and wine.

**PESTS AND DISEASES:** Plums are susceptible to black knot, a fungus that produces hard black bumps on twigs and branches. Prune out infected areas in winter by cutting the

wood well below the knots and destroying the cuttings. Sterilize your pruning tools between cuts. Use a labeled fungicide to prevent brown rot. Prune sick and damaged wood immediately, and keep the ground around trees cleaned of dropped fruit and other vegetative matter that harbors pests and encourages disease. Most diseases can be avoided by choosing resistant cultivars and practicing clean cultural habits to keep pests away. Spray dormant oil in winter to control aphids, scale, and borers. Use insecticides to control heavy infestations of plum curculio, but avoid spraying when trees are in bloom to protect bees and other beneficial pollinators. See page 37 for more information on spraying fruit trees. Use netting to protect fruit from birds, and trunk wraps in winter to prevent rodent damage.

**RECOMMENDED CULTIVARS:** Choose a self-fruitful tree if you have room for just one. To grow those that need pollenizers, be sure to choose cultivars whose bloom times overlap and at least one that bears annually. Select European *(P. ×domestica)* varieties for late-season freestone plums to dry as prunes. They are hardier than Japanese types and bloom later in spring so are safe for zones where late spring

**Use sterilized pruning tools to cut twigs and branches infected with black knot, a fungus common in plum trees.**

# PLUM
*continued*

**American plums are cold-hardy and tolerant of heat and drought but aren't as sweet as other species.**

frosts may occur. However, they fruit late in September and into October and thus may be damaged by an early autumn frost. Their freestone pits make them easy to process for canning. European prune plums include 'Bluefree', with large blue-skinned freestone fruits; 'Damson' (derived from *P. institia*), a small, self-pollinating tree with tart blue plums good for cooking; 'French Prune', a small, self-pollinating tree with very sweet, small red to purple fruits; 'Sugar', a large purple-red plum that's also good right off the tree; and 'Stanley', a vigorous annual producer of medium-size purple-blue fruits with sweet yellow flesh excellent fresh, dried, or canned. Gage plums are light green and sweet. Most are self-fruitful but will yield more heavily with a pollenizer nearby. 'Reine Claude' ripens in mid- to late summer. It can be planted in all zones because it has a low chill requirement and is cold hardy.

## SPACE-SAVING TIP

Gardeners with limited space can obtain a variety of fruits by planting trees with multiple cultivar grafts. A single plum tree, for example, can be grafted to produce both red and yellow fruits of different cultivars. Or a branch from a suitable pollenizer can be grafted to a cultivar that's not self-fertile. Just be sure to choose cultivars of similar vigor, bloom time, and disease susceptibility, and tag any individual grafts so they aren't accidentally pruned out.

Japanese plums (*P. salicina*) are shorter, spreading, early-blooming trees with sweet clingstone fruits. They have low chill requirements and not all are hardy. 'Catalina' is a self-fruitful pollinator good for home gardens with room for just one tree. 'Early Golden' and 'Abundance' (midseason) are yellow-fleshed types that tend to bear biennially. 'Omaha' is a hardy, late-season cultivar with sweet, juicy red-and-yellow-speckled fruits. 'Santa Rosa' is a hardy, midseason tree with fragrant, flavorful dark red plums with yellow flesh. 'Superior' is a Japanese × American hybrid with large, tasty red plums that can be peeled like peaches. It is hardy but needs a pollenizer such as 'Toka'. The hybrid cherry-plum is a cross of Japanese plum and western sand cherry (*P. besseyi*). The result is improved flavor in fruits from short-lived, self-sterile, frost-intolerant shrubs. Crosses of plums and apricots are discussed on page 111.

American varieties (*P. americana*) include 'Newport', 'Fairlane', and 'Manet'. All are cold hardy and tolerate heat and drought. The fruit ripens in August but is only of fair quality. Chickasaw plum (*P. angustifolia*) is faster growing than other American types, easy to prune to a central leader, and reaches 12–25' tall. The tart 1" bright red fruits ripen in September, but the tree bears biennially. Canada plum (*P. nigra*) is a native tree hardy to Zone 2. It grows to 10' and bears 1" oval red fruits that are good in preserves. Sloe plum (*P. spinosa*) is a dwarf shrub growing to 4' high and wide. It covers itself with small blue fruits that are bitter when fresh but excellent in jams and jellies and for flavoring gin.

Beach plum (*P. maritima*) grows to 6' in sandy soil and tolerates salinity. It can be used as a hedge or grown in a container. The ½–1" fruits come in black, blue, red, or yellow. 'Grant' is blue and has the largest fruits at 1". 'Red' has red skin and sweet yellow flesh. *P. maritima* ×*americana* hybrids include 'Flava', with sweet yellow-skinned fruits, and 'Dunbars', with bright red freestone fruits. They make delicious preserves.

**Choose a self-fruitful small shrub or dwarf tree cultivar to grow plums in a patio container.**

# COMMON GUAVA

*Psidium guajava*  SID-ee-um gwah-HAH-vuh

**Most guavas are self-fruitful, but yields are improved with pollenizers. Common guava is also known as tropical guava.**

**ZONES:** 9–11
**SIZE:** 6–40'h ×
8–25'w
**TYPE:** Evergreen
tree or shrub
**GROWTH:** Fast

**LIGHT:** Full sun
**MOISTURE:**
Moderate
**FEATURES:** Edible
fruits

**SITING:** Choose a sunny, protected location with soil that drains well. Plant guavas on a north-facing exposure if late spring frosts are a problem; otherwise, a south-facing slope is best. Space strawberry guavas (*P. littorale* var. *longipes*) 10–15' apart. Small cultivars can be grown in containers.

**CARE:** Guava grows best where daytime temperatures are 70–85°F. It is susceptible to frost and not tolerant of extreme heat. Water in times of drought. Most are self-fruitful but will yield more heavily when a pollenizer is planted nearby. Guavas fruit on new growth, so prune them only to shape the trees and remove suckers. Feed common guavas with balanced plant food monthly during the first year after planting and every other month thereafter. Feed strawberry guavas half that often. Use foliar sprays if soil sample analysis indicates nutritional deficiencies. Rejuvenate old trees by severe pruning.

**PROPAGATION:** Grow common guavas by grafting; grow strawberry guava from seed or cuttings.

**HARVEST:** Guavas fruit 2–4 years from planting and are productive for at least 15 years. The fruits mature 90–150 days after flowering. Leave them on the tree to ripen, but protect them from birds, bats, and fruit flies. Ripe fruits can be shaken from the tree and caught in nets, but they bruise easily. Unripe fruit is hard and gummy, but almost-ripe yellow-green guavas can be clipped from the tree and

will ripen at room temperature within 1 week. Ripe fruits covered with plastic wrap will keep in the refrigerator for up to 2 weeks. Store ripe guavas away from other fruits and vegetables that release ethylene gas.

**PESTS AND DISEASES:** Mites, thrips, aphids, fruit worms, sucking bugs, and fruit flies may cause problems. Damaged fruits are subject to rots. Avoid using insecticides when the trees are in bloom to protect pollinators. Use dormant oil spray in winter to control infestations, and keep the ground around trees clean of dropped fruit and vegetative matter that harbors pests and diseases. Control algal spots and anthracnose with labeled fungicides. Use netting and noisemakers to discourage birds and bats.

**RECOMMENDED CULTIVARS:** 'Ruby' bears red-fleshed fruits in fall and early winter in Florida and Hawaii. 'Ka Hua Kula' is a pink-fleshed dessert-type that grows well in humid climates. 'Detwiler' produces greenish-yellow fruits with sweet yellow to pink flesh. It grows well in California. Strawberry guavas bear 1–1½" red-skinned fruits with white flesh or yellow fruits.

# POMEGRANATE

*Punica granatum*  poo-NEYE-kuh gra-NAY-tum

**Pomegranates must ripen on the tree but clip them off before they crack open.**

**ZONES:** 8–11
**SIZE:** 10–30'h ×
10–30'w
**TYPE:** Evergreen or
deciduous tree or
shrub
**GROWTH:** Slow

**LIGHT:** Full sun
**MOISTURE:**
Moderate
**FEATURES:** Showy
flowers, edible
fruits

**SITING:** Choose a sunny, warm location with moist, well-drained soil. Plants may produce lower yields and fruit quality in sandy and clay soils but are tolerant of alkalinity. Plant 10–20' apart.

**CARE:** Pomegranate does best in areas with cool winters and hot, dry summers. It is

drought tolerant but yields best if the soil is consistently moist. Water young plants until they are established and mature trees with ripening fruit. Provide balanced plant food once in spring the first 2 years only. Apply a mulch each year, but keep it from touching the trunks. Plants can be pruned to a few trunks or trained as fountain-shaped shrubs for ornamental value. For multiple trunks, select five or six suckers to develop, then prune out all the others. Fruits form on the tips of the current year's growth, so prune young trees and shrubs to encourage new shoots on all sides. After the third year, prune out only dead wood and suckers.

**Train pomegranate to multiple trunks to increase its ornamental value.**

**PROPAGATION:** Grow from hardwood cuttings.

**HARVEST:** Fruits ripen 180–220 days after flowering, from July through September. Fruits ready for harvest make a slight metallic or cracking sound when tapped. Ripen fruits on the tree, but clip them off before they become overripe and crack. Their flavor improves in storage. Fruits can be kept for 6 months in cool but not freezing temperatures and high humidity.

**PESTS AND DISEASES:** Spray plants with a forceful water spray periodically to prevent spider mites. Spray flowers twice 30 days apart to control pomegranate fruit borers. Excessive moisture causes heart rot. Cover ripening fruit with netting or bags to protect fruit from birds.

**RECOMMENDED CULTIVARS:** 'Wonderful' bears large dark purple-red fruit with juicy deep red flesh. 'Granada' is darker red and sweeter than 'Wonderful' and ripens a month earlier. Both have semihard seeds. 'Sweet' is greenish with a red blush when ripe but much sweeter than other cultivars. 'Utah Sweet' has pink skin and pulp and soft seeds. Cultivars with soft seeds are often described as seedless. For container growing, try 'Nana', a dwarf pomegranate that grows to 3' tall and wide.

# PEAR

*Pyrus communis* *PY-rus kom-MEW-nis*

Select a self-fruitful pear cultivar if you have room for just one tree.

**ZONES:** 3–8
**SIZE:** 8–25'h × 8–25'w
**TYPE:** Deciduous tree
**GROWTH:** Slow
**LIGHT:** Full sun
**MOISTURE:** Average
**FEATURES:** Edible fruits

**SITING:** Choose a sunny, well-drained location. Plant in a north-facing location to delay blooming in areas with variable spring weather. Pears are deep rooted and can grow in any soil but do best in rich, heavy loam. Plant a 1-year-old whip at the same depth it grew in the nursery, then cut back the top to about 3'. Space standard cultivars 16–20' apart, dwarf varieties 10–12'. Plant pears while they are dormant in frost-free areas or in spring in cold-winter zones.

**CARE:** Pears are related to apples but more difficult to grow. Standard varieties require 800–1,110 chilling hours below 45°F; Asian pears require 400–900 hours. They are all hardy, but the flowers can be killed by a late spring frost. Most pears require cross-pollination, so plant at least two or three. Keep the soil consistently moist; lack of moisture causes fruits to drop. In areas with hot summers, shade developing fruits from sunscald and provide supplemental irrigation. Use plant food only if a soil sample analysis indicates the need; excess nitrogen encourages fire blight. After normal fruit drop, thin the remaining fruits for best size. Train standard trees to a central leader. In the dormant season head back any side branches that compete with the central leader. Dwarf cultivars can be grown as hedges or espaliered. For more information on training and pruning fruit trees, see pages 23–27.

**PROPAGATION:** Grow by grafting.

**HARVEST:** Standard pear trees begin to bear fruit in 5–6 years, dwarf trees in 3–4. The fruits—roughly the size of an elongated apple—ripen in August through September. Pick pears by hand 1–2 weeks before they are completely ripe. Lift the fruit with a twisting motion rather than pulling on it. Allow pears to ripen at room temperature, or store them in a cool, dark place and bring them out to ripen as needed. To hasten ripening place several pears together in a sealed plastic container. Unripe pears can be refrigerated for months and brought out to ripen about a week before needed. Eat them fresh out of hand, sliced into salads and baked goods, or processed for jelly, chutney, and wine.

**PESTS AND DISEASES:** Prune and destroy branches infected with fire blight, a bacterial disease for which there is no cure. Pear psylla can be controlled with a

Harvest pears a week or two before they are completely ripe and store them in cool darkness until needed.

Pears bruise and tear easily, so pick them by hand with an upward twisting motion instead of pulling down.

Remove and destroy any branches infected with fire blight, an incurable bacterial disease common in older pear cultivars.

precisely timed dormant oil spray in late winter or early spring; ask your local extension agent for help determining when treatment will be most effective. Use insecticide sprays only after the petals have fallen to avoid killing pollinating honeybees. For additional information on spraying fruit trees, see page 37. Remove water sprouts to reduce aphid populations. Rake up and destroy dropped fruits and vegetative debris to control pear scab and pests. Use hardware cloth or plastic guards around the lower part of tree trunks to prevent rabbits and mice from eating the bark.

**RECOMMENDED CULTIVARS:** Most well-known pears including 'Aurora', 'Bartlett', 'Bosc', and 'Comice' are highly susceptible to disease. Choose newer hybrids and cultivars resistant to fire blight and pear scab. Be sure to select self-fruitful types if you have room for just one tree. Otherwise, choose trees that are compatible pollenizers. 'Duchess' is self-fruitful and late bearing, a good pollinator for other trees, and grows well in northern zones. 'Moonglow' thrives in all pear-growing regions and is early, blight resistant, and good fresh or canned. Late-season 'Seckel' bears small, very sweet yellow-brown pears that are good fresh or canned. The tree is hardy, resistant to fire blight, sometimes self-fruitful, and does well everywhere but the deepest part of the South. It's a good choice for home gardens. 'Mericourt' grows well in southern zones and is good fresh or canned. 'Anjou' (sometimes 'D'anjou') does well in the cool climates of the Pacific Northwest and Great Lakes regions but not in hot-summer areas. The large fruits are green with a pink blush and have good flavor and texture fresh or cooked.

Asian pears *(P. serotina)* bear true pears that look like yellow apples. They have crisp, smooth flesh ready to eat when picked, and keep in the refrigerator for up to 6 months without becoming mushy. They grow best in cool-winter areas along the West Coast. Prune them like standard pears or train them as an espalier. Asian pears are self-fruitful but do best with pollenizers planted nearby. 'Shinseiki', an early-maturing flat yellow pear, and '20th Century', a flat green pear, may need to be cross-pollinated with a European cultivar for good fruit set annually in cooler climates.

Quince *(Cydonia oblonga)* rootstocks are used for dwarfing standard pears. Fruits of quince are good only when cooked in jelly and preserves.

# RADISH
*Raphanus sativus* *RAF-an-us sub-TY-vus*

'D'Avignon' is a tapered French cultivar ready for harvest in just a few weeks.

**ZONES:** NA
**SIZE:** 2–6"h x 2–6"w
**TYPE:** Annual
**GROWTH:** Fast
**LIGHT:** Full sun to part shade
**MOISTURE:** High
**FEATURES:** Edible roots

**SITING:** The planting area should be weed free, because emerging seedlings are difficult to distinguish and easily out-competed. Plant seeds ½" deep and 1" apart in rows 8–12" apart. Interplant with slower-developing crops such as carrots, beans, and cucumbers. Radishes are cool-weather crops; plant 3–4 weeks before the last spring frost and 6 weeks before the first fall frost in northern climates. Plant seeds in early autumn in southern zones.

**CARE:** Plant small amounts of seed every few weeks so you can pick and eat radishes at their peak. Thin the seedlings to 2" apart when they are 1" tall. Pull weeds by hand and keep the soil consistently moist.

**PROPAGATION:** Grow from seed.

**HARVEST:** Radishes are ready to pull up in 20–30 days. Those left in the ground too long crack or become pithy. Trim off the tops and roots and scrub off the dirt under running water. Radishes keep well in the refrigerator for up to 1 month. Daikon radishes are often grated and pickled for long-term storage.

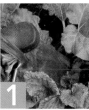

Plant Daikon radishes in midsummer for autumn harvest.

**PESTS AND DISEASES:** Choose cultivars labeled for disease resistance. Control clubroot through clean gardening practices and crop rotation in well-drained soil. Pick off harlequin bugs and cabbageworms by hand or use Bt for serious infestations. Remove and destroy leaves infested with leaf miners and use floating row covers to discourage them and cabbage maggot flies. Knock aphids off with a strong stream from the garden hose. Interplant radishes with taller crops that will provide shade to discourage flea beetles.

**RECOMMENDED CULTIVARS:** 'D'Avignon' is a 3–4" tapered, cylindrical French red radish with a white tip. It is ready in only 21 days. 'Cherry Belle' and 'Comet' are among the earliest globe radishes, ready in 20–25 days. Round bright red 'Sora' can be planted at any time of year and is ready in 25–30 days. 'White Icicle' has 4–5" slender roots ready in 25–30 days. 'Crunchy Royale' is a sweet, round red radish ready in 30 days. 'Shunkyo Semi-Long' has 4–5"-long cylindrical pink roots with white flesh, ready in 35 days. It can be sown anytime and is slow to bolt. 'Miyashige' is a traditional daikon radish for late planting only. The long, cylindrical white roots are banded in green at the top and are ready in 50 days.

# RHUBARB
*Rheum ×cultorum* *ROOM kul-TOR-um*

Cool temperatures promote the best color in red-stalked rhubarb cultivars. Rhubarb is also known as pie plant.

**ZONES:** 2–8
**SIZE:** 1–3'h x 2–4'w
**TYPE:** Herbaceous perennial
**GROWTH:** Average
**LIGHT:** Full sun
**MOISTURE:** Average
**FEATURES:** Edible petioles (stalks)

**SITING:** Choose a permanent location in a sunny space. Rhubarb needs deep, rich, well-drained soil. Plant the crowns 2" deep and 6' apart each way. Add no plant food to the holes. Set the roots so that the central bud is 2" below the soil surface.

**CARE:** Cool weather promotes the best red color in rhubarb. When daytime temperatures climb above 80°F, add 2" of organic mulch around the plants to keep the roots cool. Keep the ground around plants free of weeds and debris where pests can hide. Cut off flower stems as they appear. Use a sharp spade to divide and replant rhubarb every 6–8 years or when stalks have become thin. Divide plants in early spring or in fall if you mulch plants with straw or manure after a few frosts. Divide the crown so that each new piece has some buds and as many roots as possible. Plant the new pieces immediately. Sidedress plants with well-rotted compost or manure after the last harvest and feed with balanced plant food.

Divide rhubarb in spring or fall every 6–8 years.

Divide the crown so that each piece has stems and roots.

**PROPAGATION:** Grow by crown division.

**HARVEST:** Allow plants to grow and develop without cutting stalks the first year after planting. Begin harvesting in the second season when stalks are 8–15" tall. Take just a few stalks each week for 2 weeks. In the third season cut one-third to one-half of the thickest stalks each week for up to 4 weeks. In subsequent years harvest up to two-thirds of the stalks each week for 8–10 weeks. Cut or twist the stalks from the crown, then cut off the toxic leaf blades and compost them. Store the unwashed stalks in a plastic bag in the refrigerator for up to 2 weeks, or blanch and freeze chopped stalks for up to 1 year.

**PESTS AND DISEASES:** Purchase certified disease-free plants to avoid crown rot. Vigorous plants will not be bothered by most pests, but handpick and destroy curculio beetles, caterpillars, and Japanese beetles. Plant rhubarb in well-drained soil or raised beds to prevent verticillium wilt.

**RECOMMENDED CULTIVARS:** 'MacDonald' is a good choice for heavy soils. 'Valentine' needs less sweetening than most other cultivars. 'Canada Red' keeps its color even when cooked. 'Victoria' has green stalks.

# CURRANT, GOOSEBERRY
*Ribes* spp. *RY-beez*

**American gooseberry cultivars, such as 'Poorman', are disease resistant.**

**ZONES:** 2–9
**SIZE:** 3–6'h x 2–5'w
**TYPE:** Woody deciduous shrub
**GROWTH:** Slow
**LIGHT:** Part shade
**MOISTURE:** Average
**FEATURES:** Edible berries

**SITING:** Gooseberries and currants grow best in cool, humid regions that provide some winter chilling hours. Currants are hardy farther north than gooseberries. Both are adapted to a variety of conditions but thrive in rich, moist, well-drained, slightly acid loam that has been heavily amended with organic matter and cleared of all perennial weeds. The plants do not tolerate drought or standing water. Because they flower early, a sunny, northern exposure helps to delay blooming long enough to avoid frost damage and also provides shade for the berries from hot midday sun in summer. Plant vigorous, well-rooted 1-year-old plants in spring 4–5' apart in each direction. Spread the roots out carefully and make sure they do not touch any fresh manure or plant food, which could burn them. Set container-grown plants in the soil at the same level they were growing in the nursery. Plant bare-root stock so that the lowest branch is just above the soil surface, and cut the tops back to about 6" above ground level. *Note: Ribes is an alternate host of white pine blister rust; black currant is banned in many states. Plant all varieties at least 1,000 feet from white pine trees.*

**CARE:** Gooseberries and currants are shrubby, but in limited space they can be trained to a trellis. Prune them while they are dormant to improve air circulation and encourage new growth. Remove branches older than 3 years. Plants should have equal numbers of new, 1-year-old, and 2-year-old canes. Because they are partially self-sterile, multiple plants will result in higher yields. Thin developing fruits to increase the size of the remaining fruits. Use drip irrigation if necessary to keep the soil moist until the berries are harvested. If growing conditions are less than optimal or if plants are located near competing trees and shrubs, feed them once a year with ¼–⅓ pound of balanced plant food per plant, in early spring before they break dormancy or in autumn after all the berries have been harvested.

**PROPAGATION:** Grow from hardwood cuttings or by layering.

**HARVEST:** Gooseberries and currants grow in long clusters on the shrubs. They ripen in late summer over a period of 4–6 weeks. Pick them before they are fully ripe for best use in cooking. Let them ripen on the shrub for up to several weeks for fresh use. They sunburn easily, so keep freshly harvested ones in a shady spot while you pick. Wear gloves to pick gooseberries; most cultivars have thorns. Healthy plants may be productive for up to 20 years. Currants and gooseberries are most often used in pies, jams, and jellies but also make good sweet wine.

**PESTS AND DISEASES:** Plants are less susceptible to powdery mildew in full sun but more susceptible to fungal infections in prolonged wet weather. Spray fungicide according to label directions if needed. Prune out and destroy diseased or damaged wood, watching for signs of cane borers. Spray with insecticide to control heavy infestations of fruit fly maggots, but avoid spraying while plants are in bloom to protect beneficial pollinating insects. Remove and destroy plants infected with gall mites. Pick off any worms. Hard rain will wash off most aphids, or use a spray from the garden hose. Cover plants with netting to protect ripening fruits from birds.

**Choose only currant cultivars that are immune to white pine blister rust.**

**RECOMMENDED CULTIVARS:** Purchase certified disease-free stock. Gooseberry is divided into two groups. American gooseberry (*R. hirtellum*) cultivars have the best disease resistance. 'Red Jacket' is a nearly thornless variety. 'Poorman' is a good choice for home gardens because it is less thorny than other cultivars and its red berries are good fresh. European types (*R. uva-crispa*) are more susceptible to disease but have larger, sweeter fruit than American gooseberries. 'Fredonia' is a good late cultivar. 'Hinnomaki Yellow' is a mildew-resistant plant with pale yellow-green berries. Black currant (*R. nigrum*) is banned in many states; check with your local natural resources department before planting it. 'Consort' and 'Crusader' are

**Pick slightly unripe berries for cooking or let them ripen on the bush to eat fresh.**

rust-immune black cultivars acceptable for planting in some states. Red and white varieties are less likely to be hosts of white pine blister rust. Red currants (*R. silvestre*) are more flavorful for cooking. 'Red Lake' is a disease-resistant, late-ripening cultivar that is easy to pick. 'Wilder' is a vigorous midseason variety with large berries on long compact clusters. Because white currants have lower acidity they are better for eating fresh. 'White Imperial' bears large pale yellow berries of excellent quality. 'Gloire des Sablons' (*R. rubrum*) is a pink cultivar with an upright habit. Jostaberry (*R. nidigrolaria*) is a fast-growing hybrid of black currant and gooseberry with reddish-black fruits. Buffalo currant (*R. aureum*) is more closely related to gooseberry and has a broader, weeping habit. It is cold hardy but has low chilling hour requirements and tolerates alkaline soils. It grows well in Southern California.

# ROSEMARY
*Rosmarinus officinalis* ros-muh-RY-nus off-iss-ib-NAY-lis

**Rosemary cultivars may have spreading or upright growth habits.**

**ZONES:** (6)7–10
**SIZE:** 1–3'h x 1–3'w
**TYPE:** Woody evergreen perennial
**GROWTH:** Slow

**LIGHT:** Full sun
**MOISTURE:** Average
**FEATURES:** Edible leaves and flowers

**SITING:** Choose a sunny, protected location that drains well. Rosemary is a member of the mint family and grows well in average, neutral-pH garden soil as well as in containers indoors and out. It thrives in raised beds and is drought tolerant.

**CARE:** Plan to grow rosemary as an annual in Zones 4–6. In short-summer areas plant it in pots for easy relocation if frost is predicted. Regular harvest of a few stems throughout the season encourages bushier growth. In warm-winter areas protect rosemary from harsh winds that may dry it out.

**PROPAGATION:** Grow from cuttings or by layering.

**HARVEST:** Cut a few succulent stems above woody growth as needed throughout the growing season. Strip the resinous leaves from the stems and chop or grind them for use with meats; in recipes that include potatoes, tomatoes, eggplant, or peppers;

**Grow rosemary indoors in winter for fresh leaves year-round.**

and in soups, stews, and marinades. Insert a few stems into bottles of vinegar or olive oil to flavor them. Use the tiny flowers in salads or as a garnish. Tie harvested stems in small bunches and hang them upside down in a cool, airy space to dry. In northern climates pull the plants up before the first frost and hang them by their roots to dry. Pull the dried leaves from the stems and store in an airtight container for up to 2 years. Pulverize them before adding them to foods; the whole leaves can be chewy. Rosemary also can be frozen for long-term storage but loses its rich color.

**PESTS AND DISEASES:** None are significant.

**RECOMMENDED CULTIVARS:** Varieties with an upright growth habit include 'Madalene Hill' and 'Arp', which are hardy to Zone 6. 'Arp' has gray-green foliage and blue flowers. 'Madalene Hill' has dark green leaves and pale blue flowers. In the Midwest try 'Athens Blue Spires', a cultivar that may be hardy to Zone 6. 'Blue Boy' is a compact dwarf variety that grows well in containers. 'Majorca' has an intermediate habit—upright but spreading with some trailing stems. 'Rexford' is a warm-climate cultivar with especially good flavor.

# BLACKBERRY, RASPBERRY
*Rubus* spp.   ROO-bus

**Raspberries can be identified by their hollow cores.**

**ZONES:** 4–9
**SIZE:** To 6'h x 3'w
**TYPE:** Woody perennial shrub
**GROWTH:** Average

**LIGHT:** Full sun
**MOISTURE:** Average
**FEATURES:** Edible berries

**SITING:** Brambles grow best in areas with long, mild springs and cool summer nights. They thrive in all but the most acid soils as long as the drainage is good. They need good air circulation to ward off disease. Avoid planting them in areas where tomatoes, potatoes, eggplants, and peppers have recently grown because the site may harbor verticillium wilt. Select a site away from patios, decks, and recreational use areas where bees and dropped fruit can interfere. Plant rooted cuttings 4–6' apart in moist soil in early spring, 1 month before the last frost date. Set commercially grown canes at the same depth they were grown in the nursery.

**CARE:** Cane berries sprout new biennial canes each year. Blackberries become invasive if not pruned regularly. Because brambles bloom late in spring, frost is not a problem. Blackberries are drought tolerant; raspberries are not, but irrigation results in better yields for both. Blackberries are more tolerant of hot summer weather than raspberries, but mulch both species well to conserve soil moisture, control weeds, and increase yields. Prune unwanted blackberry canes underground. Prune out any stubs that do not sprout in spring to avoid anthracnose. Fruit is borne only on 1-year-old blackberry canes. Top new canes to 6" to promote branching; prune out 1-year-old canes immediately after they finish

**Pick ripe raspberries in the morning after the dew has dried but while the plants are still cool.**

**Prune out the current season's fruiting canes immediately after harvesting the summer crop of raspberries.**

# BLACKBERRY, RASPBERRY
*continued*

**Pinch the new cane tips of purple and black raspberry cultivars in summer to promote branching.**

fruiting. Prune trailing types to 6–10" in winter after the first growing season and train them onto trellises. Thereafter prune them like erect types. Prune everbearing raspberries twice each season. In spring remove old canes as well as any damaged, diseased, or dead canes. Then pinch the tips of canes where the fall crop was borne. The new summer crop fruits on the lower buds of the canes where the previous fall crop developed. Immediately after harvesting the summer crop, remove those canes entirely. Prune red and yellow one-crop raspberries by removing fruiting canes after harvest but do not pinch new cane tips. Pinch the tips of black and purple varieties in summer to promote branching. Remove fruiting canes immediately after harvest.

**PROPAGATION:** Grow from root or stem cuttings, new suckers, or tip-layering.

**HARVEST:** Pick in the morning when fruits and plants are dry and cool. Watch out for bees before you reach in. Carry the berries in shallow trays, because they are easily crushed. They also are highly perishable, so keep picked berries in the shade and move them to a cool location as soon as possible. Blackberries fruit the first year following planting. The fruit's green receptacle separates from the plant when the fruit is picked. The core should be small and soft. Raspberries bear a small crop the second year after planting and a full crop the third year, and remain productive for 5–8 years.

**PESTS AND DISEASES:** Purchase certified disease-free stock. Uproot and destroy virus-infected plants so that aphids don't transmit the disease to healthy plants. Black raspberries are the most susceptible of the brambles to viruses. If spider mites are a problem in hot, dry weather, dislodge them with the garden hose. Wilted tips are a sign of borers; cut out and destroy the canes. Avoid using insecticides that might harm beneficial and pollinating insects.

**RECOMMENDED CULTIVARS:** Most cane berries are self-fruitful. Blackberries require 200–800 chilling hours below 45°F. Blackberries are divided into two types, erect or trailing. The erect type grows to 6' tall. 'Brainerd' is a semihardy, drought-resistant cultivar with large black berries. 'Darrow' is a hardy, erect black-fruited cultivar that grows well in northern climates. Thornless cultivars are available but tend to be less hardy. Thorny cultivars of 'Brazos' grow best in southern climates. The trailing blackberry vine spreads to 15' and is grown mainly on the West Coast. 'Cascade' is an early variety that grows well in Pacific coastal regions. It has soft dark red berries. Boysenberry is a trailing hybrid of 'Youngberry' and blackberry that grows well in mild-winter climates. 'Dewberry' (*R. ursinus, R. canadensis)* is sometimes smaller than standard blackberries. Its flavor varies, but it grows well in southeastern and mid-Atlantic states, even in rocky soil. Prune the entire plant after harvest to reduce the possibility of disease and to give plants time to regrow in warm regions. Youngberry is a tender, trailing cross of dewberry and loganberry with fruits that resemble elongated blackberries but are red and taste like sweetened loganberries. Marionberry is a trailing, vigorous plant with mercifully few canes and does well in mild regions. Loganberry may be a cross between raspberry and dewberry. It is a late, trailing type that bears firm, blackberry-type fruits with a tart raspberry flavor. It is not hardy in the eastern United States, where 'Lucretia' grows better. Raspberries require 800–1,600 chilling hours below 45°F. They are divided by fruit colors—red, purple, yellow, and black—and by fruiting frequency—summer bearing (single crop) or everbearing (two crops). 'Heritage' is everbearing and has medium-size red fruits. 'Autumn Bliss' is everbearing and has high yields of large red berries. 'Fallgold' is a sweet yellow raspberry good for northern climates. Try 'Goldie' in warmer zones. 'Hilton' is the largest of

**Black raspberries are native to North America and therefore cold hardy.**

**Regularly prune unwanted blackberry canes underground to prevent plants from becoming invasive.**

the one-crop red raspberries (*R. idaeus).* It grows well in cold-winter areas. 'Willamette' is a midseason red berry popular in the Pacific Northwest. 'Latham' is a midseason, disease-resistant red berry commonly grown in the eastern United States. 'Pocahontas' is a hardy red raspberry bred for use in the South. 'Prelude' is an early, very hardy red berry. Black raspberries (*R. occidentalis)* are native to North America and the least tolerant of mild-winter climates. 'Cumberland' is a midseason black raspberry with large, firm fruits. 'Allen', 'Blackhawk', and 'Jewel' are popular cultivars in the Pacific Northwest. 'Bristol' grows well in the Southeast and Midwest. 'Brandywine' is an exceptionally vigorous purple raspberry. 'Royalty' has extra large purple fruits that are good fresh, frozen, or canned, and the plant is immune to raspberry aphids.

**Propagate blackberry canes by tip-layering.**

**Bend a cane over and bury it in the soil, then mulch.**

**When the tip is rooted, clip it from the mother plant.**

**Dig the rooted tip to relocate it to a new planting site.**

# GARDEN SAGE
### *Salvia officinalis* *SAL-vee-uh off-iss-ih-NAY-lis*

**Sage's pebbly-textured leaves are as ornamental as they are fragrant.**

**ZONES:** 4–10
**SIZE:** 1 ½–2'h x 2–3' w
**TYPE:** Woody perennial shrub

**GROWTH:** Average
**LIGHT:** Full sun to part shade
**MOISTURE:** Average
**FEATURES:** Edible leaves

**SITING:** Sage is adaptable to most soils but does best in rich loam that drains well. Plant it in spring where soils are heavy and in autumn in other conditions. Sage is not drought tolerant and will not thrive in standing water.

**CARE:** Trim sage to shape it after it has finished blooming, but leave the woody stems to resprout new growth. Dig plants in late autumn and pot them in containers to overwinter indoors in cold climates. Plant vigor diminishes after 4–6 years; replace old plants with new ones.

**PROPAGATION:** Grow from cuttings or division, or by layering.

**HARVEST:** Sage's pebbly-textured leaves can be cut the first year after planting. About 6–8" of succulent growth above the woody stems can be harvested two or three times before the plants bloom in summer. Take cuttings in the morning after the dew has dried; leaves cut in the heat of the day have reduced flavor. Rinse off any dust or dirt in cold water and shake off the excess. Tie cuttings together in small

**Plant rooted cuttings in rich soil that drains well. Replace plants every 4–6 years as vigor diminishes.**

bunches and hang upside down or spread out on screens in a dark, airy space to dry. Crumble the dried leaves off the stems and store in airtight jars up to 3 years. The fresh leaves are good snipped into egg and cheese dishes. The dried leaves are added to poultry stuffing and ground into a dry-rub powder for meats.

**PESTS AND DISEASES:** None are significant.

**RECOMMENDED CULTIVARS:** 'Icterina' is variegated green and gold. 'Tricolor' leaves are variegated green, cream, and purple. 'Extrakta' has smooth green leaves and is exceptionally flavorful. 'Dwarf White' is a good choice for small gardens and container growing. Its silver-white foliage and white flowers are aromatic, and the plant grows only to 12". Clary sage (*S. sclarea*) is a biennial to 5' tall that is grown for its essential oil. It can be invasive; some states ban its growth. Pineapple sage (*S. elegans*) has scarlet flowers that attract hummingbirds. It is a half-hardy perennial grown as an ornamental annual, but the leaves are edible and have a fruity aroma. Mediterranean sage (*S. fructicosa*) is often sold commercially for culinary use. White sage (*S. apiana*) is dried and bundled as "smudge sticks," a type of incense.

# SALAD BURNET
### *Sanguisorba minor* *san-gwih-SOR-buh MY-nor*

**Salad burnet, also called pimpernel and burnet bloodwort, is cold hardy.**

**ZONES:** 4–9
**SIZE:** 1–2' h x 1'w
**TYPE:** Herbaceous evergreen perennial
**GROWTH:** Fast

**LIGHT:** Full sun to part shade
**MOISTURE:** Average
**FEATURES:** Edible leaves

**SITING:** Choose a permanent location at one side of the garden or in a nearby perennial bed or border. Start seed indoors 4–6 weeks before the last frost date or direct-sow in spring in warm climates. Salad burnet is adaptable to most soils and grows well in large containers. It will thrive interplanted with peas or lettuce.

**CARE:** Use mulch around plants to conserve moisture and reduce weeds. Salad burnet may reseed itself; if so, develop new seedlings each year for the

**Grow salad burnet if there is no room for cucumbers in the garden. The leaves have a similar flavor.**

most vigorous plants. Prune off flower heads to encourage leaf growth. The plants are extremely cold hardy, but mulch them well for overwintering north of Zone 4.

**PROPAGATION:** Grow from seed.

**HARVEST:** Begin cutting salad burnet about 70 days from seeding or 30 days after setting established plants in the garden. The leaves are high in vitamin C and have a mild cucumber flavor. Use fresh leaves only; they lose their color and flavor when dried or frozen. Because salad burnet tastes like cucumber, the leaves are perfect in salads, vinegars, butters, and tomato juice. A few blooming stems make an attractive aromatic and edible plate garnish.

**PESTS AND DISEASES:** No significant disease problems affect salad burnet. Beneficial insects control most pests.

**RECOMMENDED CULTIVARS:** Salad burnet is a good herb to grow in small gardens without room for cucumbers. It is sold under its common name and also as pimpernel, burnet bloodwort, and great burnet. It also may be labeled by its alternate name, *Poterium sanguisorba*.

# SAVORY
### *Satureja* spp. *sat-yew-REE-yuh*

**Annual summer savory has a sweet flavor that goes well with beans.**

**ZONES:** 2–11
**SIZE:** 3–18"h x 2–24"w
**TYPE:** Herbaceous annual or semievergreen perennial
**GROWTH:** Average
**LIGHT:** Full sun
**MOISTURE:** Average
**FEATURES:** Edible leaves

**SITING:** Savory is adaptable to most soils. Direct-sow summer savory after the last frost date in spring in northern climates or anytime during the growing season in mild-winter zones. It does not transplant easily. Plant the seeds ½" deep and 1" apart. Interplant with beans, beets, eggplant, or cucumbers. Start winter savory seed indoors 4–6 weeks before the last frost date or plant rooted cuttings after the soil warms.

**CARE:** Keep the soil consistently moist but not waterlogged. Hand-weed around young plants. Trim annual savory regularly to encourage new growth. Prune perennial savory to a miniature hedge.

**PROPAGATION:** Grow either type from seed; grow the perennial from cuttings.

**HARVEST:** Summer savory is ready to harvest in 60–70 days from sowing seeds.

**Perennial winter savory has a stronger piney scent and taste.**

Winter savory can be trimmed the first time 50 days after planting cuttings or 75–100 days after planting seed. Cut stems from either plant for drying when flowers begin to form. Spread them on screens or tie them in small bunches and hang upside-down in a dark, airy space. When the leaves are completely dry, strip them from the stems, making sure to remove any woody parts. Store the leaves in airtight containers for up to 2 years.

**PESTS AND DISEASES:** None are significant. Savory's essential oil repels some insects.

**RECOMMENDED CULTIVARS:** Summer savory *(S. hortensis)* is a sweet-flavored, upright annual with tiny white or pink flowers. 'Aromata' is a peppery cultivar bred for high leaf yields. Winter savory *(S. montana)* is a semievergreen spreading perennial with trailing stems and petite purple flowers. Its pine scent and flavor are stronger than summer savory's. 'Nana' is an extremely cold-hardy dwarf variety only 3" tall that spreads to 2'. African savory *(S. biflora)* has a spicy lemon aroma and flavor that blends well in sweet or savory dishes, but it is a tropical plant suitable only for Zones 9–11.

# EGGPLANT
### *Solanum melongena* *so-LAY-num mel-on-GEE-nuh*

**Eggplant thrives in heat and humidity and needs lots of plant food. It is also sometimes called aubergine.**

**ZONES:** NA
**SIZE:** 1–3'h x 1–2'w
**TYPE:** Annual
**GROWTH:** Average
**LIGHT:** Full sun
**MOISTURE:** Moderate
**FEATURES:** Edible fruits

**SITING:** Direct-sow eggplant in hot climates. In northern zones, start seeds indoors 8 weeks before the last frost date and transplant at least 2 weeks after the last frost. Use black plastic to warm the soil before planting in cool climates. Eggplant does best in rich, slightly acid, well-draining soil with compost added.

**CARE:** Eggplant thrives in high heat and humidity. Grow eggplant under tunnels, cloches, or row covers in cool climates to increase the temperature around the plants. Plants will not set fruit where nighttime temperatures are consistently below 65°F. Eggplant is a heavy feeder. Sidedress plants with well-rotted compost or manure and feed once a month with soluble plant food. Keep the area free of weeds, and mulch around the plants in hot weather to conserve soil moisture.

**PROPAGATION:** Grow eggplant from seed or transplants.

**HARVEST:** Cut fruits from the plant when they reach full cultivar color and are firm and glossy, about 60–90 days from transplanting.

**PESTS AND DISEASES:** Pick off and destroy any beetles, worms, and caterpillars. Shake or knock Colorado potato beetles off plants and onto a sheet early in the morning, then destroy them. Protect young plants from flea beetles with floating row covers. Choose virus-resistant cultivars. Use fungicide to prevent anthracnose. Follow clean cultural practices to avoid blights.

**RECOMMENDED CULTIVARS:** 'Ichiban' bears elongated purple fruits in 65 days. 'Neon' bears medium-size bright pinkish-purple fruits. 'Black' is a dark purple cultivar with 4–6" fruits ready in 70–75 days. 'Rosa Bianca' is an almost round Italian white eggplant blushed with purple. 'Black Beauty' is a plump heirloom variety with large fruits ready for harvest in 80–85 days.

**Eggplant is ready to harvest when firm and glossy.**

**Clip ripe fruits regularly to promote new ones.**

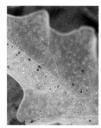

**Use row covers to protect plants from flea beetles.**

# POTATO
*Solanum tuberosum* *so-LAY-num too-ber-OH-sum*

**Potatoes come in a variety of shapes, sizes, and colors.**

**ZONES:** NA
**SIZE:** 1 ½'h x 1 ½'w
**TYPE:** Annual
**GROWTH:** Average

**LIGHT:** Full sun to part shade
**MOISTURE:** Average
**FEATURES:** Edible tubers

**SITING:** Choose a sunny location with well-drained, acid soil amended with lots of organic matter but where no lime has been added previously. If possible, grow an autumn green manure crop where potatoes will grow and turn it under before planting in spring. In small gardens grow potatoes in their own raised bed. Potatoes grow best planted in cool climates 2–4 weeks before the last frost date. Use commercial seed tubers; grocery store potatoes are usually treated to inhibit sprouting. Cut whole seed potatoes into pieces, each with one or two eyes and some fleshy tuber attached. Dry the pieces overnight before planting them to help protect them from rot. Plant the pieces eyes up in trenches dug 4" deep in heavy soil and 6" deep in light soil. Space them 12-15" apart in rows 20-24" apart, depending on the mature size of the cultivar, and cover with 2–4" of soil. Presprouted seed potatoes will lead to faster development of the tubers.

**CARE:** Keep the soil consistently moist but not waterlogged until the plants emerge. Thereafter water in periods of high heat or when rainfall is inadequate. Tubers develop best when the daytime air temperature is 60–65°F and nighttime temperatures are about 10 degrees cooler, but there are cultivars available for warm climates. Potatoes are heavy feeders; provide plant food higher in phosphorus and potassium than in nitrogen, which reduces plant vigor and can lead to disease. Begin hilling soil around the bottoms of the stems when the plants are 6–8" tall and repeat frequently as they grow taller. Hilling builds up the area where the tubers will develop. When the plants reach full height, add mulch on top of the hills to conserve moisture and hold weeds down. Cover any tubers that poke through

the surface with more mulch. Tubers exposed to the sun turn green and develop a mild toxin. Work around and harvest potatoes when the plants and soil are dry.
**PROPAGATION:** Grow from seed "eyes" or pieces of sprouting tubers.
**HARVEST:** Potatoes are a universal culinary ingredient good boiled, baked, fried, mashed, roasted, and scalloped, added to soups and stews and meat hash, and dried and ground into flour. New potatoes are delicious cooked with spring peas. Early varieties are best suited for use as new potatoes, which can be harvested as soon as they reach usable size. Check them about a week after the plants flower to see if they are ready. Carefully loosen the soil with a digging fork and reach in by hand to pull those you want away from the parent plant. Continue harvesting until the plant tops have died back, then pull up the entire plants with a garden fork to get those that remain. You can leave potatoes to cure in the ground for up to a few weeks after the tops die if you garden in a warm, dry climate. Pest- or disease-damaged tubers are still edible once the bad spots are removed but won't store well. Potatoes that have frozen in the ground are inedible. Brush any loose dirt off harvested potatoes and cure them unwashed in a dark, humid spot at 65–70°F for about 2 weeks. Then move them to a cool, dark, humid garage, shed, or cellar for storage at 35–40°F for up to 9 months. Potatoes bruise easily; handle them gently.
**PESTS AND DISEASES:** Keeping the soil pH acidic helps to prevent scab disease. Use a fungicide to prevent anthracnose. Follow clean cultural practices to avoid blights; destroy vegetative debris where pests may overwinter. Rotate crops each year. Choose virus-resistant cultivars. Pick off and destroy any beetles, worms, and caterpillars. Shake or knock Colorado potato beetles off plants and onto a sheet early in the morning, then destroy them. Use Bt or a neem-based insecticide if

infestations are severe. Control leafhoppers with insecticidal soap. Use floating row covers to protect young plants from flea beetles. Interplant potatoes with taller crops that provide some shade, which flea beetles do not tolerate. If gophers are a problem, catch them in traps.
**RECOMMENDED CULTIVARS:** Early-maturing varieties ready to harvest in 55–75 days include 'Adora', 'Charlotte', and 'Yukon Gold', all yellow fleshed. 'Shepody' is a blocky white-skinned potato good for French fries. 'Red Pontiac' is a highly adaptable, easy-to-grow red potato. 'Purple Peruvian' is a medium to large fingerling potato with purple skin and flesh. Fingerling 'Red Thumb' has red skin and red flesh. Midseason varieties mature in 80–90 days. 'Bellisle' is a Canadian white cultivar good for mashed potatoes. 'Ida Rose' is an Idaho potato with rose-red skin and white flesh. 'Island Sunshine' is a yellow-skinned potato with yellow flesh. It's resistant to late blight. 'Kennebec' is the well-known Maine potato with tan skin and white flesh. It's an especially good baking potato and stores well. 'Pink Wink' is a floury-textured Irish potato with pink eyes. 'Red Gold' has red skin and yellow flesh. It sprouts in storage. 'Saginaw Gold' is a virus-resistant yellow potato that keeps well until midspring. 'Sieglinde' is an old German heirloom yellow potato popular for its thin skin and good flavor. 'Viking Red' is a fast-growing, heat-resistant red-skinned variety. 'Anna Cheeka' is an Ozette fingerling potato with pale gold skin and creamy yellow flesh best cooked only lightly to bring out its nutty flavor. Late-maturing potatoes are ready to harvest in 90 or more days. 'Butte' is a russet variety resistant to scab and late blight. 'German Butterball' is an award-winning yellow cultivar. Try 'Nooksack', a russet baker, in coastal regions. 'Russian Banana' is an easy-to-grow fingerling potato with excellent disease resistance. For information on sweet potatoes, see page 88.

**1** **Cut seed potatoes into pieces that each have eyes.**

**2** **Dry them overnight and then plant them eyes-up in trenches.**

**3** **Loosen soil with a digging fork to harvest potatoes.**

**4** **Brush off loose dirt and cure them in a cool, dark spot.**

# SPINACH
## *Spinacea oleracea* spin-ACH-ee-uh oh-ler-AY-see-uh

**Semi-savoyed spinach cultivars are bred for cultivation in warm weather.**

**ZONES:** NA
**SIZE:** 3–8"h x 2–8"w
**TYPE:** Annual
**GROWTH:** Fast
**LIGHT:** Full sun to part shade
**MOISTURE:** Average
**FEATURES:** Edible leaves

**SITING:** Soak spinach seed overnight and sow it directly into fertile, moist, well-drained soil. Broadcast the seed in a patch, or plant it ¼" deep and 1" apart in rows 12" apart. Spinach seed will germinate at soil temperatures as low as 35°F, so begin planting 4–6 weeks before the last spring frost date in northern climates.

**CARE:** Thin plants to 6" apart when they reach 3" tall. Keep the soil consistently moist and mulch to keep the roots cool. Water in the morning so that plants have time to dry and keep them thinned for good air circulation to avoid rust. Make successive sowings of spinach every few weeks to extend the harvest until late spring. In warmer weather plant cultivars slow to bolt. You can grow spinach year-round in mild-winter climates and even through the winter in a cold frame in all but the coldest northern zones.
**PROPAGATION:** Grow from seed.
**HARVEST:** Leaves are large enough to harvest in 35–50 days.
**PESTS AND DISEASES:** Cover young plants with floating row covers to protect them from leaf miners and flea beetles. Aphids can be knocked off by a strong spray from the garden hose. Handpick and destroy caterpillars. Choose cultivars that are resistant to downy mildew and mosaic virus.
**RECOMMENDED CULTIVARS:** Smooth-leaf spinaches such as 'Olympia' grow best in cool weather. Semi-savoyed cultivars such as 'Tyee', 'Space', and 'Melody' are slow to bolt. Savoyed types such as 'Winter Bloomsdale' are deeply crinkled and grow best in autumn and winter. 'Nordic' is a smooth-leaf type that thrives in cold weather. Grow heat- and drought-resistant spinach look-alikes in extremely hot climates. Malabar spinach (*Basella alba* 'Rubra'), is a tropical, tender perennial usually grown as an annual in the United States. New Zealand spinach (*Tetragonia expansa*) is a succulent annual slow to germinate but extremely heat-tolerant.

**Grow spinach in a coldframe for winter harvest.**

# THYME
## *Thymus vulgaris* TY-mus vul-GARE-is

**Creeping thyme forms a low ground cover that is ornamental as well as flavorful.**

**ZONES:** 4–9
**SIZE:** 3–12"h x spreading
**TYPE:** Herbaceous perennial
**GROWTH:** Average
**LIGHT:** Full sun to part shade
**MOISTURE:** Average
**FEATURES:** Edible leaves

**SITING:** Plant divisions in spring in average, well-drained soil. Space plants 8–12" apart, or interplant with Solanaceae family rops—tomatoes, potatoes, eggplant, and peppers. Thyme can also be grown in containers indoors or out.
**CARE:** Water when needed to maintain soil moisture, but do not overwater. Clear weeds by hand. Shear off the tiny flowers after plants finish blooming to keep energy concentrated in the leaves. Plants may lose vigor and need replacing in a few years.
**PROPAGATION:** Grow by division or from cuttings or layering.
**HARVEST:** Strip the leaves from the stems and use in salads, soups, stews, stuffings, vinegars, and vegetables. Thyme blends well with almost any beef, pork, poultry, or seafood dish and adds a sophisticated flavor to cheese and egg dishes. Harvest handfuls of the stems and tie small bundles together. Hang them upside down in a cool, airy room to dry. When the leaves are completely dry, crumble them off the stems and store in airtight glass jars for up to 2 years.
**PESTS AND DISEASES:** None are significant. Roots may rot if plants are overwatered.
**RECOMMENDED CULTIVARS:** Thymes labeled French or English are intended for cooking, but many of the creeping *T. serpyllum* and *T. pulegioides* ground cover cultivars can do double duty in the kitchen. Of the common varieties, 'German Winter' is an especially hardy thyme good for cold-winter climates. Grow 'Summer Thyme' as an annual above Zone 6. It is smaller than average with a spicier flavor. Try 'Orange Balsam Thyme' straight from the plant on fish and vegetable dishes. It is hardy to Zone 5. 'Hi Ho Silver' is a green and white variegated cultivar, hardy to Zone 4. 'Italian Oregano Thyme' tastes like the name implies and is hardy to Zone 5. 'Lemon' and 'Lime' thymes (*T. ×citriodorus*) have a citrusy fragrance but the flavor is lost in cooking. They are hardy to Zone 4.

**Thyme thrives interplanted with peppers, potatoes, tomatoes, and eggplants.**

# HIGHBUSH BLUEBERRY

*Vaccinium corymbosum* *vak-SIN-ee-um kor-im-BOH-sum*

Tasty blue fruits and colorful red fall foliage make blueberries outstanding additions to the landscape.

**ZONES:** 3–9
**SIZE:** 1½–7'h x 2–10'w
**TYPE:** Woody perennial shrub
**GROWTH:** Slow

**LIGHT:** Full sun
**MOISTURE:** Moderate
**FEATURES:** Edible berries

**SITING:** Choose a sunny, breezy location in well-drained, sandy, acid loam with a pH of 4.5–5.5. Have the soil tested before planting to determine pH and what amendments are needed. If possible, grow a green manure cover crop on the site and till it under before planting blueberries. Plant them in spring in northern zones and in late fall in the South, in holes spaced 6' apart for highbush plants, 2' apart for lowbush, and 3–4' for dwarf or hedge highbush varieties. No plant food should be added to the holes. Keep the plants continuously moist before planting them. Carefully spread the roots out and firm the soil around them, then water well. Set bare-root stock at the same depth it was grown in the nursery, then cut the plants back by half to remove buds.

**CARE:** Because blueberry roots lack root hairs, they are sensitive to changes in soil moisture. Keep the plants consistently moist. They need 1–2" of good-quality water low in mineral salts each week. Harvested fruits retain their stems if drought stressed. Spread mulch 6–8" deep and 2–4' wide along the row. Feed plants each year at flowering with acidic compost or plant food for acid-loving plants. Excessive nitrogen causes low yields. Blueberries fruit on 1-year-old wood. Pinch off developing fruits until plants are 3–4 years old, to encourage the bush to grow. Blueberries tend to overbear, which wears out the plants in just a few years if left unchecked. Prune them with loppers when they are fully dormant in late winter. Flower

buds will be visible on 1-year-old wood. Heavy pruning results in earlier ripening, which may be especially desirable in the South, and also yields larger berries. Renewal-prune annually to remove old canes. In the first 2 years of growth, remove weak, diseased, or damaged canes only. In subsequent years remove weak, diseased, or damaged canes along with some of the oldest canes. Remove excess young canes to encourage the growth of others, and prune to reduce the density of the branches at the tops of plants. Careful selection of canes to prune helps to balance the fruit load on the plant in the next season. Each mature plant should have 15–25 canes of varying ages. Canes decline in productivity after 5–6 years.

**PROPAGATION:** Grow from rooted cuttings.

**HARVEST:** Blueberries are ready to pick 2–4 months after flowering, from July to September. Hold a container in one hand and use your other hand to gently loosen berries from the cluster so they drop into the container. Ripening berries turn from green to pinkish red to blue, but not all blue ones are fully ripe. Blueberries are extremely perishable. Store them unwashed in the refrigerator for up to 1 week. Enjoy them fresh out of hand or on cereals and in fruit salads, or cooked in baked goods, jams, and preserves. They also make delicious sweet wine. Rinse and dry berries and freeze them in single layers in plastic for long-term storage. Blueberries can also be dried and stored in airtight containers for up to 3 years.

**PESTS AND DISEASES:** Choose cultivars bred for resistance to viruses. Use labeled fungicides according to directions to control phomopsis canker, root rot, mummyberry, and twig blight. Japanese beetles may bother blueberries in the home garden. Keep the ground clean of dropped fruit and vegetative debris to discourage fruit flies and maggots. Use insecticidal sprays if needed to control them and fruit worms, curculios,

leafhoppers, scale, and borers, but avoid spraying when plants are in bloom to protect beneficial insect pollinators such as bumblebees and southeastern blueberry bees. Use reflective tape or balloons, noisemakers, or netting that covers the plants all the way to the ground to protect ripening fruits from birds.

**RECOMMENDED CULTIVARS:** The most commonly grown blueberry is the highbush (*V. corymbosum*). It is native to the eastern United States and grows to 8' where soil is highly acid and drains well. Highbush is a hardy blueberry species, requiring 650–850 chilling hours and 160 frost-free days. The buds are hardy to –20°F, the stems to –30°F, and the flowers to 25–30°F. 'Earliblue', 'Bluetta', and 'Duke' are early cultivars. 'Spartan' is a good choice for regions with late spring frosts; it blooms late but ripens early. Late-ripening cultivars include 'Blueray', a large-fruited variety good for hot climates, and 'Berkeley', which grows well in light soils. 'Olympia' has good flavor and freezes well. 'Coville' is resistant to phomopsis canker. 'Lateblue' and 'Elliott' are medium-size berries good for eating fresh. 'Sierra' is an interspecific hybrid of *V. darrowi, V. corymbosum, V. ashei*, and *V. constablaei* that requires 1,000 chilling hours. Rabbit-eye blueberry (*V. ashei*) is a highbush species native to the southeastern United States that can reach 20' tall. It needs only 250 chilling hours, tolerates heat and dry weather, and is hardy to Zone 7. It ripens later than northern highbush types, and the fruits are not as sweet off the vine but are good for baking. Because it is partially or completely self-sterile, rabbit-eye blueberry requires pollenizers. The fruits are sometimes shiny; frequent harvests promote their ripening. 'Climax' is an early cultivar with good flavor. 'Premier' is a large, early- to midseason cultivar with superior flavor. 'Centurion' is adapted to heavy soils; it blooms late and ripens late. It is a good dessert fruit. Southern

Choose cultivars resistant to canker.

**1** Test the soil before planting to determine pH and what amendments are needed.

**2** Plant bare-root stock at the same depth it was grown in the nursery.

# HIGHBUSH BLUEBERRY
*continued*

Highbush blueberry is a hardy and common species, with cultivars available for a variety of regions.

Rabbit-eye is a highbush blueberry for southern climates. The berries are tart and good for baking.

highbush cultivars include crosses of *V. australe* and *V. corymbosum* with *V. darrowi* as well as crosses of highbush and lowbush called half-high blueberries, bred to create southern-type fruits on plants that are hardy to –20°F. They are self-sterile and require pollenizers. 'Sapphire', 'Sharpblue', and 'Gulf Coast' are popular in Florida. 'Northland' and 'St. Cloud' are early cultivars; 'Northblue' is midseason; and 'Northcountry' is good for northern zones. It has the naturally sweet flavor of its lowbush ancestor. Lowbush blueberry (*V. angustifolium*) is the native species that thrives in the northeastern United States. *V. myrtilloides* is the lowbush species of eastern Canada. The wild plants are managed with sprays and pruning for best yields. Multiple plants are necessary for successful pollination. They are hardy to –20°F and need 1,000 chilling hours below 45°F. The branches spread like a ground cover to 2'. Huckleberry (*V. ovatum* and others) is a related evergreen plant with small, edible blue berries. It grows best in cool, dry climates. Lingonberry (*V. vitis-idaea*), also called cowberry, is a creeping evergreen hardy to Zone 2 that bears small, sour, cranberrylike fruits. Bilberry (*V. myrtillus*) is a deciduous shrub that thrives in the Pacific Northwest. Its aromatic purple berries are used in jam, jelly, and wine.

# CRANBERRY
*Vaccinium macrocarpon* vak-SIN-ee-um mak-roh-KAR-pon

Cranberries thrive in the acidic soil of swamps, bogs, and shorelines.

**ZONES:** 3–8
**SIZE:** 1'h x 4'-6'w
**TYPE:** Woody evergreen perennial shrub
**GROWTH:** Slow

**LIGHT:** Full sun to part shade
**MOISTURE:** High
**FEATURES:** Edible berries

**SITING:** Cranberry grows best in cool climates, planted in weed-free acid soil in the standing water of swamps and bogs or along wet shorelines. Plant 6–8"-long cuttings 18" apart in peat or sandy acid loam where the top 6" of soil can be kept constantly moist year-round to prevent wind desiccation in freezing temperatures.

**CARE:** Cranberry is not truly hardy and is susceptible to fungal diseases in warm climates. Because the roots have no root hairs, the plants won't tolerate drought. Cranberry plants self-pollinate but yield bigger crops if pollinated by bumblebees. Keep the planting area weed free. Pruning is required only to reduce the density of upright branches on vigorous plants.
**PROPAGATION:** Grow from rooted cuttings.
**HARVEST:** Use a berry scoop to pick the shiny berries in mid- to late autumn when they turn red. Rinse them thoroughly and discard any that are shriveled or damaged. Cranberries are too tart to eat raw, but the sweetened fruits are used in juice cocktail, baked goods, stuffings, relishes, gelatin salads, citrus fruit salads, chutneys, marinades, and condiments for meat, poultry, and fish. Fresh unwashed berries keep in the refrigerator for up to 3 weeks but can be frozen for long-term storage or dried to use like raisins. Cranberries are traditionally strung together in strands to use as holiday decorations in December.
**PESTS AND DISEASES:** Cranberries are largely untroubled in the home garden. Keep the dropped fruit and vegetative debris where pests can hide picked up and destroyed. Use insecticidal sprays if needed to control serious insect infestations, but avoid spraying when plants are in bloom to protect beneficial pollinators. Pick off and destroy Japanese beetles. Pests in commercial plantings are controlled with periodic flooding; try that at home only if your plants are located in a suitable low-lying spot where you can add sand to cover the roots afterward. Flooding in winter also protects plants from cold injury. Use reflective tape or balloons, noisemakers, or netting to protect ripening fruits from birds.
**RECOMMENDED CULTIVARS:** Cranberry is native to North America, where it thrives in swampy areas primarily in the northeastern United States, upper Midwest, and Pacific Northwest. They are closely related to blueberries and huckleberries. 'HyRed', 'Franklin', and 'Beaver' are early cultivars; 'Ben Lear', 'Crowley', 'Stevens', and 'Bergman' are all midseason varieties; and 'Pilgrim' is late. Highbush cranberry (*Viburnum* spp.) is unrelated. It bears small, tart, cranberrylike fruits used in jam, syrup, and wine.

# MÂCHE, CORN SALAD

*Valerianella locusta* *vuh-lair-ee-uh-NEL-luh loh-KOO-stuh*

**Mâche, also called corn salad or lamb's lettuce, is the smallest mesclun-mix leaf.**

**ZONES:** NA
**SIZE:** 2–4"h x 4–8"w
**TYPE:** Annual
**GROWTH:** Fast
**LIGHT:** Full sun to part shade
**MOISTURE:** Average
**FEATURES:** Edible leaves

**SITING:** Mâche is often included in mesclun salad seed mixes but is easier to manage by itself because of its small size. Sow anytime in early spring or autumn. Broadcast seed in a small, moist patch of rich soil at least 1' square that has been cleared of all weeds, or in clearly marked rows 6" apart so that seedlings will be distinguishable from weeds. Mâche, also called lamb's lettuce because sheep graze on it in Europe, looks much like a broadleaf weed and can get lost among true weeds in the garden. Cover the seeds with ¼" of fine soil or sand and gently water.

**CARE:** Begin thinning plants when the rosettes of leaves are large enough to grasp—about 3". Use the thinnings in salads. Make successive plantings every 3 weeks for a continuous supply. Water as necessary to maintain soil moisture. Mâche is a cold-weather plant hardy to 5°F and easy to grow throughout the winter. Even in northern zones you can grow it in a cold frame or in the open garden with just some straw mulch. Cold weather enhances the flavor. It tastes good even if it has been frozen.

**PROPAGATION:** Grow from seed.

**HARVEST:** Mâche is ready to harvest about 50 days from planting. Pinch off leaf clusters or pull entire plants when they are 3–4" tall. When the plants send up flower stalks in hot weather, harvest the whole crop and sow new seed if daytime temperatures are still below 80°F. The spoon-shaped leaves add a mildly nutty flavor to salads and sandwiches. They can also be steamed or boiled and prepared like cole-crop greens or added to soups and stews a few minutes before serving. Store the unwashed leaves in the crisper drawer of the refrigerator for up to 2 weeks. Rinse leaves well before eating to remove any sand or dirt.

**PESTS AND DISEASES:** None are significant.

**RECOMMENDED CULTIVARS:** 'Jade' holds its elongated dark blue-green leaves upright and is resistant to mildew and yellows. 'Vit' also has an upright habit and a mild, minty flavor. 'Broad Leaved' is heat tolerant and a good choice for temperate climates. 'Gross Graine' is a slightly larger plant popular in Europe. 'Verte D'Etampes' has crinkly leaves like savoy cabbage.

# FAVA BEAN

*Vicia faba* *VEE-see-uh FAY-buh*

**Grow fava beans, also known as broad beans or horse beans, on a trellis to support the long vines and pods.**

**ZONES:** NA
**SIZE:** 12–72"h x 6–24"w
**TYPE:** Annual
**GROWTH:** Fast
**LIGHT:** Full sun
**MOISTURE:** High
**FEATURES:** Edible seeds

**SITING:** Choose a sunny location where legumes have not been grown in the last 3 years. Dust dampened seeds with rhizobial inoculant before planting to fix nitrogen in the soil. *Vicia* is adaptable and more tolerant of acidity than other beans but does best in rich loam. Sow seed 4–8 weeks before the last frost date, 2–4" deep and 6" apart in rows 18–24" apart. Fava bean also can be grown as a winter annual in subtropical zones that have no frost.

**CARE:** Fava beans do best in areas with a long, cool growing season. The long, vining plants require staking or trellising to support the developing pods. Beans prefer daytime temperatures of 70–80°F and may drop their blossoms above 85°F. They are also sensitive to frost. Temperatures below 35°F kill the flowers and pods. Bean plants are tender and easily damaged by garden tools, so weed by hand if possible. Keep the soil consistently moist, but water only in the morning so the plants dry quickly, which reduces the potential for disease. Extremes in soil moisture result in malformed pods. To avoid injury to the plants and the spread of fungal spores, work around and harvest beans only when they are not wet. Beans supply their own nitrogen but benefit from a monthly application of soluble plant food high in phosphorus and potassium.

**PROPAGATION:** Grow from seed.

**HARVEST:** The beans mature 90–200 days after planting. Pull up the plants when the lower pods are full and dry and the upper ones are developed but still green. Use a sheet under the plants to catch any seeds that fall when dry pods shatter. The seeds can be canned when fully developed but not dry. Pinch the beans from their protective coatings before use.

**PESTS AND DISEASES:** Choose cultivars bred for resistance to blights, rust, and anthracnose and pretreated with fungicide. Practice crop rotation to avoid diseases that live in the soil. All beans are attacked by a host of damaging insects, including aphids, thrips, beetles, weevils, mites, stinkbugs, and tarnished plant bugs. The Mexican bean beetle is the main pest in home gardens; it lays its eggs on the underside of bean leaves. Handpick and destroy eggs and larvae, or use neem oil for heavy infestations. Ask your local extension agent which other pests are most common in your locale and how to deter them. Avoid using insecticides when the plant is in bloom; fava bean flowers attract beneficial ladybugs and predatory wasps and are pollinated by bumblebees.

**RECOMMENDED CULTIVARS:** Windsor cultivars, also called broad beans, horse beans, or English beans, have short pods containing four large seeds each. 'Aprovecho' is ready for harvest in 75–85 days or 140–180 days if planted in fall. Longpod or tick types contain up to eight smaller seeds. 'Banner' is a cold-tolerant variety good for overwintering in areas with mild winters. It is ready for harvest in 80–90 days, or 200–240 days if fall planted.

# COWPEA
### Vigna unguiculata *VIG-nuh un-gwih-kew-LAH-tuh*

Cowpea, also known as black-eyed pea or Southern pea, is actually a type of bean grown for green shelling or dried use.

**ZONES:** NA
**SIZE:** 8–36"h x 6–24"w
**TYPE:** Annual
**GROWTH:** Average
**LIGHT:** Full sun
**MOISTURE:** Average
**FEATURES:** Edible seeds

**SITING:** Choose a sunny location where legumes have not been grown in the last 3 years. Dust dampened seeds with rhizobial inoculant before planting to fix nitrogen in the soil for the crop that follows the cowpeas. Plant cowpeas 1–1½" deep and 2–4" apart in rows 12–24" apart in well-drained, acid, sandy, loam when the soil temperature is at least 65°F. Seeds may rot in cool, wet soils. Strongly determinate bush types can be planted closer together than indeterminate vines.

**CARE:** Cowpea has a long taproot and is more drought resistant than common beans. It is a warm-season crop that does best in humidity but is also adapted to dry conditions. Keep the soil consistently moist from planting through bloom and control weeds. Remove and destroy any plants showing signs of infection or infestation.

**PROPAGATION:** Grow from seed.

**HARVEST:** Cowpea can be used at any stage of development but is most often used as a green-mature bean in western cooking, ready for harvest 70–90 days after planting. Store the shelled seeds in the warmest part of the refrigerator and use them within a few days.

**PESTS AND DISEASES:** Choose cultivars bred for resistance to bacteria and viruses and pretreated with fungicide for prevention of blights, rots, rusts, and anthracnose. Practice crop rotation to avoid diseases that live in the soil. All beans are visited by a host of damaging insects, including cowpea curculio, aphids, thrips, beetles, mites, stinkbugs, and tarnished plant bugs. The Mexican bean beetle is the main pest in home gardens; it lays its eggs on the underside of bean leaves. Handpick and destroy eggs and larvae or use neem oil for heavy infestations. Ask your local extension agent which pests are most common in your locale and how to deter them. Avoid using insecticides; cowpea flowers attract beneficial insects.

**RECOMMENDED CULTIVARS:** There are vining, semivining, and bush types; all grow well in humid climates, but bush types do best in northern climates. Seed coats may be speckled or have a distinctive spot or "eye." Pods are 6–10" long and can be green, yellow, or purple as the seeds reach green maturity but turn tan or brown when dry. 'Whippoorwill' is a climbing type grown for its dried seeds. 'California Blackeye' is good for green-mature cooking. Adzuki bean (*V. angularis*), bears small, oval dark red beans used to make sweet bean paste, a popular ingredient in Asian cuisines. Another related species, mung bean (*V. radiata*), is grown primarily for bean sprouts.

# ASPARAGUS BEAN
### Vigna unguiculata ssp. *sesquipedalis* *VIG-nuh un-gwih-kew-LAH-tuh seh-skwih-peh-DAY-lis*

Asparagus or yard-long beans will grow to 3' but aren't tender at that length.

**ZONES:** NA
**SIZE:** 6–12'h x 1½–2½'w
**TYPE:** Annual
**GROWTH:** Average
**LIGHT:** Full sun
**MOISTURE:** Moderate
**FEATURES:** Edible seeds and immature pods

**SITING:** Choose a sunny location where legumes have not been grown in the last 3 years. Dust dampened seeds with rhizobial inoculant before planting. Plant seeds 1–2" deep and 12" apart in rows 3–4' apart after all danger of frost has passed and the soil temperature is at least 65°F.

**CARE:** Plants require support on poles or trellises. Train the vines on their supports; if needed attach them loosely with figure-eight loops of soft twine. To encourage fruiting pinch out the terminal ends of vines when they reach the top of the supports. Consistent soil moisture keeps the pods from turning tough and fibrous. Yard-long beans thrive in high heat and do not tolerate frost or cool temperatures.

**PROPAGATION:** Grow from seed.

**HARVEST:** The pods are ready to harvest when they are 10–12" long but before the

Yard-long beans are related to cowpeas and are grown for the immature pods, which are eaten like snap beans.

seeds have filled out, about 7–10 days from flowering. Pick pods every few days for maximum tenderness. Yard-long beans will live up to their name if allowed to mature, but at 3' long the pods are too tough to eat and the beans should be shelled out and used like cowpeas. Keep freshly harvested pods moist and cool to prevent rusty-looking patches from developing. Store them in the refrigerator for up to 1 week.

**PESTS AND DISEASES:** Plants will outgrow thrip infestations, but black bean aphids and Mexican bean beetles may require treatment with a labeled insecticide. Avoid using insecticides when the plants are in bloom to protect beneficial insects that pollinate the flowers. Choose cultivars bred for resistance to bacteria and viruses and pretreated with fungicide to prevent blights, rots, rusts, and anthracnose.

**RECOMMENDED CULTIVARS:** 'Liana' vines grow vigorously to 12' if not pinched back. 'Orient Extra Long' thrives in the heat and humidity of tropical zones. 'Red Stripe' is a good choice for home gardens and will tolerate cool temperatures. The seeds have red and white stripes.

# GRAPE

*Vitis* spp. *VY-tis*

**American grapes, also called fox or Concord grapes, must be sprayed.**

**ZONES:** 4–10

**SIZE:** 4–10'h x 6–12'w

**TYPE:** Woody perennial vine

**GROWTH:** Fast

**LIGHT:** Full sun

**MOISTURE:** Moderate

**FEATURES:** Edible berries

**SITING:** Choose a south- or east-facing slope in an area with good air circulation to prevent mildew and rot. Grapes adapt to all soils but do best in deep, well-drained, light, slightly acid to neutral soil. Table grapes grow best in areas with long, hot, dry summers and mild winters. Wine and muscadine grapes thrive in humid temperate climates, but muscadines need a longer growing season and milder winter than Concord grapes. In late winter or early spring, dig the holes 1' in diameter, leaving adequate room to place a stake, post, or trellis before the roots are positioned. Position the lowest bud on the trunk even with the soil line. Tamp soil lightly over the roots and flood the hole with water, repeating until the soil settles at ground level.

**CARE:** Test the soil every 3–5 years. Highly fertile soil detracts from the flavor of wine grapes. Irrigation also may be harmful and even illegal for wine grapes but is beneficial for table and raisin grapes. Spread mulch around the base of the vines for protection in cold-winter areas. In extremely cold winter zones, untie the vines and bend them to the ground, then cover them with soil or straw. Provide

windbreaks in exposed areas. Rake back the mulch in spring, add new well-rotted compost or manure, and replace the mulch.

To train a grapevine to a wire trellis, begin the winter after planting. Prune off all shoots but the strongest cane to train as the trunk. Tie it loosely to an upright support pole. When the trunk grows as tall as the first wire (3' above ground) in the next season, prune out all but two branches to form two main lateral arms, and tie those in either direction along the wire. Each year cut fruiting growth back to three nodes. When the main trunk reaches the height of the second wire (5½' above ground), select another pair of strong canes to train as arms like the first ones, then cut off the top of the trunk above the wire. In each following spring prune out all other canes coming off the trunk and suckers growing from the base.

Spurs and canes grow from the permanent trunk and arms (called cordons) trained to the trellis. Grapes fruit on lateral shoots from the current season's woody growth. All grapes should be pruned each year as close to the arms as possible to produce the best fruit. Without pruning, the grapes grow increasingly far from the main trunk on the ends of long canes. Wine grapes and muscadines are cane- or spur-pruned after the first three growing seasons; American grapes and 'Thompson Seedless' are cane-pruned only. To spur-train grapes, cut all side branches on lateral arms to two buds in winter. Two new shoots will grow on each remaining spur, and each of those will yield one to three fruit bunches. The spurs should be spaced 6" apart. Keep some one-bud renewal spurs to develop for next year's fruiting wood.

Cane pruning leaves two whole canes from the previous season and two additional canes near the head of the trunk, cut back to buds. Gather fruiting canes upward and tie them together toward the tip. Let growth from the

renewal buds trail. The Kniffen two-arm system leaves canes only on the top wire; the four-arm and six-arm systems leave canes at two or three levels. Use the four-arm and six-arm systems only where vigorous top growth on the higher wire will not shade out the canes on the bottom one. Growing grapes on an arbor is a good way to use vertical space in a small garden for ornamental as well as edible purposes. To grow vines on an arbor, train and tie one strong cane up a post as a trunk and prune out the side canes. When the trunk reaches the top of the arbor in the second or third season, select a single cane from it to develop as a cordon across the top of the framework. Then begin pruning to train two-bud spurs across the top. Head back all the vines in late winter to a few buds per cane. (Prune muscadines in early winter to reduce bleeding.) For very large arbors, grow vines up opposite posts and train canes to cross one another over the framework. Vigorous vines overproduce; thinning fruit bunches helps the remaining grapes to become sweet.

**PROPAGATION:** Grow by grafting, rooted cuttings, or layering.

**HARVEST:** Vines bear the second or third year after planting. American and table grapes are ready when they have reached full cultivar size and color, in about 150–165 days. Leave raisin grapes on the vines to ripen completely before picking. The best time to pick wine grapes depends on the type of wine to be made. Both the Brix (sugar) level and the pH are determining factors. Concord juice grapes are ready to harvest when the Brix level is about 15°. Use a digital wine refractometer to measure the Brix level. Muscadine grapes are ready for harvest in about 200 days. Clip grape clusters from the vines with sharp scissors and handle them as little as possible to avoid damage. Picking bunches with grapes of varying degrees of ripeness is desirable for making jelly and jam. Pick grapes for fresh eating and juice two or three times over a period of several

**Prune out all but two branches to form the lateral cordons (arms).**

**Tie grapevines loosely to a trellis or other strong support. Untie in winter to mulch.**

**Healthy vines bear too many bunches. Thin some to make the remaining fruits sweeter.**

**Cover ripening grapes with netting to protect them from hungry birds.**

# GRAPE

*continued*

weeks as the grapes ripen. Store them in the refrigerator for up to 2 weeks.

**PESTS AND DISEASES:** Many grape diseases can be prevented with good air circulation and clean cultural practices. Black rot overwinters on infected vines, leaves, and unpicked grapes. Keep vines pruned and trellised so that air circulates well. Choose cultivars resistant to botrytis bunch rot, downy mildew, and powdery mildew. Remove and destroy infected plants immediately. Copper and sulfur fungicides are effective controls but may damage the vines. Choose cultivars resistant to gall phylloxera and pretreated for crown gall. Pick and destroy grape berry moth cocoons and infested grapes and leaves. Spray labeled insecticide for heavy infestations of whiteflies and leafhoppers. Use sticky bands around trunks to control ants. Pick and destroy Japanese beetles. Scrape off loose bark to expose mealybugs. Keep old wood pruned out to control scale. Use netting, reflective tape, or balloons to discourage birds, or enclose whole bunches of ripening grapes in paper bags.

**RECOMMENDED CULTIVARS:** Most grapes are self-fruitful and self-pollinating. If you have pruned and maintained healthy plants in a sunny location but the fruits never sweeten, replant with another type. Ask your local extension agent which grapes are better suited to your area.

American grapes *(V. labrusca)*, also called fox grapes or Concord grapes after the main cultivar, grow well in all but the hottest climates and are adaptable to many soils. The fruits are slipskin type—a tough skin that separates easily from the pulpy flesh. American grapes are susceptible to disease and require spraying to obtain high yields of good-quality berries. 'Catawba' is a hardy red grape but more susceptible to fungal diseases than 'Concord'. 'Niagara' is not as cold hardy as 'Concord' and ripens earlier. The low-acid white grapes are eaten fresh or used in wine and juice. 'Delaware' is an early-ripening red grape. It does not thrive in heavy soils. Hybrids of American and riverbank grapes *(V. labrusca × V. riparia)* are especially cold hardy.

Muscadines *(V. rotundifolia)* are the best choice for gardens in the Deep South. They are not as hardy as other grapes but are highly disease resistant. 'Southland' is a large purple grape that grows well in the Gulf Coast states. 'Yuga' has sweet reddish bronze fruits of excellent quality that ripen late. 'Scuppernong' is an old cultivar with fruits good for eating fresh or making into wine.

**Hybrids of American and riverbank grapes are cold-hardy.**

To grow common or European grapes *(V. vinifera)* for wine, choose certified virus-free planting stock grafted to American grape rootstock. Most varieties are hardy to Zone 7 but few are grown outside of California. 'Chardonnay' is the most commonly grown white wine grape in the eastern United States. It is cold hardy but susceptible to botrytis bunch rot. 'Riesling' and 'Cabernet Franc' are more cold hardy but also susceptible. 'Pinot Blanc', the white-fruited form of 'Pinot Noir', has more resistance, as does 'Pinot Gris', although they are not as cold hardy. They grow well in the Pacific Northwest. 'Cabernet Sauvignon' is among the most cold-hardy and disease-resistant red wine grapes but ripens late. 'Pinot Noir' is fairly cold hardy and ripens early but is susceptible to bunch rot. 'Merlot' needs a long season to fully develop and tends to produce heavy canopies that shade the fruit and encourage bunch rot. 'Zinfandel' grapes are the most adaptable and can be used for white or red wine.

French-American hybrid grapes are grown primarily for making wine but also are good eaten fresh. 'Chambourcin', a late-ripening medium blue grape, needs a long growing season in a mild-winter climate. 'St. Croix' is a comparable grape that is very hardy and disease resistant. 'Maréchal Foch' and 'Léon Millot' are early, hardy, small black grapes that grow well in the Midwest. 'Cayuga White' is a popular

**Muscadine grapes grow well in the Deep South and are disease-resistant.**

dessert grape in the eastern United States. 'Ravat' is an early, hardy, disease-resistant vine with pink to red grapes used in white wines. 'Villard Blanc' requires a long growing season but produces good dessert grapes when fully ripe. 'Seyval' is commonly grown in dry climates east of the Rockies. 'LaCrosse' was derived from 'Seyval' but is earlier and more cold hardy.

Table grape clusters must be thinned to produce large grapes free from rot and insect damage. 'Kay Gray' is perhaps the hardiest seeded grape available (to Zone 3). 'Buffalo' has medium blue grapes with a fruity flavor but is susceptible to powdery mildew. 'Edelweiss' is a very cold hardy American white grape. 'Golden Muscat' has large amber fruits that ripen late. 'Price' is an early-ripening, small to medium Concord-type grape. 'Sheridan' is a hardy, late-ripening Concord. Hardy 'Steuben' is a good choice for home gardens. Its spicy-sweet blue-black fruits grow in long clusters that are attractive on an arbor. 'Yates' is a hardy, late-ripening, sweet red grape. 'Thompson Seedless' grows well only in hot climates. The mild-flavored green berries are excellent fresh or dried

**European or common grapes are usually not cold-hardy or disease-resistant.**

as raisins. 'Himrod' is a cross of 'Thompson Seedless' and labrusca grapes that is moderately hardy and produces large bunches of honey-flavored pale green fruits that are good fresh or as raisins. 'Canadice' is a hardy red grape derived from 'Himrod'. It grows best in dry climates. 'Einset' is an early, hardy red grape with strawberry flavor. 'Interlaken' is similar, but the smaller amber fruits ripen earlier. 'Glenora' is a hardy, disease-resistant, seedless variety recommended for home gardens. The large dark blue grapes have a spicy flavor that's good fresh or in Riesling wine. 'Mars' is a cold-hardy and disease-resistant seedless blue grape used in pies and preserves. 'Saturn' has red fruits and grows best in hot climates. 'Reliance' is a very cold hardy red grape.

# SWEET CORN
*Zea mays*   ZEE-uh MAYZ

**Plant bicolor corn in small gardens to get the best of both yellow and white types.**

**ZONES:** NA
**SIZE:** 3–8'h x 1–3'w
**TYPE:** Annual
**GROWTH:** Average

**LIGHT:** Full sun
**MOISTURE:** High
**FEATURES:** Edible seeds (kernels)

**SITING:** Corn needs warm soil to germinate. It will grow in any well-drained, deeply dug soil but does best in rich, loose, slightly acid soil and especially well where legumes have grown previously. Direct-sow about 2 weeks after the last frost date ½" deep in moist soils or 1–1½" deep in dry soils. Use fresh seed each year; its quality declines quickly. Space the seeds 8–12" apart, using the closest spacing for early cultivars and in small gardens. Because corn is pollinated by the wind, plant the seeds in blocks of three or more in each direction instead of in rows. Planting in blocks also protects shallow-rooted corn from toppling over in high winds. Don't reseed where some seeds in a block fail to germinate. The taller plants will shade the younger ones and they won't all be ready for pollination at the same time.

**CARE:** Choose cultivars carefully for home gardening. Yellow and white varieties will easily cross-pollinate and turn white corn yellow; this does not affect the taste. In a small garden, plant all yellow, all white, or all bicolor cultivars. Remove weeds by hand or hoe shallowly to avoid damaging roots. Water during periods of drought, especially when ears are developing. To hand-pollinate, place pollen from tassels into an envelope, then sprinkle the pollen on the silks. Corn is a heavy feeder. Side dress plants with 33-0-0 plant food at the equivalent of 3 pounds per 100 foot row when they are 12–18" tall.

Sugar-enhanced (se and se+) varieties are more tender and sweeter than standard corn. Super-sweet (sh2) varieties are much sweeter and more tender than standard and sugar-enhanced varieties and have special cultural requirements. They will cross-pollinate with standard (su) and sugar-enhanced types, which results in starchy kernels in all plants. To avoid this problem in a small garden, plant cultivars that do not form silks at the same time. Supersweet varieties need very warm soil—at least 60°F—and more moisture than standard types in order to germinate. To preserve the high sugar content, cool the ears immediately after picking and store them in the refrigerator.

**PROPAGATION:** Grow from seed.

**HARVEST:** Pick sweet corn ears in the milk stage—when kernels are fully formed but not mature, about 20 days after the first silks appear. The silks will be starting to dry and turn brown, and the ears will feel full and firm. Carefully peel back the husk on an ear to see if it is ready. The kernels should be plump and squirt a milky juice when punctured. Most types remain in the milk stage for less than a week, so pick frequently. Immature kernels will have watery juice; overmature ones will be tough and doughy. Use a sharp, downward, twisting motion to break the shank (stem) below the ear without tearing the shank from the stalk. Eat or process the corn as soon as possible. Even in the sweetest cultivars, the sugar in corn turns to starch—especially in warm summer weather. Store ears in their husks in the refrigerator if you can't use them immediately. Pull off the silks and roast unhusked ears on a grill or in an open pit for 10–15 minutes, turning them a bit every few minutes. The silks will come off when you remove the husks. Or remove the husks and silks and cook the corn wrapped in aluminum foil. To prepare corn for eating fresh on the cob, first remove the husks and gently scrub away the silks under cool water. Cut away any discolored or wormy areas. Drop into boiling water for just 3 or 4 minutes or steam ears for 8 minutes. Enjoy as is or with melted butter or lemon juice. Ears blanched in boiling water can be cooled and frozen whole or the kernels stripped and frozen or pressure-canned. Dried kernels can be ground into cornmeal, hominy (grits), and flour.

Leave popcorn and ornamental corn to dry on the stalks until the first frost in dry climates. In areas with rainy weather, cut the stalks when the corn is mature and hang them to dry in a well-ventilated area protected from rain and animals. Remove the husks when they are dry and cure the cobs in the sun or in the oven at the lowest setting. Store the dried cobs whole or strip the kernels off. Keep both in airtight containers in cool storage.

**PESTS AND DISEASES:** Choose cultivars resistant to leaf blight, smut, and bacterial wilt. Use floating row covers on young plants to prevent infection by flea beetles, which cause bacterial wilt. Use seed pretreated with fungicide to control seed rot and seedling blight. Control earworm on early and midseason varieties with regular applications of labeled insecticide spray. Use fencing around the garden to keep out deer and raccoons.

**RECOMMENDED CULTIVARS:** Sweet corn is most often grown in home gardens for eating fresh on the cob or for freezing and canning. Hybrids of 'Seneca' are popular in

**1** Collect pollen from corn tassels into a cup or an envelope.

**2** Sprinkle the pollen from the tassels onto the corn silks.

**3** Carefully peel back the husk to check for ripeness for picking.

**4** Mature ears are plump and squirt a milky juice when punctured.

Control earworms with regular applications of labeled pesticide spray.

# SWEET CORN
### continued

Grow popcorn in large, long-season gardens for fun and food.

northern zones. The 7–8" yellow, white, or bicolor ears grow on stalks up to 6' tall and are ready to harvest in 60–65 days. 'Kandy' cultivars grow well in warmer climates. Choose from early, midseason, and late varieties. Try 'Golden Midget' in small gardens, where its 3' stalks and 4" ears take up little room and are ready in 60 days. 'Fleet' bears bicolor ears on

5' plants in 65 days. 'Northern Xtra Sweet' yields 8–9" yellow ears on 5' plants in 70 days. It germinates well in cool soil.

The larger ears of midseason cultivars may be worth waiting for another couple of weeks if space permits the 6–7' stalks. 'True Platinum' produces only two long white ears per stalk, but the dark burgundy husks add ornamental value in the garden. 'Butter and Sugar', a bicolor type, and 'Merit', a traditional yellow corn with good disease resistance, and 'Silver King', a white type, are good choices ready in 75–85 days. 'Double Standard' is an open-pollinated bicolor sweet corn with 7" ears on 5' stalks ready in 75 days.

'Silver Queen' has long been a favorite late-season white corn. The 8" ears are ready to harvest in 95 days. 'Golden Bantam' is an open-pollinated yellow heirloom variety known for its sweetness. The slender ears are ready in 80 days and should be cooked within a few hours of harvest to retain the best flavor. 'Stowell's

Evergreen' is an heirloom variety that gets its name from white kernels that stay in the milk stage a long time. The 8–9" ears grown on 8' stalks and are ready in 100 days.

Some cultivars can be enjoyed fresh in the milk stage or dried for cornmeal. 'Mandan Red Flour' has 4–5' stalks with 6" ears of pale yellow kernels that mature to deep red when dry. It is ready in 80–85 days. 'Oaxacan Green Dent' has 5–6' stalks with 6" ears of emerald green, dented kernels. It thrives in cool climates and is ready in 70–75 days.

Where space and climate permit, popcorn is a fun and often ornamental food crop. 'Ruby Red' and 'Shaman's Blue' have 8–9" ears of colorful kernels that are ornamental as well as tasty when popped. They are ready in 110–115 days. 'Robust' is a high-yielding yellow variety with tender kernels ready in 100–115 days. The hulls of 'Japanese Hulless' almost disappear when popped and the flavor is nutty and sweet. Three to six 4" ears grow on 4–5' plants ready in 95–105 days. Try 'Tom Thumb' where space is limited. Larger cultivars bear more tender corn, but the 3–4" ears of this miniature variety grow on stalks 3–4' tall and are ready in just 85 days.

# GINGER
### *Zingiber officinale*   ZIN-jih-ber off-fib-sih-NAY-lay

Grow ginger as an annual in northern zones and overwinter it indoors.

**ZONES:** 8–11
**SIZE:** 2–4'h x 2–4'w
**TYPE:** Herbaceous perennial
**GROWTH:** Average
**LIGHT:** Full sun to part shade
**MOISTURE:** Average
**FEATURES:** Edible rhizomes

**SITING:** Plant ginger in rich, well-drained, slightly acid soil that has been deeply worked to be loose and free of rocks or organic debris.
**CARE:** Keep the soil consistently moist. Ginger goes dormant in winter in tropical climates, although the stems may remain

green. Grow it as an annual in cold-winter climates, and pot one or more rhizome pieces after harvest for overwintering indoors. Keep the plants in a sunny window and water just enough to keep the soil moist but not wet. Replant the rhizomes outdoors in spring after the last frost date. Lay the pieces horizontally 1–1½" deep. Each piece should have two or more growth nodes.
**PROPAGATION:** Grow by division.
**HARVEST:** Dig the rhizomes in autumn. They should be firm and feel heavy. Wrinkled rhizomes are old or dry and will taste bitter. Cut away the stalks and fibrous roots. Peel and grate or slice ginger into salads, stir-fries, curries, marinades, and baked goods. It combines particularly well with chicken and fish, sweet potatoes, carrots, winter squash, pumpkin, carrots, lemons, peaches, and apricots. Diced dried ginger is sugared and served as a sweet with tea. Ground dried ginger is used as a cooking condiment. Pickled ginger is a popular condiment in Japanese cuisine. Store fresh, unpeeled ginger wrapped in

damp paper towels in a plastic bag in the crisper drawer of the refrigerator for up to 3 weeks. To keep it longer, peel it, break it into pieces, and store the pieces in the refrigerator covered with sherry or vodka in a glass jar.
**PESTS AND DISEASES:** Bacterial soft rot and Pythium fungus may develop in waterlogged soil. Rotate ginger to new locations in the garden to avoid root-knot nematodes. Protect new shoots from cutworms with cardboard or aluminum collars pressed an inch into the soil. Keep the ground around plants cleaned of decaying vegetative matter, which might encourage fusarium rhizome rot.
**RECOMMENDED CULTIVARS:** In addition to common ginger, there are several related plants cultivated for similar culinary use. Thai ginger or galangal (*Alpinia galanga*) is a tropical perennial herb grown for its flowers and young shoots as well as its underground stems. Japanese woodland ginger (*Zingiber mioga*) is grown for its edible shoots and flowers, which taste like bergamot.

# INDEX

Note: Page references in bold type refer to Encyclopedia entries. Page references in italic type refer to additional photographs, illustrations, and information in captions. Plants are listed under their common names.

# RESOURCES FOR
## PLANTS & SUPPLIES

### VEGETABLES AND HERBS

Abundant Life Seed Foundation
P.O. Box 772
Port Townsend, WA 98368
360/385-5660
www.abundantlifeseed.org

Bountiful Gardens
18001 Shafer Ranch Rd.
Willits, CA 95490-9626
707/459-6410
www.bountifulgardens.org

Burgess Seed & Plant Co.
905 Four Seasons Rd.
Bloomington, IL 61701
309/663-9551
www.cometobuy.com/burgess

Comstock, Ferre & Co.
263 Main St.
Wethersfield, CT 06109
800/733-3773
www.comstockferre.com

D. Landreth Seed Co.
P.O. Box 6398
Baltimore, MD 21230
800/654-2407
www.landrethseeds.com
Catalog: $2

DeGiorgi Seeds & Goods
6011 N St.
Omaha, NE 68117
800/858-2580
www.degiorgiseed.com

Earl May Seed & Nursery
Shenandoah, IA 51603
800/831-4193
www.earlmay.com.

Evergreen Y.H. Enterprises
P.O. Box 17538
Anaheim, CA 92817
714/637-5769
www.evergreenseeds.com

Farmer Seed & Nursery Co.
818 NW. 4th St.
Fairibault, MN 55021
507/334-1623

Ferry-Morse Seed Co.
P.O. Box 1620
Fulton, KY 42041
800/283-3400
www.ferry-morse.com

Irish Eyes—Garden City Seeds
P.O. Box 307
Thorp, WA 98946
509/964-7000
www.irish-eyes.com

J.L. Hudson, Seedsman
Star Route 2, Box 337
La Honda, CA 94020
www.jlhudsonseeds.net

Johnny's Selected Seeds
955 Benton Ave.
Winslow, ME 04901
207/861-3900
www.johnnyseeds.com.

J.W. Jung Seed Co.
335 S. High St.
Randolph, WI 53957-0001
800/297-3123
www.jungseed.com.

Native Seeds/SEARCH
526 N. 4th Ave.
Tucson, AZ 85705-8450
520/622-5561
www.nativeseeds.org

Nichols Garden Nursery
1190 Old Salem Rd. NE
Albany, OR 97321-4580
800/422-3985
www.nicholsgardennursery.com

Ornamental Edibles
3272 Fleur de Lis Ct.
San Jose, CA 95132
408/929-7333
www.ornamentaledibles.com

Papa Geno's Herb Farm
6005 West Roca Rd.
Martell, NE 68404
402/794-0400
www.papagenos.com

Park Seed Co.
1 Parkton Ave.
Greenwood, SC 29649
800/213-0076
www.parkseed.com

Pinetree Garden Seeds
P.O. Box 300
New Gloucester, ME 04260
207/926-3400
www.superseeds.com

Renee's Garden
888/880-7228
www.reneesgarden.com

Ronniger's Seed Potatoes
Moyie Springs, ID 83845
208/267-7938
Catalog $2

Sand Mountain Herbs
321 County Road 18
Fyffe, AL 35971
256/528-2861
www.sandmountainherbs.com

Sandy Mush Herb Nursery
Rt. 2, Surrett Cove Rd.
Leicester, NC
704/683-2014
www.brwm.org/sandymushherbs
Catalog $4

Seeds of Change
P.O. Box 15700
Santa Fe, NM 87506
888/762-7333
www.seedsofchange.com

Seeds West Garden Seeds
317 14th St. NW
Albuquerque, NM 87104
505/843-9713
www.seedswestgardenseeds.com
Catalog: $2

Stokes Seeds Inc.
P.O. Box 548
Buffalo, NY 14240-0548
800/396-9238
www.stokesseeds.com

Territorial Seed Co.
P.O. Box 157
Cottage Grove, OR 97424
541/942-9547
www.territorial-seed.com

The Cook's Garden
P.O. Box 5010
Hodges, SC 29653-5010
800/457-9703
www.cooksgarden.com

Thompson & Morgan, Inc.
P.O. Box 1308
Jackson, NJ 08527-0308
800/274-7333
www.thompson-morgan.com

Tomato Growers Supply Co.
P.O. Box 2237
Ft. Myers, FL 33902
888/478-7333
www.tomatogrowers.com

Vesey's Seeds Ltd.
P.O. Box 9000
Calais, ME 04619-6102
800/363-7333
www.veseys.com

W. Atlee Burpee & Co.
300 Park Ave.
Warminster, PA 18991
800/888-1447
www.burpee.com

**Fruits, Nuts, and Berries**
Adams County Nursery, Inc.
26 Nursery Rd.
P.O. Box 108
Aspers, PA 17304
717-677-8105
www.acnursery.com

Aesthetic Gardens
P.O. Box 1362
Boring, OR 97009
503/663-6672 fax
www.agardens.com

Ames' Orchard and Nursery
18292 Wildlife Rd.
Fayetteville, AR 72701
501/443-0282

Ahrens Strawberry Nursery
RR1
Huntingburg, Indiana 47642
812/683-3055

W. F. Allen, Co.
Box 1577
Salisbury, Maryland 21801

Bergenson Nursery
Rt. 1, Box 84
Fertile, MN 56540
218/945-6988

Blossomberry Nursery
Route 2
Clarksville, AR 72830
501/754-6489

Brittingham Plant Farms
P.O. Box 2538
Salisbury, MD 21801
301/749-5153

Burnt Ridge Nursery & Orchards
432 Burnt Ridge Rd.
Onalaska, WA 98570
360/985-2873
landru.myhome.net/burntridge

Columbia Basin Nursery
P.O. Box 458
Quincy, WA 98848
800-333-8589
www.cbnllc.com

Edible Landscaping
P.O. Box 77
Afton, VA 22920
804/361-9134
www.eat-it.com

England's Orchard and Nursery
316 S.R. 2004
McKee, KY 40447-9616
877/965-2228
www.nuttrees.net

Fedco Trees
P.O. Box 520
Waterville, ME 04903-0520
207/873-7333

Foster Nursery Co., Inc.
69 Orchard St.
Fredonia, NY 14063

Four Winds Nursery
www.FourWindsGrowers.com
Mail-order dwarf citrus

Garden of Delights
14560 SW 14th St.
Davie, Florida 33325-4217
800/741-3103
www.gardenofdelights.com

Greenmantle Nursery
3010 Ettersburg Rd.
Garberville, CA 95542
707/986-7504

Hartmann's Plantation Inc.
P.O. Box E
Grand Junction, MI 49056
616/253-4281
www.hartmannsplantcompany.com

Henry Leuthardt Nurseries
Montauk Hwy., Box 666
East Moriches, NY 11940
516/878-1387
www.henryleuthardtnurseries.com

Indiana Berry & Plant Co.
5218 West 500
South Huntingburg, IN 47542-9724
800/295-2226
berryinfo@inberry.com
www.inberry.com

Ison's Nursery & Vineyards
Route 1, Box 191
Brooks, GA 30205
800/733-0324
www.isons.com

Johnson Nursery
5273 Hwy. 52E
Ellijay, GA 30540
888/276-3187
www.johnsonnursery.com

Just Fruits Nursery
30 St. Frances St.
Crawfordville, FL 32327
850/926-5644

Kelly Nurseries
P.O. Box 800
Dansville, NY 14437
800/325-4180
www.kellynurseries.com

Lawson's Nursery
2730 Yellow Creek Rd.
Ball Ground, GA 30107
770/893-2141

Logee's Greenhouses
55 North St.
Danielson, CT 06239
888/330-8038
www.logees.com

Mellingers, Inc.
2310PP W. South Range Rd.
North Lima, OH 44452
330/549-9861
www.mellingers.com

Miller Nurseries
5060 W. Lake Rd.
Canandaigua, NY 14424-8904
800/836-9630
www.millernurseries.com

New York State Fruit Testing Cooperative
Association, Inc.
P.O. Box 462
Geneva, NY 14456
315/787-2205
$10 refundable membership fee

Nolin River Nut Tree Nursery
797 Port Wooden Rd.
Upton, KY 42784
270/369-8551
www.nolinnursery.com

Nourse Farms Inc.
41 River Rd.
South Deerfield, MA 01373
413/665-2658
www.noursefarms.com

One Green World
P.O. Box 1080
Molalla, OR 97038
503/651-3005
www.onegreenworld.com

Oregon Exotics Rare Fruit Nursery
1065 Messinger Rd.
Grants Pass, OR 97527
541/846-7578
www.exoticfruit.com
Catalog $4

Pacific Tree Farms
4301 Lynwood Dr.
Chula Vista, CA 91910
619/422-2400
www.kyburg.com/ptf/index.html

Paradise Nursery
6385 Blackwater Rd.
Virginia Beach, VA 23457-1040
757/421-0201
www.paradisenursery.com

Raintree Nursery
391 Butts Rd.
Morton, WA 98356
360/496-6400
www.raintreenursery.com

Saint Lawrence Nurseries
RD 2
Potsdam, NY 13676
315/265-6739
www.sln.potsdam.ny.us

Southmeadow Fruit Gardens
P.O. Box 211
Baroda, MI 49101
269/422-2411
www.southmeadowfruitgardens.com

Spring Hill Nurseries
110 W. Elm St.
Tipp City, OH 45371
513/354-1509
www.springhillnursery.com

Stark Brothers Nurseries & Orchards
P.O. Box 10
Louisiana, MO 63353
800/325-4180
www.starkbros.com

The Banana Tree, Inc.
715 Northampton St.
Easton, PA 18042
610/253-9589
www.banana-tree.com

Van Well Nursery
2821 Grant Rd.
Wenatchee, WA 98807
800/572-1553
www.vanwell.net

# USDA PLANT HARDINESS ZONE MAP

This map of climate zones helps you select plants for your garden that will survive a typical winter in your region. The United States Department of Agriculture (USDA) developed the map, basing the zones on the lowest recorded temperatures across North America. Zone 1 is the coldest area and Zone 11 is the warmest area.

Plants are classified by the coldest temperature and zone they can endure. For example, plants hardy to Zone 6 survive where winter temperatures drop to –10°F. Those hardy to Zone 8 die long before it's that cold. These plants may grow in colder regions but must be replaced each year. Plants rated for a range of hardiness zones can usually survive winter in the coldest region as well as tolerate the summer heat of the warmest one.

To find your hardiness zone, note the approximate location of your community on the map, then match the color band marking that area to the key.

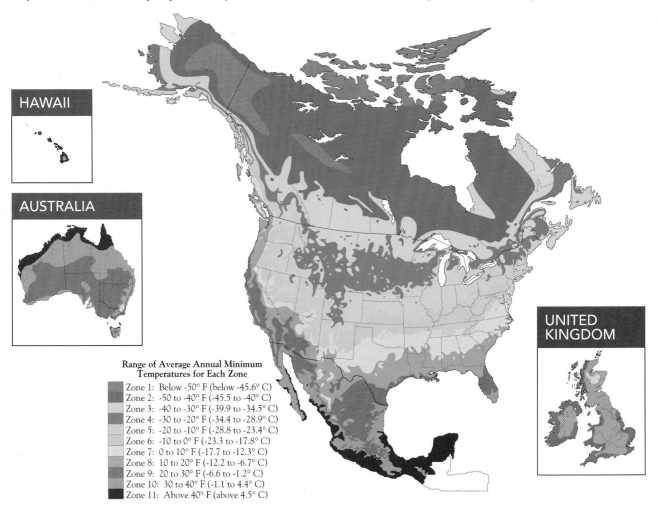

HAWAII

AUSTRALIA

UNITED KINGDOM

**Range of Average Annual Minimum Temperatures for Each Zone**

Zone 1:  Below -50° F (below -45.6° C)
Zone 2:  -50 to -40° F (-45.5 to -40° C)
Zone 3:  -40 to -30° F (-39.9 to -34.5° C)
Zone 4:  -30 to -20° F (-34.4 to -28.9° C)
Zone 5:  -20 to -10° F (-28.8 to -23.4° C)
Zone 6:  -10 to 0° F (-23.3 to -17.8° C)
Zone 7:  0 to 10° F (-17.7 to -12.3° C)
Zone 8:  10 to 20° F (-12.2 to -6.7° C)
Zone 9:  20 to 30° F (-6.6 to -1.2° C)
Zone 10:  30 to 40° F (-1.1 to 4.4° C)
Zone 11:  Above 40° F (above 4.5° C)

## METRIC CONVERSIONS

| U.S. Units to Metric Equivalents | | | Metric Units to U.S. Equivalents | | |
| --- | --- | --- | --- | --- | --- |
| To Convert From | Multiply By | To Get | To Convert From | Multiply By | To Get |
| Inches | 25.4 | Millimeters | Millimeters | 0.0394 | Inches |
| Inches | 2.54 | Centimeters | Centimeters | 0.3937 | Inches |
| Feet | 30.48 | Centimeters | Centimeters | 0.0328 | Feet |
| Feet | 0.3048 | Meters | Meters | 3.2808 | Feet |
| Yards | 0.9144 | Meters | Meters | 1.0936 | Yards |

To convert from degrees Fahrenheit (F) to degrees Celsius (C), first subtract 32, then multiply by ⅚.

To convert from degrees Celsius to degrees Fahrenheit, multiply by ⅚, then add 32.